THE ULTIMATE Bible FACT AND QUIZ BOOK

CHARTWELL
BOOKS

Inspiring | Educating | Creating | Entertaining

Brimming with creative inspiration, how-to projects, and useful information to enrich your everyday life, Quarto Knows is a favorite destination for those pursuing their interests and passions. Visit our site and dig deeper with our books into your area of interest: Quarto Creates, Quarto Cooks, Quarto Homes, Quarto Lives, Quarto Drives, Quarto Explores, Quarto Gifts, or Quarto Kids.

Copyright © Arcturus Holdings Limited
26/27 Bickels Yard, 151–153 Bermondsey Street,
London SE1 3HA

First published in 2018 by Chartwell Books, an imprint of The Quarto Group,
142 West 36th Street, 4th Floor, New York, NY 10018, USA
T (212) 779-4972 F (212) 779-6058 www.QuartoKnows.com

Chartwell Books titles are also available at discount for retail, wholesale, promotional, and bulk purchase. For details, contact the Special Sales Manager by email at specialsales@quarto.com or by mail at The Quarto Group, Attn: Special Sales Manager, 401 Second Avenue North, Suite 310, Minneapolis, MN 55401, USA.

Scripture quotations are taken from the Holy Bible, New International Version Copyright NIV Copyright 1973, 1978, 1984 by International Bible Society.
Used by permission of Zondervan Publishing House. All rights reserved.

Extracts marked as KJV are from the Authorized Version of the Bible (The King James Bible), the rights in which are vested in the Crown, are reproduced by permission of the Crown's Patentee, Cambridge University Press.

10 9 8 7 6 5 4 3 2 1

ISBN: 978-0-7858-3642-1
AD006536UK

Compilers: Andy Bianchi, Debra K. Reid, Lee Simmons, W. M. Stamp, Drake Williams
Associate Editor: W. M. Stamp
Design: Chris Smith
Typeset by MATS, Southend-on-Sea, Essex
Illustrations by Jim Hansen

Printed in China

CONTENTS

Foreword

The Bible is one of the world's greatest books. It is a bestseller, has had a far-reaching impact on human civilization, and has encouraged and inspired millions of people throughout history.

The Ultimate Bible Fact and Quiz Book is a new and exciting way to discover the Bible. It can be used in community and church groups, Sunday School classes, family games and devotions, or simply for entertaining reading.

What's unique about this collection of quizzes and facts is its variety. Topics covered include Jesus Christ, important Bible characters, significant events, geography, music, food, love, war, money, gardening, animals, crime, punishment, miracles, angels, dreams… the list is virtually endless!

The quizzes are designed to challenge every age and ability. Some questions may seem easy, such as, *'In which town was Jesus born?'* or *'Who was said to be the wisest King in the Bible?'* Others may be a bit more challenging, like *'How old was Joash when he began to reign in Judah?'* or *'What was the name of King David's third son?'*

There are hundreds of fascinating facts included. Did you know that one of the words for 'miracles' in the New Testament is *'dunamis',* from which we get our word *'dynamite'?* You'll find this and many more interesting nuggets of information – all about this amazing book called the Bible. Enjoy!

Martin H. Manser

The Light of the World

Quiz #1

1. To which bereaved woman did Jesus say, "Don't cry!"?

2. When Dr. Luke described the healing of a man on the Sabbath, he diagnosed the man's illness, using a medical term found nowhere else in the New Testament. What was the illness?

3. Only one of Jesus' miracles is recorded in all four Gospels. Which miracle?

4. What is the Bible reference for the famous verse which begins, "For God so loved the world that he gave his one and only Son..."?

5. After meeting Jesus, who said that he would give away half of his possessions to the poor?

6. Which Gospel starts with the words, "The beginning of the gospel about Jesus Christ, the Son of God"?

7. True or false? Chapter 17 of John's Gospel contains Jesus' longest recorded prayer.

8. To which woman did Jesus say, "Daughter, your faith has healed you. Go in peace and be freed from your suffering"?

9. What was unusual about the place where Jesus healed a little girl who was possessed by an evil spirit?

10. True or false? There is only one mention in the Gospels of a meeting between Jesus and the apostle Paul.

11. Which top Jewish religious leader visited Jesus at night?

12. True or false? A blind beggar kept calling out to Jesus, but the people told him to be quiet.

13. Which Gospel opens with the words, "In the beginning was the Word..."

14. How old was Jesus when his parents took him to the temple in Jerusalem for the Passover?

15. Where did Jesus attend a wedding reception?

Answers

1. The widow of Nain who was about to bury her son **2.** Dropsy, which is an accumulation of fluid
3. The feeding of the 5,000 **4.** John 3:16 **5.** Zacchaeus **6.** Mark's Gospel
7. True **8.** To a woman who had been suffering from bleeding for twelve years
9. The miracle took place outside Palestine in the region of Tyre and Sidon
10. False. There is no record of such a meeting **11.** Nicodemus **12.** True (Mark 10:47-48)
13. John's Gospel **14.** 12 years old **15.** Cana

Quiz #2

1. True or false? Jesus prayed in public but it is never recorded that he prayed by himself in private.

2. To which ill woman did Jesus say on the Sabbath, "Woman, you are set free from your infirmity"?

3. When Jesus rode into Jerusalem amid cheering crowds, on what was he riding?

4. Which Old Testament book has a verse in it which is taken as a prophecy about the birth place of Jesus?

5. To whom did Jesus say, "Get up, take your mat and go home"?

6. Which Old Testament book has a verse in it which is taken as a prophecy that Jesus would be born of a virgin?

7. To whom did Jesus say, "Did I not tell you that if you believed you would see the glory of God?"?

8. To which would-be disciple did Jesus say, "Foxes have holes and birds of the air have nests, but the Son of Man has no place to lay his head"?

9. True or false? The last verse in the Bible says, "And surely I am with you always, to the very end of the age."

10. When Jesus told the professional mourners that the ruler's daughter was "not dead but asleep" how did they react?

11. Who asked Jesus, "How is it that we and the Pharisees fast, but your disciples do not fast?"?

12. What did Jesus promise he would give to the weary and burdened if they came to him?

13. True or false? Jesus had half-sisters as well as half-brothers.

14. Jesus had four half-brothers. James and Joseph were two of the brothers. Name one of the other two.

15. Who said, "Where is the one who has been born king of the Jews?"?

Answers

1. False (Matthew 14:23) 2. A woman who had been crippled for 18 years 3. A donkey 4. Micah 5:2
5. To the paralyzed man who had been let down through the roof of a house to reach Jesus 6. Isaiah 7:14
7. Martha 8. A teacher of the law who said, "I will follow you wherever you go."
9. False. This is the last verse of Matthew's Gospel 10. They laughed at Jesus
11. John the Baptist's disciples 12. Rest 13. True (Mark 6:3).
14. Judas and Simon 15. The wise men

Quiz #3

1. How old was Jesus when he began his ministry?

2. What memorable act did Jesus do immediately before eating the last supper with his disciples on the day we now call Maundy Thursday?

3. True or false? Jesus rebuked a storm on Lake Galilee and it obeyed him.

4. Which Old Testament book has a verse in it which is taken as a Messianic prophecy about the slaughter of the innocents?

5. On what occasion did Jesus say, "I have not found such great faith even in Israel"?

6. True or false? As he looked at the Roman soldiers, Jesus said they were like sheep without a shepherd.

7. To whom did Jesus point and say, "Here are my mother and my brothers"?

8. How old was the daughter of Jairus when Jesus brought her back to life?

9. In which town was Jesus born?

10. What was Jesus' one-word reply to Peter when Peter said, "Tell me to come to you on the water"?

11. When did Jesus say, "Open your eyes and look at the fields! They are ripe for harvest"?

12. When Jesus said to a deaf and dumb man, "Be opened!", what, according to Mark's Gospel, was the actual Aramaic word that Jesus used?

13. Which Old Testament book has a verse in it which is taken as a Messianic prophecy about Jesus being called out of Egypt?

14. To whom did Jesus say, "I was sent only to the lost sheep of Israel"?

15. What had the disciples been arguing about not long before Jesus asked them, "What were you arguing about on the road?"?

Answers

1. About 30 years old **2.** Jesus washed his disciples' feet **3.** True (Mark 4:39) **4.** Jeremiah 31:15
5. When a centurion asked Jesus to heal his servant, not by visiting his home, but by giving a command.
6. False. Jesus was talking about the crowds (Matthew 9:36) **7.** His disciples
8. 12 years old **9.** Bethlehem **10.** Come
11. When Jesus' disciples returned to the well and found him talking to a Samaritan woman
12. Ephphatha **13.** Hosea 11:1 **14.** The Canaanite woman **15.** About who should be greatest

Quiz #4

1. True or false? Jesus said to his disciples, "I will not leave you as orphans."

2. About whom was Jesus speaking when he said, "Have I not chosen you, the Twelve? Yet one of you is a devil"?

3. Jesus once healed ten lepers. How many came back to thank him?

4. Which Old Testament book has a verse in it which is taken as a Messianic prophecy about Jesus' ministry being in Galilee?

5. To which group of people did Jesus say, "The harvest is plentiful, but the workers are few"?

6. Who said of Jesus, "You are the Christ, the Son of the living God"?

7. To whom did Jesus say, "Get behind me, Satan"?

8. What did Jesus say is the second greatest commandment?

9. True or false? Immediately after Jesus was baptized he chose his twelve apostles.

10. When did Jesus' clothes become as white as light?

11. What was the name of the devout and righteous man who met Jesus in the temple when he was circumcised?

12. True or false? Jesus regularly attended a synagogue on the Sabbath.

13. Which Old Testament book has a verse in it which is taken as a Messianic prophecy about Jesus riding into Jerusalem on a donkey?

14. About which dead man did Jesus say, "This sickness will not end in death"?

15. True or false? Moses and Elijah were seen at Jesus' ascension.

Answers

1. True (John 14:18) **2.** Judas Iscariot **3.** 1 **4.** Isaiah 9:1-2 **5.** The 72 disciples sent out two by two **6.** Peter **7.** Peter **8.** "Love your neighbor as yourself" **9.** False (Matthew 4:1) **10.** At the transfiguration **11.** Simeon **12.** True (Luke 4:44) **13.** Zechariah 9:9 **14.** Lazarus **15.** False. They were seen at Jesus' transfiguration (Matthew 17:3)

Quiz #5

1. When Jesus said that "Elijah has already come", to whom was he referring?

2. To whom did Jesus say, "You are in error because you do not know the Scriptures or the power of God"?

3. True or false? After Jesus spat on a blind man's eyes, the man said he could see people but they all looked tiny, like very young children.

4. Who did Jesus tell that he must be born again?

5. About whom did Jesus say, "Satan has asked to sift you as wheat"?

6. True or false? When Jesus was arrested, Peter helped him to escape.

7. To the nearest five years, which year is it traditionally thought that Jesus started his ministry?

8. True or false? Jesus never married.

9. What are the first recorded words of Jesus in Mark's Gospel?

10. How many different miracles of Jesus do the four Gospels record: to the nearest five?

11. How many different parables of Jesus do the four Gospels record: to the nearest five?

12. About whom did Jesus say, "Take off the grave clothes and let him go"?

13. When Jesus, Mary and Joseph left Egypt, which town did they go to?

14. How many of Jesus' disciples witnessed his transfiguration?

15. Who did Jesus say were like white-washed tombs?

Answers

1. John the Baptist 2. The Sadducees
3. False. The people looked like trees walking around (Mark 8:24) 4. Nicodemus
5. Simon (Peter) 6. False. Peter ran away (Mark 14:50) 7. A.D. 26/27 8. True
9. "The time has come, the kingdom of God is near" 10. 35 miracles 11. 40 parables 12. Lazarus
13. Nazareth 14. 3 15. The Pharisees

Quiz #6

1. True or false? Jesus walked on the water of the Sea of Galilee.

2. Which Gospels state that Jesus taught with authority and not like the teachers of the law?

3. Who said to Jesus, "What do you want with us, Jesus of Nazareth? Have you come to destroy us?"?

4. True or false? When Jesus needed money to pay the temple tax, he told Peter to go fishing and to look in the mouth of the first fish he caught. There Peter found the money he needed.

5. Where was Jesus when he said, "I and the Father are one"?

6. Jesus told people not to focus on the speck of sawdust in their brother's eye when they had what in their own eye?

7. True or false? Jesus spent about ten years teaching and performing miracles with his disciples.

8. Where did Jesus make his base in Galilee?

9. In which of the Gospels is Jesus called "the Lamb of God"?

10. Who was the only person to call Jesus "the Lamb of God"?

11. There is one saying of Jesus which is not found in the four Gospels but comes in another book in the New Testament. Which New Testament book does the saying come in?

12. To which group who opposed him did Jesus say, "At the resurrection people will neither marry nor be given in marriage"?

13. True or false? Jesus said he was the good farmer.

14. Who did Jesus take in his arms and bless?

15. True or false? Jesus' first miracle took place at a wedding.

Answers

1. True (John 6:19) 2. Matthew 7:29 and Mark 1:22 3. A man possessed by evil spirits
4. True (Matthew 17:24-27) 5. Solomon's Colonnade, in the temple 6. A plank
7. False. It was about 3 years. 8. Capernaum 9. John's Gospel 10. John the Baptist 11. The book of Acts
12. The Sadducees 13. False. Jesus said he was the good shepherd (John 10:11).
14. Little children 15. True (John 2:11)

Quiz #7

1. True or false? Jesus spoke Aramaic.

2. When did Jesus make a whip of cords?

3. What did Jesus say it is hard for a rich man to do?

4. What was the name of the Pharisee who invited Jesus for a meal?

5. Which Gospel was written by a doctor?

6. Before Jesus started his ministry, what work did he do?

7. What were the first words of Jesus recorded by Matthew?

8. To whom did Jesus say, "Do not put the Lord your God to the test"?

9. In what town could Jesus perform very few miracles because of the people's lack of faith?

10. According to the Pharisees, Jesus broke the law when he healed on the Sabbath. What other Sabbath law did he break?

11. True or false? Jesus was so pure that he was never tempted.

12. Complete the first beatitude, "Blessed are the poor in spirit..."

13. True or false? Jesus' mother and brother wanted to take charge of him because they thought he was out of his mind.

14. What percentage of the 1,071 verses in Matthew's Gospel contain the spoken word of Jesus; to the nearest 10%?

15. Who asked Jesus, "How many times shall I forgive my brother when he sins against me? Up to seven times?"?

Answers

1. True (John 6:41) **2.** When he threw the money-changers out of the temple
3. Enter the kingdom of heaven **4.** Simon **5.** Luke's Gospel **6.** He was a carpenter
7. "Let it be so now; it is proper for us to do this to fulfil all righteousness" (Matthew 3:15) **8.** The devil
9. Nazareth **10.** He allowed the disciples to pluck and eat corn on the Sabbath
11. False. Jesus was often tempted, but never gave in to temptation. **12.** "...for theirs is the kingdom of heaven"
13. True (Mark 3:20-21) **14.** 60 per cent **15.** Peter

Quiz #8

1. Who asked Jesus for a drink at a well?

2. True or false? When Jesus was a teenager, baseball was his favorite sport.

3. Complete the second beatitude, "Blessed are those who mourn..."

4. What did Jesus say about a city on a hill?

5. True or false? Jesus spoke more about heaven and hell than anyone else in the Bible.

6. To whom did Jesus say, "...with God all things are possible"?

7. True or false? In chapter 4 of John's Gospel Jesus is seen as the soul-winner as he speaks with Zacchaeus.

8. Fill in the missing word: "The people were amazed at his teaching, because he taught them as one who had ____."

9. Complete the third beatitude, "Blessed are the meek..."

10. Lazarus had two sisters: Martha was one sister. Who was the other?

11. What special request did James and John ask of Jesus?

12. What trick question did the disciples of the Pharisees and the Herodians ask Jesus?

13. What reply did Jesus give to the trick question posed by the disciples of the Pharisees and the Herodians?

14. In Jesus' parable about the man who was mugged, who were the two people who ignored him?

15. True or false? In chapter five of John's Gospel Jesus heals a man who had been ill for eight years.

Answers

1. A Samaritan woman 2. False. The Gospels give no details about Jesus' teenage years
3. "...for they will be comforted" 4. It cannot be hidden 5. True 6. His disciples
7. False. Jesus spoke to the woman of Samaria 8. Authority 9. "...for they will inherit the earth" 10. Mary
11. To sit at his right hand and left hand when he comes in his glory 12. "Is it right to pay tax to Caesar or not?"
13. "Give to Caesar what is Caesar's, and to God what is God's" 14. A priest and a Levite
15. False. The man had been ill for 38 years (John 5:5)

Quiz #9

1. Complete the fourth beatitude, "Blessed are those who hunger and thirst for righteousness..."

2. True or false? In chapter 6 of John's Gospel Jesus is depicted as the water of life.

3. True or false? Jesus said that anyone who marries a divorced woman commits adultery.

4. What was the one exception that Jesus made when he said that anyone who divorces his wife makes her an adulteress?

5. In Jesus' Parable of the Ten Virgins, what did the five foolish girls neglect to do?

6. Who did Jesus say would be remembered wherever the gospel was preached throughout the world?

7. Complete the fifth beatitude, "Blessed are the merciful..."

8. Which Gospel was written by an ex tax-collector?

9. True or false? The Gospels describe one visit Jesus made to Malta.

10. Who gave to God all the money she had to live on?

11. What is the name given to Jesus' most famous prayer which begins, "Our Father in heaven"?

12. At what Feast did Jesus stand up and say, "If anyone is thirsty, let him come to me and drink"?

13. What are the final words of Jesus, as recorded in Acts?

14. Complete the sixth beatitude, "Blessed are the pure in heart..."

15. In whose house was Jesus when he said, "I have not come to call the righteous, but sinners"?

Answers

1. "...for they will be filled" **2.** False **3.** Jesus is depicted as the bread of life. **3.** True (Mark 10:11)
4. Except for marital unfaithfulness **5.** Take extra oil with them
6. The woman who poured expensive perfume on Jesus' head **7.** "...for they will be shown mercy."
8. Matthew's Gospel **9.** False. No such visit is mentioned **10.** A poor widow **11.** The Lord's Prayer
12. The Feast of Tabernacles **13.** In Acts 1:7-8, Jesus said, "You will be my witnesses... to the ends of the earth"
14. "...for they will see God" **15.** Levi's (Matthew)

Quiz #10

1. Jesus said that the Queen of the South would condemn the people of his generation for their lack of faith. What group of people would also stand up in condemnation?

2. To whom did Jesus say, "Sell everything you have and give to the poor"?

3. Complete the seventh beatitude, "Blessed are the peacemakers..."

4. Why did Jesus say, "The Sabbath was made for man, not man for the Sabbath"?

5. Who said of Jesus, "He is possessed by Beelzebub!"?

6. What happened to the house built on sand?

7. How many times is Jesus called "Son of David" in Matthew's Gospel?

8. Which Gospel was written by a man who never mentions himself in it by name, but refers to himself as "the disciple whom Jesus loved"?

9. True or false? In chapter 9 of John's Gospel Jesus says he is the light of the world.

10. Fill in the missing word: Jesus said, "Heaven and earth will pass away, but my _____ will never pass away."

11. What sin was Jesus condemning in his parable about the Pharisee and the tax-collector?

12. What animals went rushing over a cliff into the sea?

13. When did Peter fall at Jesus' feet and say, "Go away from me, Lord, I am a sinful man"?

14. True or false? Jesus was sold into slavery by his brothers.

15. When healing a little girl Jesus said, "Talitha koum." What do these words mean?

Answers

1. The men of Nineveh 2. The rich young ruler 3. "...for they will be called the sons of God"
4. Because the Pharisees condemned him for allowing his disciples to eat corn on the Sabbath
5. The teachers of the law 6. It fell down 7. 10 times 8. John's Gospel
9. True (John 9:5) 10. Words 11. Pride 12. Pigs
13. After Jesus told Peter to drop his nets into the sea, and they caught a large number of fish
14. False. That was Joseph in the Old Testament. 15. "Little girl, I say to you, get up!"

Quiz #11

1. True or false? Jesus told a story about a housewife who lost her ring.

2. Jesus only once gave someone a name in his parables. Who was it?

3. How many loaves of bread did Jesus use to feed the 4,000?

4. How many baskets full of leftovers were collected after the feeding of the 4,000?

5. How many baskets full of leftovers were collected after the feeding of the 5,000?

6. Complete the eighth beatitude: "Blessed are those who are persecuted because of righteousness..."

7. To whom did Jesus say, "Follow me, and let the dead bury their own dead"?

8. Fill in the missing word, from the healing of the two blind men: "According to your _____ will it be done to you."

9. In John's Gospel Jesus gave himself a name by saying "I am..." seven times. What was the first name?

10. In John's Gospel Jesus gave himself a name by saying "I am..." seven times. What was the second name?

11. In John's Gospel Jesus gave himself a name by saying "I am..." seven times. What was the third name?

12. In John's Gospel Jesus gave himself a name by saying "I am..." seven times. What was the fourth name?

13. In John's Gospel Jesus gave himself a name by saying "I am..." seven times. What was the fifth name?

14. In John's Gospel Jesus gave himself a name by saying "I am..." seven times. What was the sixth name?

15. In John's Gospel Jesus gave himself a name by saying "I am..." seven times. What was the seventh name?

Answers

1. False. It was a coin (Luke 15:8) 2. Lazarus the beggar 3. 7 loaves 4. 7 baskets 5. 12 baskets 6. "...for theirs is the kingdom of heaven" 7. The disciple who said to Jesus, "First let me go and bury my father." 8. Faith 9. The bread of life 10. The light of the world 11. The gate (door) 12. The good shepherd 13. The resurrection and the life 14. The way and the truth and the life 15. The true vine

 # Facts 1

We don't know the date of Jesus' birth. Jesus' birthday is celebrated on December 25 because that was the date of the Jewish Festival of Lights, called the Festival of Hanukkah, which fell on 25 to 30 Kislev (our November to December).

The present era was calculated to begin with the birth of Jesus Christ, that is A.D. 1. The initials A.D. stand for Anno Domini "in the year of our Lord."

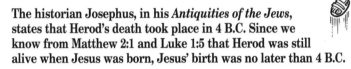

In the sixth century Abbot Dionysius Exigutus fixed the present Christian era. He calculated that this occurred 754 years after the founding of the city of Rome. Today scholars say that it was 750 B.C., which places the birth of Jesus at 4 B.C.

The historian Josephus, in his *Antiquities of the Jews*, states that Herod's death took place in 4 B.C. Since we know from Matthew 2:1 and Luke 1:5 that Herod was still alive when Jesus was born, Jesus' birth was no later than 4 B.C.

The wise men depicted on Christmas cards as kings, are traditionally called Melchior, Caspar and Balthazar. Matthew says that these visitors were following a star, so it is likely that they were astrologers rather than kings. The Bible doesn't give their names.

When the baby Jesus was presented in the temple (Luke 2:24), Joseph gave the offering allowed for a poor man, which was a pair of doves, rather than a lamb.

When Jesus was born, Mary "wrapped him in cloths" (Luke 2:7). Jewish mothers believed that if they wrapped up their babies firmly in bandages, then the baby's limbs would grow straight.

Jesus was circumcised, as were all other Jewish male babies, on the eighth day after his birth. This Jewish custom dated back to Abraham's time: "You are to undergo circumcision, and it will be the sign of the covenant" (Genesis 17:11-12).

Since Jesus was sinless, why was he baptized? Jesus was "born under law" (Galatians 4:4) and so it was right for him to be baptized "to fulfil all righteousness" (Matthew 3:15). This included being consecrated for his work.

In the Old Testament, priests were consecrated to God when they first started their ministry. This included washing, clothing and anointing the priests as described in Exodus 29:4-7.

Facts 2

Jesus told his disciples that they should preach the gospel to all nations and baptize believers. In the early church, baptism became a sign of being a follower of Jesus (Acts 16:33).

In the Bible, names were highly significant and gave information about the person. The name "Jesus" was chosen by God (Matthew 1:21). It means "the Lord saves".

In the Old Testament, God the Father was never called by the name which Jesus used of him, "Abba". Originally "Abba" was the Aramaic word used by a small child, which is equivalent to "Dad" or "Daddy".

Matthew's genealogy of Jesus, Matthew 1:1-17, shows that the blessing brought by Jesus, the Son of David, was not restricted to one race. Four women, all Gentiles (non-Jews) are mentioned: Tamar, Rahab, Ruth and Bathsheba.

Early Christians saw the "magi from the east," who were Gentiles, as a fulfilment of the words of Isaiah 60:3, "Nations will come to your light, and kings to the brightness of your dawn."

The Bible does not say how many wise men came to see Jesus. The traditional number of three came about because three gifts are mentioned.

King Herod was infamous for his cruelty and paranoia. He had any potential rival murdered. His favorite wife, Mariamne, all her male relatives, and some of his own sons were executed on his instructions.

At his birth, Jesus was put to sleep "in a manger" (Luke 2:7). The second century Christian writer, Justin Martyr, who was born in Palestine, said that Joseph found a cave which was used as a stable.

Shepherds still tend their flocks of sheep around Bethlehem. It has been pointed out that shepherds do not spend the night in the fields during winter. This indicates that Jesus may have been born in spring or summer.

To show that Jesus really was the promised and long-awaited Messiah, Matthew emphasizes Jesus' credentials and qualifications. He does this with over a hundred quotations from and allusions to the Old Testament.

Facts 3

In his Gospel, Mark portrays Jesus as the active and obedient Servant of God. Jesus' constant obedience is seen in the 47 occurrences in Mark's Gospel of the Greek word euthus, which means "immediately", "at once".

At his baptism, Jesus was publicly declared as God's Messiah (John 1:31-34). He identified himself with our sin in his baptism. Jesus had no sin of his own and so could become the substitute for the sins of humankind (2 Corinthians 5:21).

The four symbols in Ezekiel 1:10 and Revelation 4:7 have been applied to the four Gospels in the following way: the lion has been linked with Matthew's Gospel, the ox with Mark's Gospel, the man with Luke's Gospel, and the eagle with John's Gospel.

John's Gospel includes no parables, but has many metaphors about ordinary things, such as water, harvest, bread, light, a shepherd and a grain of wheat. These are used to convey spiritual truth.

The woman in Jesus' parable who lost one coin (Luke 15:8-10), would have been greatly upset since it was probably part of her dowry. A set of coins with holes drilled through them were strung together and worn on the forehead.

No one knows the precise date of Jesus' return. He said that this date was not known by the angels or even by himself, but only by the Father (Matthew 24:36).

Jesus knew the Scriptures (our Old Testament) thoroughly. But then so did most Jews. All Jewish boys (but not girls) went to the village school, held in the synagogue.

The level of literacy among the Jews was among the highest in the Roman Empire.

The record of Jesus' temptations in the desert (Matthew 4:1-11) must have originated with Jesus himself, as no one else was present. From this we deduce that Jesus knew that Satan was no illusion.

Jesus experienced temptation in a more profound and deeper way than anybody else. He alone endured every temptation right through to its depths without giving in part way through (Hebrews 4:15).

Facts 4

The Gospels tell us that Passover fell on a Friday in the year of Jesus' death. This fits the astronomical data for either A.D. 30 or A.D. 33, but not for A.D. 31 or A.D. 32.

Jesus' healing miracles were usually performed with a word of command. He had the kind of authority over disease that an officer has over subordinates. Twice Jesus "gave the order" without even seeing the patient.

Jesus never touched a patient in exorcisms, as he did in other healings. Exorcisms were done by word alone. The conflict was between the demon and Jesus, with the patient the battleground.

Outside Jesus' many healing miracles, the Gospels record a total of only eight other miracles. Five of these supplied food or drink to meet a real shortage. According to the Old Testament prophecy, the future Messiah would feed the hungry.

When Jesus silenced the storm at sea, he was proclaiming his divinity. The Jews were afraid of the sea, regarding it as out of human control and only God could control it (Psalm 89:9).

To the Jews, wealth was a sign of God's blessing. Thus, the disciples were astounded by Jesus' statement that it is extremely difficult for a wealthy man to enter heaven.

In John's Gospel, the Greek word for sign, semeion, is used to describe a miracle. The miracles were signs that the Messiah had come (Isaiah 35:5).

The Gospels record that Jesus had "compassion" on people. The Greek word used *splagchnizesthai* refers to the entrails, which were thought to be the seat of the emotions. When Jesus saw a widow's grief or a leper's deformity he was churned up inside with love and pity.

The strict rabbis (teachers) did not allow a rabbi to speak to a woman in public. A rabbi could not greet his own wife or daughter in a public place.

When Jesus spoke of a "good Samaritan," his words would have sounded absurd to all Jews. Jews believed that the only good Samaritan was a dead Samaritan.

Three Days that Changed the World

Quiz #1

1. Which Old Testament book has a verse in it which is taken as a Messianic prophecy about Jesus being betrayed by a friend?

2. In Matthew's Gospel, which two women were the first people to see Jesus alive again?

3. When Jesus said, "Eloi, Eloi, lama sabachthani?" which psalm was he quoting from?

4. True or false? As Jesus was being arrested, a disciple seized his sword and cut off the high priest's servants thumb and Jesus healed it.

5. True or false? Jesus was crucified between two criminals.

6. Pilate had a notice fastened to the cross stating the charge against Jesus: JESUS OF NAZARETH, THE KING OF THE JEWS. In what three languages was it written?

7. Why did the Jewish leaders object to this notice?

8. Which Old Testament book has a verse in it which is taken as a Messianic prophecy about Jesus being betrayed for 30 pieces of silver?

9. When Jesus cried out from the cross, "Eloi, Eloi, lama sabachthani?" who did the people think he was calling to?

10. According to Mark's Gospel, after the Sanhedrin condemned Jesus for blasphemy, what did the guards do?

11. True or false? After Jesus died there was an earthquake in Jerusalem.

12. Who taunted Jesus by saying that if he was the Son of God he should come down from the cross?

13. Who mocked Jesus by saying that they would believe in him if he came down from the cross?

14. Fill in the missing word uttered by those taunting Jesus: "He saved others, but he can't _____ himself."

15. True or false? Pilate's wife referred to Jesus as an "innocent man."

Answers

1. The book of Psalms (41:9) 2. Mary Magdalene and the other Mary 3. Psalm 22:1
4. False. The disciple cut off his ear (Matthew 26:51-52) 5. True (Mark 15:27) 6. Latin, Greek, and Aramaic
7. They wanted the notice to say, "This man claimed to be King of the Jews" 8. Zechariah 9. Elijah
10. They beat him 11. True (Matthew 27:51) 12. Those who passed by
13. The chief priests, the teachers of the law, and the elders 14. Save 15. True (Matthew 27:19)

Quiz #2

1. During the first Lord's Supper, who said, "Take and eat; this is my body"?

2. In the Garden of Gethsemane, which of his three disciples did Jesus tell to watch with him in prayer?

3. Which Old Testament book has a verse in it which is taken as a Messianic prophecy about Jesus being accused by false witnesses?

4. When the soldiers mocked Jesus, what did they put on his head?

5. When Jesus died, what was torn in two from top to bottom?

6. According to Matthew's Gospel, who rolled a big stone in front of the tomb after Jesus had been laid inside?

7. On what day of the week was Jesus crucified?

8. Who does Matthew say watched Jesus die "from a distance"?

9. True or false? Whenever the New Testament speaks of the "blood" of Jesus, it is referring to his death.

10. Who washed his hands in front of a crowd to show that he was not responsible for Jesus' death?

11. When the soldiers mocked Jesus, what item of clothing did they put on him?

12. Where was Jesus when a large crowd came to arrest him, armed to the teeth with clubs and swords?

13. After Jesus died, who thrust a spear into Jesus' side?

14. As well as blood, what also came out of Jesus' side after it had been pierced with a spear?

15. Name three of the five friends of Jesus who were standing at the foot of the cross.

Answers

1. Jesus 2. Peter, James, and John 3. The book of Psalms
4. A crown of thorns 5. The inner curtain of the temple 6. Joseph of Arimathea 7. Friday
8. Many women who had followed Jesus from Galilee 9. True 10. Pilate 11. A (scarlet) robe
12. The Garden of Gethsemane 13. A soldier 14. Water
15. His mother, his mother's sister, Mary, the wife of Clopas; Mary Magdalene; the apostle John

Quiz #3

1. When Judas and the guards came to the Garden of Gethsemane, by what prearranged sign did Judas identify Jesus in the darkness?

2. Which Old Testament book has a verse in it which is taken as a Messianic prophecy about Jesus being beaten?

3. Why did Jesus' enemies not arrest him when he was preaching in the temple?

4. True or false? As Jesus was dying, three soldiers divided Jesus' clothes between them.

5. Why did the soldiers cast lots to decide who should have Jesus' tunic?

6. When Jesus was praying in the Garden of Gethsemane, what did his disciples do?

7. What is the Thursday before Jesus' death now called?

8. What is the Friday when Jesus died now called?

9. Who said, "What I have written, I have written"?

10. During the Last Supper, what did Jesus give to Judas Iscariot?

11. In Acts, who preached a sermon which said that Jesus was nailed to a cross?

12. True or false? Jesus warned his disciples that they would all fall away and lose faith in him.

13. To whom did Jesus say, "Do not weep for me; weep for yourselves and for your children"?

14. According to Paul's letter to the Corinthians, what do those who are perishing think of the message of the cross?

15. How many silver coins did Judas receive for betraying Jesus?

Answers

1. By a kiss 2. Isaiah 53:4-5 3. Because they were afraid it would cause a riot 4. False. It was four (John 19:23) 5. Because they didn't want to tear it 6. Sleep 7. Maundy Thursday 8. Good Friday 9. Pontius Pilate 10. A piece of bread dipped in the wine 11. Peter 12. True (Mark 14:27) 13. The "daughters of Jerusalem" who were following him and crying as he walked through Jerusalem on the way to be crucified 14. They think it is foolishness 15. 30

Quiz #4

1. Who said, "I have betrayed innocent blood"?

2. True or false? At Jesus' trial the false witnesses against Jesus could not agree with each other.

3. Who said that it was expedient that one man should die for the people?

4. Which Old Testament book has a verse in it which is taken as a prophecy about Jesus being offered vinegar for his thirst?

5. In which of his letters does Paul mention the "offence" of the cross?

6. Why did the Jews ask Pilate to give orders for the soldiers to break the legs of the men on the crosses?

7. Who was the first person to see Jesus alive?

8. Which group of people who did not believe in any resurrection did Jesus rebuke, saying that they were in error and did not know the Scriptures or God's power?

9. Which Old Testament book has a verse in it which is taken as a Messianic prophecy about Jesus having his side pierced?

10. In which of his letters does Paul say that he longs to know the power of Christ's resurrection?

11. According to Luke's Gospel, when Jesus was first brought before Pilate, he was accused of subverting the nation. Name one of the two specific crimes he was said to have committed.

12. After the Lord's Supper, before going into the Garden of Gethsemane, what did Jesus and his disciples do?

13. True or false? John says in his Gospel that when Judas went to betray Jesus "it was night."

14. To whom did Jesus say, "You will see the Son of Man sitting at the right hand of the Mighty One"?

15. Name one of the two sons of the man who was forced to carry Jesus' cross.

Answers

1. Judas Iscariot 2. True (Mark 14:59) 3. Caiaphas 4. The book of Psalms 69:21 5. Galatians 5:21 6. To hasten their death, because they did not want the bodies to be on the crosses during the Sabbath, which began at six o'clock 7. Mary Magdalene 8. The Sadducees 9. Zechariah (12:10) 10. Letter to the Philippians 3:10 11. Opposing payment of taxes and proclaiming himself as King 12. They sang a hymn 13. True (John 13:30) 14. To the high priest 15. Alexander and Rufus

Quiz #5

1. When did Jesus say that his blood was poured out for the forgiveness of sins?

2. Fill in the missing words from Paul's first letter to the Corinthians: "If Christ has not been raised, your faith is _____ and you are still in your _____."

3. True or false? No event in ancient history is as well documented as Jesus' death and resurrection.

4. Who said to Jesus, "Even if all fall away on account of you, I never will".

5. True or false? Jesus said to Peter, "Before the owl hoots, you will disown me three times".

6. Name one of the two friends who invited a stranger to a meal and found it was the risen Jesus.

7. Where did Judas fling the money he had been given to betray Jesus?

8. Who picked up the money Judas returned?

9. What name was given to the field bought with the money Judas returned?

10. Which Old Testament book has a verse in it which is taken as a Messianic prophecy about lots being cast for Jesus' clothes?

11. Which prisoner was released instead of Jesus at the Passover Festival?

12. True or false? Jesus' body was placed in a new tomb.

13. What did the crowd say when Pilate asked them what he should do with Jesus?

14. Why did Jesus' disciples meet in a locked room after his death?

15. What was the first thing that happened to Jesus after he was condemned to death?

Answers

1. At his institution of the Lord's Supper 2. Futile, sins 3. True 4. Peter
5. False. Jesus said, "Before the rooster crows" (Matthew 26:34) 6. Cleopas 7. In the temple
8. The chief priests 9. The Field of Blood 10. The book of Psalms (22:18) 11. Barabbas
12. True (Matthew 27:59) 13. They yelled, "Crucify him!"
14. They were afraid of the leaders of the Jews 15. He was flogged

Quiz #6

1. When Pilate found that Jesus came from Galilee, what did he do, in an attempt to evade responsibility?

2. According to Mark's Gospel, what did Mary Magdalene, Mary the mother of James, and Salome bring to Jesus' tomb?

3. Who said, when he met the risen Jesus, "My Lord and my God"?

4. Why is Thomas often called "Doubting Thomas"?

5. When the soldiers mocked Jesus, what did they put in his hand?

6. What did the soldiers say to Jesus as they knelt in front of him and ridiculed him?

7. What had Jesus just been doing when he asked his disciples if they were still sleeping?

8. Which psalm has a verse in it which is taken as a Messianic prophecy about none of Jesus' bones being broken?

9. A man called Simon was forced to carry Jesus cross. Where did Simon come from?

10. Jesus was crucified at the third hour: what time was this?

11. For how many hours did Jesus hang on the cross?

12. What came over all the land from the sixth hour to the ninth hour?

13. When Jesus called out "My God, my God, why have you forsaken me?" what drink was he offered?

14. Where was Jesus when he told his disciples that the spirit was willing but the flesh was weak?

15. Why did Jesus' friends wait till Sunday before coming to anoint Jesus' body with spices?

Answers

1. Pilate sent Jesus to Herod Antipas, tetrarch (ruler) of Galilee **2.** Spices to anoint Jesus' body **3.** Thomas **4.** Because he said he would not believe Jesus was alive until he had seen and touched him **5.** A staff **6.** "Hail, King of the Jews" **7.** Praying **8.** Psalm 22 **9.** Cyrene **10.** Nine o'clock in the morning **11.** 6 hours **12.** Darkness **13.** Vinegar/wine vinegar **14.** In the Garden of Gethsemane **15.** Because to anoint with spices was regarded as work, and all work was forbidden on the Saturday, because it was the Sabbath

Quiz #7

1. Who helped Joseph of Arimathea take Jesus' body from the cross?

2. On the afternoon Jesus rose from the dead, he joined two friends as they were walking from Jerusalem to what village?

3. True or false? This village was five miles from Jerusalem.

4. Who said that he was certain that Jesus was a righteous man?

5. When three women went to visit Jesus' tomb, what question did they discuss on the way?

6. Which Old Testament figure did Jesus mention in connection with the Son of man being in the heart of the earth for three days and nights?

7. At Jesus' trial before the Sanhedrin, what accusation did the witnesses make?

8. Which Old Testament book has a verse in it which is taken as a Messianic prophecy about Jesus being buried with the rich?

9. When Judas went up to Jesus in the Garden of Gethsemane, how did Jesus address him?

10. After Jesus was laid in the tomb, why did his enemies go to Pilate?

11. True or false? According to Mark's Gospel, the women went to the tomb just after sunrise?

12. Peter and John both ran to Jesus' tomb, who reached it first?

13. Who was the first disciple to enter the tomb?

14. Who was the first disciple to believe that Jesus was alive?

15. Which two enemies became friends as a result of the arrest and trial of Jesus?

Answers

1. Nicodemus 2. Emmaus 3. False. It was about 7 miles (Luke 24:13) 4. A centurion 5. Who would roll the stone away from the tomb for them 6. Jonah 7. That Jesus would destroy the Temple of God and rebuild it in 3 days 8. Isaiah 9. Friend 10. They wanted a guard put on the tomb in case the disciples stole the body 11. True (Mark 16:2) 12. John 13. Peter 14. John 15. Pilate and Herod Antipas

Quiz #8

1. Who were the two disciples who followed at a distance after Jesus was arrested?

2. Where was Peter when a maid said to him, "You also were with that Nazarene"?

3. What was Peter doing when the maid spoke to him?

4. True or false? Peter twice denied knowing Jesus.

5. True or false? Peter's northern accent gave him away.

6. When Mary of Magdalene first saw the risen Jesus who did she think he was?

7. Who wrote about Jesus dying on a "tree"?

8. When Mary of Magdalene recognized the risen Jesus, what single Aramaic word did she say to him?

9. Name one of the two ways in which the tomb was made secure against thieves.

10. Who rolled back the stone at the entrance to the tomb and sat on it?

11. Complete these words of Jesus: "Simon, Simon, Satan has asked to…"

12. To make the disciples understand that dangerous times were facing them, what did Jesus tell them to sell in order to buy a sword?

13. The prophecy of which Old Testament prophet was fulfilled when a field was bought with the money Judas returned?

14. What did Jesus say to Herod Antipas?

15. After Jesus was arrested, how did John gain entry into the high priest's house?

Quiz #9

I. What was the first saying of Jesus from the cross?

2. What was the second saying of Jesus from the cross?

3. What was the third saying of Jesus from the cross?

4. What was the fourth saying of Jesus from the cross?

5. What was the fifth saying of Jesus from the cross?

6. What was the sixth saying of Jesus from the cross?

7. What was the seventh saying of Jesus from the cross?

8. In which of his letters did Paul write that Christ was raised from the dead through the glory of the Father?

9. According to Luke, what did Jesus tell his disciples to pray for as they arrived at the Garden of Gethsemane?

10. Who strengthened Jesus as he prayed in the Garden of Gethsemane?

11. True of false? As Jesus prayed in the Garden of Gethsemane sweat like drops of blood fell from him.

12. Who wrote that Jesus was a lamb without blemish or defect?

13. After Peter disowned Jesus three times, who turned and looked straight at him?

14. What is the Sunday on which Jesus rose from the dead now called?

15. How many legions of angels did Jesus say he could call to his assistance?

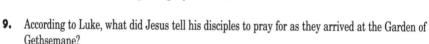

Answers

1. "Father, forgive them; for they do not know what they are doing" (Luke 23:34).
2. "I tell you the truth, Today you will be with me in paradise" (Luke 23:43).
3. "Dear woman here is your son," and to the disciple, "Here is your mother!" (John 19:26).
4. "My God, My God, why have you forsaken me?" (Mark 15:34). **5.** "I am thirsty." (John 19:28).
6. "It is finished" (John 19:30). **7.** "Father, into your hands I commit my spirit" (Luke 23:46). **8.** Romans
9. Pray not to fall into temptation **10.** An angel **11.** True (Luke 22:44) **12.** Peter **13.** Jesus **14.** Easter Day **15.** 12

32

Quiz #10

1. Which Old Testament book has a verse in it which is taken as a Messianic prophecy about Jesus being killed with sinners?

2. After Peter denied knowing Jesus, what did he do?

3. After Judas betrayed Jesus and returned the money, what did he do?

4. Which Old Testament book was Jesus quoting from when he spoke about a shepherd being struck and the sheep being scattered?

5. True or false? Luke records that Jesus was blindfolded when the soldiers mocked him.

6. Who declared that Jesus had done nothing to deserve death?

7. According to Luke, who told the women who visited Jesus' grave that he was not there but had risen?

8. When the women passed on the message, why did the disciples not believe them?

9. Who stood outside Jesus' tomb crying?

10. True or false? On the day he rose from the dead, Jesus appeared to Peter, and spoke to him privately.

11. Who did the risen Jesus tell to feed his lambs?

12. Which psalm has a verse in it which is taken as a Messianic prophecy about Jesus having his hands and feet pierced?

13. What did Jesus do to prove to his disciples that he was not a ghost?

14. Fill in the missing word from the angels' message to the women: "Why do you look for the living among the _____?"

15. True or false? The Roman soldiers reported to Pilate that an angel had petrified them.

Answers

1. Isaiah 53:12 **2.** Peter went out and cried bitterly **3.** Judas killed himself **4.** Zechariah 13:2 **5.** True (Luke 22:64)
6, 7. 2 angels **8.** "Their words seemed like nonsense" **9.** Mary Magdalene
10. True (Luke 24:34) **11.** Peter **12.** Psalm 22 **13.** He ate of a piece of cooked fish **14.** Dead
15. False. The Jewish leaders bribed them and they reported that the disciples had stolen the body (Matthew 28:13)

33

Quiz #11

1. What did John note about the strips of linen that had been around Jesus' body and the burial cloth that had been around his head?

2. What were Jesus' first words when he greeted his disciples on the evening of the day he rose from the dead?

3. When did Mary realize that the man in the garden was Jesus?

4. When did the two disciples in Emmaus realize that the stranger was Jesus?

5. How long did Thomas have to wait before he saw Jesus for himself?

6. In his conversation with Thomas, who did Jesus say are the blessed people?

7. What were the disciples arguing about during the Last Supper?

8. According to Mark, why did the women say nothing about the angels' message?

9. Fill in the missing words from Jesus' conversation with the two friends on Sunday afternoon: "He explained to them what was said in all the _____ concerning himself."

10. According to Mark's Gospel, as Jesus was being nailed to the cross, what was he offered?

11. To whom did Jesus say, "Today you will be with me in Paradise"?

12. Who was the high priest who condemned Jesus?

13. The Sanhedrin found Jesus guilty of what crime?

14. According to Jewish law, what was the punishment for this crime?

15. What relation was Annas to Caiaphas?

Answers

1. The burial cloth was folded up by itself, separate from the strips of linen 2. "Peace be with you" 3. When Jesus said her name 4. When he sat down for a meal with them, said grace, and broke the bread 5. A week 6. "Those who have not seen and yet have believed" 7. Which of them was the greatest 8. Because they were afraid 9. Scriptures 10. Wine mixed with myrrh 11. To the thief who said, "Remember me when you come into your kingdom" 12. Caiaphas 13. Blasphemy 14. Death 15. Father-in-law

Facts 1

Isaiah chapter 53 gives astonishing details about the death of Jesus. The servant is pierced and wounded, taken away by oppression and led as a lamb to the slaughter. His grave is "with the rich".

Gethsemane, which means "oil-press," was a garden, perhaps an enclosed olive orchard, on the slopes of the Mount of Olives. It was a favorite rendezvous for Jesus and his disciples.

In biblical times, the table at which people ate a meal was in a U shape, with the host in the middle of the U. The guests reclined on couches, leaning on their left elbow, with their right hand free.

At the Last Supper, John, reclining at Jesus' right hand, would have been very close to him, close enough to speak privately without anyone hearing (John 13:25).

If the host wanted to show special friendship to a guest, he gave a piece of food taken from the main dish. It has been suggested that in this way Jesus was making a last appeal to Judas (John 13:26).

When Jesus shouted out from the cross "It is finished," it was not a cry of loneliness or defeat, but a cry of achievement. He had accomplished what he had been born to do.

The Old Testament prefigures the cross of Jesus. God provided the Old Testament sacrifices (Leviticus 1–7) as a pointer to the way of salvation. The New Testament writers often refer to Jesus' death as a "sacrifice."

When Jesus told Peter and John to prepare for the Passover meal, they were to look out for a man carrying a jar of water. This was a prearranged secret sign. Carrying water was women's work, so men very rarely carried a jar of water.

Crucifixions were commonplace in Roman times. Because it was a dishonorable form of death Roman citizens were not crucified, except for treason.

Before being crucified, criminals were scourged (beaten) with a whip. The thongs of the whip were barbed with pieces of lead or bone. This punishment caused considerable bleeding and sometimes death.

Criminals facing crucifixion walked through the city carrying the cross-piece. A placard giving the reason for the conviction was hung around the neck, or carried on ahead, and then fastened to the cross.

Facts 2

One of the objections raised against the resurrection appearances of the risen Jesus is that they could have been hallucinations. Hallucinations, however, are not experienced by over 500 people at the same time (1 Corinthians 15:6).

Jerusalem was transformed during the time of the Passover. The population of Jerusalem may have been about 30,000, but there were six times as many people in Jerusalem during the Passover.

As a terrible warning to other would-be criminals, people were crucified outside the walls of cities, in public places. Hence the reference in Mark's Gospel to "those who passed by."

Sometimes a victim took days to die. This accounts for Pilate's surprise when Joseph asked for Jesus' body.

The Roman writer, Cicero, wrote, "Crucifixion is indeed one of the most abominable torments that the very inventive genius of torture has imagined."

To speak of the "trial" of Jesus is an oversimplification. The Gospels record five different examinations of Jesus.

Jesus first "trial" was held in the home of Annas, before a hastily gathered group of members of the Sanhedrin. The witnesses did not agree, so Annas asked Jesus directly if he was the Son of God. His reply was taken to be blasphemy.

Jesus' second hearing was held at dawn, before the full Sanhedrin, the supreme court of the Jews, presided over by Caiaphas. At this trial, Jesus was officially condemned to death.

Since Roman law did not allow the Jews to carry out the death sentence, Jesus was taken to Pilate for the third hearing. Blasphemy was not a crime under Roman law, so the Jews submitted the charge of revolutionary activity.

Faced with Jesus' obvious innocence, Pilate tried to avoid responsibility by sending Jesus to Herod Antipas, the tetrarch of Galilee, who was in Jerusalem for the Passover. This fourth hearing was a farce. No judicial proceedings are recorded.

Herod returned Jesus to Pilate. After further questioning, Pilate's verdict was that Jesus was innocent but when the Jews threatened to report Pilate to Caesar, he ordered Jesus' execution.

Facts 3

Jewish law required that there had to be a 24 hour delay between the passing of a verdict of guilty and the sentence of death. This law was broken by the Sanhedrin.

Jewish law did not allow the charge to be altered when a case was passed on to the Roman authorities. But the charge against Jesus was changed from blasphemy to insurrection.

It was also laid down that trials requiring the death penalty should not be held on a feast day or the day preceding a feast day.

Annas was the father-in-law of the high priest. He himself had been high priest until a Roman prefect had deposed him 15 years earlier. Many Jews still regarded him as high priest.

The "scarlet robe" of Matthew 27:28, a parody of the emperor's purple robe, would have been a soldier's red cape. The "staff" represented a royal scepter and the "crown of thorns" a royal crown.

In dreadful mockery, the soldiers knelt in front of Jesus. Their "Hail, king of the Jews!" (Matthew 27:29) parodied the formal greeting "Ave Caesar".

Most victims of crucifixion eventually fell into unconsciousness, but Jesus remained fully conscious until the end. He died suddenly with a prayer.

The wine mixed with myrrh which was offered to Jesus and which he declined (Mark 15:23) was a narcotic drink. According to the Babylonian Talmud, kind ladies from Jerusalem provided this drink to numb the senses of the victim.

Each new Jewish day begins, not at dawn, but at sunset. The Sabbath would therefore have started at six in the evening on the day Jesus was crucified, hence the haste.

Pilate had his headquarters at Caesarea. He was in Jerusalem for the Passover Festival, a time of potential unrest.

When in Jerusalem, Pilate stayed in the Praetorium, the official Jerusalem residence of the procurator, and the Roman military headquarters (Matthew 27:27).

Facts 4

It was not usual to bury the bodies of criminals. They were left for the dogs and vultures to eat.

The word "paradise" comes from a Persian word meaning "a walled garden." In Persia, it was a special honour to be invited to walk in the garden with the king.

A letter from the first century by a non-Christian Syrian writer, Mara bar Serapion, a Syrian sage, refers to the folly of the Jews in "executing their wise king."

If the body of Jesus was really in the tomb all the time, the authorities would not have needed to say that the disciples had stolen the body. They could simply have produced it.

Jesus' resurrection was quite different from the coming back to life of Lazarus. Lazarus had to die again. Jesus' resurrection shows that he had passed through into another dimension of life.

When the risen Jesus met with his disciples, he told them to look at his feet as well as his hands, indicating that his feet had also been nailed to the cross.

In the time of Jesus, a dead body was laid on a stone shelf in a cave with a stone in front of the entrance. After about a year, when only the bones were left, they were collected and put into an ossuary (a stone box).

Jewish law did not allow women to act as witnesses in a law court. But the first witnesses to Jesus' resurrection, with instructions to pass on the message, were women. No Jew would have invented this.

Eye-witness accounts of an incident usually differ slightly as witnesses pick out different details. This is a mark of authenticity. In modern police investigations, detectives are suspicious of stories that are too similar. This applies to the accounts of the resurrection given in the Gospel.

The "curtain of the temple" separated the Holy Place from the Most Holy Place. Under Jewish law, only the high priest could go through, and then only once a year.

The tearing of the curtain symbolizes the destroying of the barrier between God and men.

100 Key Events

Quiz #1

1. *The Creation* On what day did God create man?

2. *The Creation* True or false? God made the fish, the birds and the animals on day five.

3. *The Creation* Fill in the missing word: "God said, 'Let us make man in our ___.' "

4. *The Fall* From which tree in the garden were Adam and Eve not allowed to eat?

5. *The Fall* Which creature tempted Eve?

6. *The Fall* Eve was persuaded to eat the fruit for three reasons: name two.

7. *Sin Is Passed On* Who hated his brother?

8. *Sin Is Passed On* What offering did Abel make?

9. *Sin Is Passed On* Fill in the missing word: God said, "Your brother's ___ cries out to me."

10. *The Flood* Who was described as "a righteous man, blameless among the people of his time, and he walked with God"?

11. *The Flood* Fill in one of the missing words: "Now the earth was ___ in God's sight and full of ___."

12. *The Flood* How many humans were kept safe in the ark?

13. *The Tower of Babel* Before the tower of Babel was built how many languages were there in the world?

14. *The Tower of Babel* What was the name of the plain in Babylonia where the tower of Babel was built?

15. *The Tower of Babel* Fill in the missing words: "They used ___ instead of stone, and ___ for mortar."

Answers

1. The sixth day **2.** False. God made the fish on day 5, and birds and animals on day 6
3. Image (Genesis 1:26) **4.** The tree that gives knowledge of what is good and bad (Genesis 2:17)
5. A serpent **6.** The fruit of the tree was good for food; pleasing to the eye; desirable for gaining knowledge (Genesis 3:6) **7.** Cain **8.** A firstborn lamb **9.** Blood **10.** Noah **11.** Corrupt and violence
12. 8 **13.** "The whole world had one language" **14.** Shinar **15.** Brick and bitumen

Quiz #2

1. *Abraham's Call* Who was Abraham's father?

2. *Abraham's Call* Where was Abraham living when God told him to leave his country?

3. *Abraham's Call* True or false? Abraham took Lot, who was his cousin, with him when he left his country.

4. *The Covenant* Fill in one of the missing words: "Do not be afraid, Abram. I am your ___, your very great ___."

5. *The Covenant* The Lord told Abraham to count the stars. Why?

6. *The Covenant* What was the sign of God's covenant (agreement) with Abraham?

7. *Sacrifice of Isaac* Who said, "God himself will provide the lamb for the burnt offering"?

8. *Sacrifice of Isaac* When Abraham prepared to sacrifice Isaac, he bound Isaac and placed him on the altar. What was between Isaac and the altar?

9. *Sacrifice of Isaac* After Abraham sacrificed a ram in place of his son Isaac, what name did Abraham give to that place?

10. *Isaac and Rebekah* Who did Abraham entrust with the responsibility of finding a wife for his son Isaac?

11. *Isaac and Rebekah* Where did this person place his hand as Abraham made him swear that he would not let Isaac marry a daughter of the Canaanites?

12. *Isaac and Rebekah* What did Abraham's servant pray that the girl who met him and his camels would do if she was the one who was going to become Isaac's wife?

13. *Birth of Esau and Jacob* What did God say to Rebekah when she asked, "Why is this happening to me?" when the babies jostled within her?

14. *Birth of Esau and Jacob* Which of the twin boys was born first: Esau or Jacob?

15. *Birth of Esau and Jacob* Fill in the missing words: "Isaac, who had a taste for wild game, loved ___, but Rebekah loved ___."

Answers

1. Terah **2.** Haran **3.** False. Abraham did take Lot, but Lot was Abraham's nephew
4. Shield and reward **5.** Because that would be the number of his offspring **6.** Circumcision
7. Abraham, answering Isaac's question, "Where is the lamb for the burnt offering?" **8.** Wood **9.** The Lord Will Provide
10. Abraham's servant **11.** Under Abraham's thigh **12.** She would offer to water his camels
13. "Two nations are in your womb" (Genesis 25:23) **14.** Esau **15.** Esau, Jacob

Quiz #3

1. ***Jacob Gets The Blessing*** What type of stew did Esau sell his birthright for?

2. ***Jacob Gets The Blessing*** True or false? Jacob tricked his father into giving him his blessing by allowing him to feel his smooth skin.

3. ***Jacob Gets The Blessing*** Fill in the missing words: "Esau ___ ___ ___ against Jacob because of the blessing his father had given him."

4. ***Jacob's Sons*** What did Jacob's sons became the founders of?

5. ***Jacob's Sons*** When Jacob thought that Laban had given him his daughter Rachel to marry, which of Laban's daughters had in fact been given to Jacob?

6. ***Jacob's Sons*** True or false? Reuben was Jacob's firstborn son.

7. ***Joseph's Dreams*** When Joseph told his brothers about his first dream, how did they react?

8. ***Joseph's Dreams*** In Joseph's second dream, what replaced the eleven sheaves of corn?

9. ***Joseph's Dreams*** In Joseph's second dream, what did the sun and the moon stand for?

10. ***Joseph Into Egypt*** Which of Joseph's brothers tried to stop Joseph from being sold?

11. ***Joseph Into Egypt*** For how many shekels of silver did Joseph's brothers sell him?

12. ***Joseph Into Egypt*** True or false? The Ishmaelites took Joseph to Israel.

13. ***Joseph's Family Go To Egypt*** Pharaoh dreamt of the same number of fat cows, thin cows, good ears of corn and thin ears of corn. How many were there each time?

14. ***Joseph's Family Go To Egypt*** Which of Jacob's sons did Joseph keep in Egypt when his remaining brothers returned to Jacob?

15. ***Joseph's Family Go To Egypt*** For how long did the Egyptians mourn Jacob?

Answers

1. Lentil stew 2. False. Jacob had the smooth parts of his skin covered with goatskin, so Isaac would think he was Esau 3. Held a grudge 4. The 12 tribes of Israel 5. Leah 6. True 7. They hated Joseph even more 8. 11 stars 9. His father and his mother 10. Reuben (Genesis 29:32) 11. 20 shekels of silver 12. False. The Ishmaelites took Joseph to Egypt (Genesis 37:28) 13. 7 14. Benjamin 15. 70 days

Quiz #4

1. **Birth of Moses** Why was Moses hidden among the reeds along the bank of the River Nile?

2. **Birth of Moses** What was Moses' waterproof basket made out of?

3. **Birth of Moses** Who discovered the baby among the reeds?

4. **Moses Kills A Man** Why did Moses kill the Egyptian?

5. **Moses Kills A Man** On the following day who did Moses stop a fight between?

6. **Moses Kills A Man** True or false? Moses ran away from Pharaoh and fled to Jerusalem.

7. **The Burning Bush** Fill in the missing words: "I am the God of your father, the God of ___, the God of ___ and the God of ___."

8. **The Burning Bush** True or false? Moses saw that the bush was on fire but it did not burn up.

9. **The Burning Bush** When Moses heard the Lord speaking to him and saw the burning bush why did he hide his face?

10. **The Plagues and Passover** What relation of Moses did the Lord provide to speak for Moses to the Israelites?

11. **The Plagues and Passover** What was the first plague?

12. **The Plagues and Passover** As a result of the second plague, what would Pharaoh find in his ovens and kneading troughs?

13. **Crossing The Red Sea** Why did the Israelites eat unleavened bread (bread without yeast) on the eve of the Exodus?

14. **Crossing The Red Sea** A pillar of fire shed light for the Israelites by night, what guided them by day?

15. **Crossing The Red Sea** True or false? The Israelites crossed through the sea on dry ground, with a wall of water on both sides.

Answers

1. Because Pharaoh had ordered that all Hebrew baby boys should be killed at birth **2.** Papyrus
3. Pharaoh's daughter **4.** Because he was beating the Hebrew slave **5.** 2 Hebrews
6. False, Moses fled to Midian (Exodus 2:15) **7.** Abraham, Isaac and Jacob **8.** True (Exodus 3:2)
9. Because Moses was afraid to look at God **10.** His brother Aaron **11.** A plague of blood **12.** Frogs
13. Because they did not have time to prepare food for themselves (Exodus 12:39) **14.** A pillar of cloud
15. True (Exodus 14:29)

Quiz #5

1. **Receiving The Law** What is the eighth commandment in the Ten Commandments?

2. **Receiving The Law** Where was Moses when he received the Ten Commandments?

3. **Receiving The Law** On how many stone tablets were the Ten Commandments written?

4. **The Tabernacle** True or false? The upright frames of the tabernacle were made from mahogany.

5. **The Tabernacle** Fill in the missing word: "Make the tabernacle with ten ___ of finely twisted linen and blue, purple and scarlet yarn."

6. **The Tabernacle** Why did the Israelites have to bring clear oil of pressed olives to the tabernacle?

7. **Food In The Wilderness** What meat did the Israelites eat in the desert?

8. **Food In The Wilderness** True or false? The Israelites were allowed to collect enough manna for two days on the sixth day, so they did not have to collect any on the Sabbath.

9. **Food In The Wilderness** Except for the manna collected on the sixth day, what happened to any manna that was not eaten on the day it was collected?

10. **Spies Enter and Return** Name two of the three kinds of fruit which the spies brought back from Canaan.

11. **Spies Enter and Return** Most of the spies who returned from Canaan said they felt like what, in their own eyes, and in the eyes of the Nephilim?

12. **Spies Enter and Return** Who were the only two spies to say to Moses that they should enter Canaan and attack the people?

13. **Joshua** Who did Joshua take over from as the commander-in-chief of the Israelites?

14. **Joshua** Fill in the missing words: "Do not let this ___ ___ ___ ___ depart from your mouth; meditate on it day and night, so that you may be careful to do everything written in it."

15. **Joshua** How many spies did Joshua secretly send in to Jericho to spy out the land?

Answers

1. You shall not steal **2.** On Mount Sinai **3.** 2
4. False. The upright frames were made of acacia wood (Exodus 26:15) **5.** Curtains
6. The oil was used to light the lamps **7.** Quails **8.** True (Exodus 16:22) **9.** The manna became full of maggots
10. Grapes, figs and pomegranates (Numbers 13:23) **11.** Grasshoppers (Numbers 13:33)
12. Caleb and Joshua **13.** Moses **14.** Book of the Law **15.** 2 spies

Quiz #6

1. **David and Jonathan** True or false? The deep friendship and love David and Jonathan had for each other was said to surpass that of a man for a woman.

2. **David and Jonathan** Fill in the missing words: "And Jonathan made David reaffirm his oath out of ____ for him, because he ____ him as he ____ himself."

3. **David and Jonathan** True or false? David said to Jonathan, "Whatever you want me to do, I'll do for you."

4. **David as King** At which town was David anointed king over Judah?

5. **David as King** How old was David when he became king over Israel as well as Judah?

6. **David as King** For how many years did David reign in Jerusalem?

7. **Capture of Jerusalem** Who said to David about Jerusalem: "You will not get in here; even the blind and the lame can ward you off"?

8. **Capture of Jerusalem** Fill in the missing words: "Anyone who conquers the Jebusites will have to use the ____ ____."

9. **Capture of Jerusalem** Who was the father of the following children, and where were they born? Shammua, Shabob, Nathan, Solmon, Ibhar, Elishua, Nepheg, Japhia, Elishama, Eliada and Eliphelet.

10. **The Ark Taken to Jerusalem** What happened to Uzzah after touching the ark of God?

11. **The Ark Taken to Jerusalem** When Michal, Saul's daughter, saw David leaping and dancing before the Lord as the ark of God entered Jerusalem, how did she react?

12. **The Ark Taken to Jerusalem** What did the ark symbolize?

13. **Bathsheba** True or false? David did not know the name of the beautiful woman who he watched bathing.

14. **Bathsheba** To whom was Bathsheba married?

15. **Bathsheba** What happened to Uriah in the next battle after David had ordered that he should be left alone in the front line?

Answers

1. True (2 Samuel 1:26) **2.** Love, loved, loved **3.** False. This was said by Jonathan to David (1 Samuel 20:4)
4. Hebron **5.** 30 years old (2 Samuel 5:4) **6.** 33 years **7.** The Jebusites **8.** Water shaft
9. They were all David's children who were born in Jerusalem
10. God struck him down and he died beside the ark **11.** Michal despised David **12.** The presence of God
13. True (2 Samuel 11:2-3) **14.** Uriah the Hittite **15.** Uriah was killed

Quiz #7

1. *Elijah on Mount Carmel* Who opposed Elijah on Mount Carmel?

2. *Elijah on Mount Carmel* The true God was the one who answered by what?

3. *Elijah on Mount Carmel* Fill in the missing words: "A cloud as small as a ____ ____ is rising from the seas."

4. *The Still Small Voice* On which mountain was Elijah when God said, "Go and stand on the mountain in the presence of the Lord"?

5. *The Still Small Voice* What was the first thing that Elijah heard on the mountain?

6. *The Still Small Voice* The second thing that Elijah observed on the mountain was an earthquake, what was the third thing?

7. *Elisha and Naaman* What was Elisha doing as Elijah threw his cloak over him?

8. *Elisha and Naaman* What was the matter with commander Naaman?

9. *Elisha and Naaman* Who said, "If only my master would see the prophet who is in Samaria! He would cure him"?

10. *Hezekiah* Who said, "The god of Hezekiah will not rescue his people from my hand"?

11. *Hezekiah* Which prophet advised Hezekiah to trust God?

12. *Hezekiah* What happened to Sennacherib when he returned home in disgrace?

13. *Isaiah's Vision of God* As a result of his vision of God, Isaiah became a prophet: Isaiah dates it by the death of which king?

14. *Isaiah's Vision of God* Fill in the missing words: "____, ____, ____ is the Lord Almighty; the whole earth is full of his glory."

15. *Isaiah's Vision of God* What touched Isaiah's lips in this vision?

Answers

15. A live coal from the altar.
12. Some of his sons murdered him in the temple of his god **13.** King Uzziah **14.** Holy, holy, holy
10. An officer in King Sennacherib's army **11.** Isaiah
9. A young Israelite maidservant of Naaman's wife who had been captured from Israel
4. Mount Horeb (Sinai) **5.** A strong wind **6.** A fire **7.** Driving a yoke of oxen **8.** He had leprosy
1. The prophets of Baal **2.** The God who answered by fire **3.** man's hand

Quiz #8

1. *Josiah Finds the Law* How old was Josiah when the Book of the Law was found?

2. *Josiah Finds the Law* What was the name of the high priest who discovered the Book of the Law?

3. *Josiah Finds the Law* True or false? When Josiah heard the Book of the Law read he tore his robes.

4. *Amos Thrown Out of Bethel* Where was Amos living when God told him to prophecy in Israel?

5. *Amos Thrown Out of Bethel* Fill in the missing words: "I will turn your religious feasts into ____ and all your singing into ____."

6. *Amos Thrown Out of Bethel* To show the people how crooked they had become, Amos pictured God as a builder, holding what?

7. *Hosea and His Wife* What was the name of Hosea's wife?

8. *Hosea and His Wife* About whom did Hosea complain, "There is no faithfulness, no love, no acknowledgment of God in the land"?

9. *Hosea and His Wife* Fill in the missing words: "I will ____ their waywardness and ____ them freely."

10. *Samaria Destroyed* True or false? Samaria was the capital of the southern kingdom of Judah.

11. *Samaria Destroyed* What was the name of the King of Assyria who defeated Samaria in 722 B.C.?

12. *Samaria Destroyed* Fill in the missing words: "They sacrificed their ____ and ____ in the fire."

13. *Fall of Jerusalem* Which king captured Jerusalem in 587 B.C.?

14. *Fall of Jerusalem* To which land were the people of Judah deported?

15. *Fall of Jerusalem* Which exile from Jerusalem interpreted dreams for the king of Babylon?

---

13. King Nebuchadnezzar 14. Babylon 15. Daniel

10. False. Samaria was capital of the northern kingdom of Israel 11. Sennacherib 12. Sons, daughters

6. A plumb line 7. Gomer 8. The Israelites 9. Heal, love

1. 26 years old 2. Hilkiah 3. True (2 Kings 22:11) 4. Tekoa (in southern Judah) 5. Mourning, weeping

Answers

Quiz #9

1. ***Birth of Jesus*** How many children had Mary had before she gave birth to Jesus?

2. ***Birth of Jesus*** Who said, to whom, "Today in the town of David a Savior has been born to you; he is Christ the Lord"?

3. ***Birth of Jesus*** Fill in the missing words: "So they hurried off and found ___ and ___, and the ___, who was lying in the manger."

4. ***Visit of Wise Men*** True or false? There were only three wise men.

5. ***Visit of Wise Men*** Where were the wise men when they asked, "Where is the one who has been born king of the Jews?"?

6. ***Visit of Wise Men*** What were the three gifts the wise men gave to Jesus?

7. ***Death of Herod*** How did Joseph know that Herod was set to kill Jesus?

8. ***Death of Herod*** Where did Joseph, Mary and Jesus flee to as refugees?

9. ***Death of Herod*** After Joseph heard that Herod was dead, where did he settle down with Mary and Jesus?

10. ***Jesus at Twelve in the Temple*** True or false? Jesus stayed behind in Jerusalem because he wanted to have a good look at Herod's magnificent temple.

11. ***Jesus at Twelve in the Temple*** To whom did Jesus say: "Didn't you know I had to be in my Father's house?"

12. ***Jesus at Twelve in the Temple*** Fill in the missing words: "And Jesus ___ in wisdom and stature, and in favor with ___ and ___." (Luke 2:52)

13. ***John the Baptist*** To whom did this fiery preacher say, "You brood of vipers!"?

14. ***John the Baptist*** Fill in the missing words: "He will baptize you with the ___ ___ and with ___." (Matthew 3:11)

15. ***John the Baptist*** True or false? John wore clothes made of sheepskin.

Answers

1. None. She was a virgin 2. The angel, to the shepherds 3. Mary, Joseph, baby
4. False. We are not told how many wise men there were 5. In Jerusalem
6. Gold, frankincense (incense) and myrrh 7. The Lord warned him in a dream 8. Egypt 9. Nazareth
10. False. Jesus listened to and asked questions of the teachers in the temple courts (Luke 2:41-50)
11. Mary 12. Grew, God, men 13. The Pharisees and Sadducees (religious leaders) 14. Holy Spirit, fire
15. False. They were made of camel's hair (John 3:4)

Quiz #10

1. **Jesus' Baptism** Did John the Baptist baptize Jesus, or did Jesus baptize John the Baptist?

2. **Jesus' Baptism** What did people see coming down on Jesus after he was baptized?

3. **Jesus' Baptism** Where did the voice come from which said, "This is my Son, whom I love; with him I am well pleased"?

4. **Jesus' Temptations** True or false? In Jesus' first temptation, the devil offered him some roast lamb to eat.

5. **Jesus' Temptations** Fill in the missing word which Jesus spoke to the devil: "Do not put the Lord your God to the ___."

6. **Jesus' Temptations** In the third temptation, did the devil take Jesus up a very high mountain or out in a boat on the Sea of Galilee?

7. **John The Baptist Arrested** True or false? After his temptation, Jesus stayed in the south; he only moved to Galilee when John was arrested.

8. **John The Baptist Arrested** Why was John arrested?

9. **John The Baptist Arrested** Why did King Herod keep John in prison instead of immediately killing him?

10. **Call of First Disciples** Which of Jesus' twelve disciples was Peter's brother?

11. **Call of First Disciples** About whom did Jesus say: "Here is a true Israelite, in whom there is nothing false"?

12. **Call of First Disciples** Who is the only disciple whose martyrdom is recorded in the pages of the Bible?

13. **First Miracle** True or false? Mary was not present at the marriage feast in Cana.

14. **First Miracle** What instruction did Jesus give to the servants concerning the lack of wine?

15. **First Miracle** Fill in the missing words: "He thus revealed his ___, and his disciples put their ___ in him."

Answers

1. John the Baptist baptized Jesus **2.** The Holy Spirit in the form of a dove **3.** It was "a voice from heaven" **4.** False. Jesus was tempted to turn stones into bread **5.** Test **6.** A very high mountain **7.** True (Mark 1:14) **8.** Because John told Herod Antipas that his marriage to his brother's wife was wrong **9.** Herod was afraid to kill him because he was a righteous man **10.** Andrew **11.** Nathanael (Bartholomew) **12.** James the brother of John: he was beheaded by Herod Agrippa I **13.** False. It was Mary who told Jesus that the hosts had run out of wine (John 2:1-3) **14.** "Fill the jars with water." **15.** Glory, faith

49

Quiz #11

1. **Jesus in Nazareth** True or false? When Jesus visited his home town of Nazareth during his public ministry he was driven out of the town.

2. **Jesus in Nazareth** Fill in the missing words: "He has anointed me to preach ___ ___ to the poor."

3. **Jesus in Nazareth** Where did Jesus go on the Sabbath "As his custom was"?

4. **Sermon on the Mount** Are there six, eight, or twelve beatitudes in the Sermon on the Mount?

5. **Sermon on the Mount** Fill in the missing words: "___ your enemies and ___ for those who persecute you."

6. **Sermon on the Mount** When Jesus told people not to worry, what did he tell people to look at?

7. **Jesus Heals on the Sabbath** Which group of people were furious with Jesus when he healed a man with a shriveled arm on the Sabbath?

8. **Jesus Heals on the Sabbath** Who said, "There are six days for work. So come and be healed on those days, not on the Sabbath"?

9. **Jesus Heals on the Sabbath** Fill in the missing word: "You ___! Doesn't each of you on the Sabbath untie his ox to give it water?"

10. **Feeding of 5,000** When Jesus fed 5,000 people, how many loaves of bread and how many fish did the disciples have to start with?

11. **Feeding of 5,000** Did the figure "five thousand" include women and children, or did it just refer to men?

12. **Feeding of 5,000** After everyone had eaten, how many baskets full of leftovers were there?

13. **Peter's Declaration** When Peter said to Jesus, "You are the Christ, the Son of the living God," what question had Jesus just asked his disciples?

14. **Peter's Declaration** Fill in the missing words spoken by Jesus to Peter: "I will give you the keys of the ___ of ___."

15. **Peter's Declaration** Just after Peter's declaration, to whom did Jesus say, "Get behind me, Satan!"?

Quiz # 12

1. **Transfiguration** How many of Jesus' disciples witnessed his transfiguration?

2. **Transfiguration** Which two people from the Old Testament were seen at Jesus' transfiguration?

3. **Transfiguration** Fill in the missing word: "His face shone like the ___."

4. **Private Teaching** When the disciples argued about which of them was the greatest whom did Jesus stand beside him as he taught his disciples about true greatness?

5. **Private Teaching** Fill in the missing word: "For he who is ___ among you all—he is greatest."

6. **Private Teaching** True or false? When John told Jesus that they had tried to stop a man from driving out demons in his name because he was not one of them, Jesus replied, "Do not stop him."

7. **Raising of Lazarus** Fill in the missing words: "I am the resurrection and the ___. He who believes in me will ___, even though he dies."

8. **Raising of Lazarus** Was Lazarus the brother of Mary and Martha, or the brother of James and John?

9. **Raising of Lazarus** For how many days had Lazarus been dead when Jesus arrived at his tomb?

10. **Palm Sunday** On which animal did Jesus ride as he went into Jerusalem on the day we now call Palm Sunday?

11. **Palm Sunday** Which articles of clothing did some of the crowd throw on the ground in front of Jesus?

12. **Palm Sunday** Fill in the missing word: "Blessed is the ___ who comes in the name of the Lord!"

13. **Judas Goes to the Priests** True or false? Judas Isacariot, who betrayed Jesus, was one of his twelve disciples.

14. **Judas Goes to the Priests** Did Judas go to the chief priests and say he could betray Jesus, or did the chief priests ask Judas to do this?

15. **Judas Goes to the Priests** Finish the sentence: "[Judas] watched for an opportunity to betray Jesus ___ ___ ___ ___ ___."

Answers

1, 3: Peter, James and John 2. Moses and Elijah 3. sun 4. A child 5. Least 6. True (Mark 9:39) 7. Life, live 8. Lazarus was the brother of Mary and Martha 9. 4 days 10. A donkey 11. Cloaks 12. King 13. True (Mark 3:19) 14. Judas went to the chief priests and said he would betray Jesus to them 15. when no crowd was present

Quiz #13

1. **Last Supper** Which of Jesus' disciples protested when Jesus came to wash his feet?

2. **Last Supper** Which is the only Gospel to record the event of Jesus washing his disciples' feet?

3. **Last Supper** Fill in the missing word: "I have set you an ____ that you should do as I have done for you."

4. **Eating the Meal** What did Jesus say the bread he gave his disciples represented?

5. **Eating the Meal** What did Jesus say the wine he gave his disciples represented?

6. **Eating the Meal** Fill in the missing word: "Do this in ____ of me."

7. **Gethsemane** While Jesus prayed in Gethsemane, what did Peter, James and John keep on doing?

8. **Gethsemane** True or false? In Gethsemane Jesus prayed, "My Father, if it possible, may this cup be taken from me."

9. **Gethsemane** Fill in the missing words: "The ____ is willing, but the body is ____."

10. **Crucifixion** True or false? Jesus was crucified inside the boundary of the temple.

11. **Crucifixion** Who were the two people Jesus was speaking to when he said from the cross, "Dear woman, here is your son... Here is your mother"?

12. **Crucifixion** Who arranged for the wording of the notice on the cross to read: "JESUS OF NAZARETH, THE KING OF THE JEWS"?

13. **Resurrection** On which day of the week did Jesus' disciples discover that his tomb was empty?

14. **Resurrection** Which of the eleven disciples was not with the other disciples when the risen Jesus appeared to them on the evening of the day he rose?

15. **Resurrection** To whom did the risen Jesus say, "Take care of my sheep"?

Answers

1. Peter 2. John's Gospel 3. Example 4. His body 5. His blood 6. Remembrance
7. They kept on falling asleep 8. True 9. Spirit, weak 10. False. Jesus was crucified just outside
Jerusalem (John 19:17-18) 11. To his mother Mary and to "the disciple whom he loved," John
12. Pilate 13. Sunday 14. Thomas 15. Peter

Facts 1

The opening verse of the Bible states that, "In the beginning God created..." In the Old Testament the Hebrew word used for "create" is only used of God's actions and never of human actions.

Genesis 3:1 says that "the serpent was more crafty" than any of the other animals that God had made. He used his cunning to sell a lie to Eve and to entice her to rebel against God. The devil, or Satan, is referred to as "that ancient serpent" in Revelation 20:2.

The tower of Babel was probably modeled on Mespotamian temple-towers, which were known as ziggurats. Built on a square base, it had stepped, sloping sides which led to a small shrine at the top.

God told Noah to build an "ark" (Genesis 6:14). The only other time the word for "ark" is used in the Old Testament is for the basket which the baby Moses was placed on the bank of the River Nile. That "ark" was also made watertight by being coated with pitch.

When God called Abraham, he promised to bless him in seven ways (Genesis 12:2-3). The seventh promise, that "all peoples on earth would be blessed through you" (Genesis 12:3), is mentioned in the New Testament and referred to Abraham's physical descendants (Acts 3:25) and spiritual descendants (Galatians 3:8).

When Abraham was told to count the stars, God promised him "So shall your offspring be" (Genesis 15:5), Abraham must have realized that God was saying that he would have countless descendants. Eight thousand stars can be seen in the Near-Eastern night sky.

When, at the very last moment, a ram was sacrificed in place of Isaac, the idea that one life being given for another (substitutionary sacrifice) is mentioned for the first time in the Bible. In Mark 10:45, Jesus' life is said to be a ransom for (that is, "instead of") many.

The girl who met Abraham's servant as he was looking for a wife for Isaac, was the daughter of Bethuel, son of the wife of Abraham's brother (Genesis 24:15). So when Isaac married Rebekah he married his father's great-niece.

The Lord told Rebekah an unusual thing when he said of her unborn twin boys, "the older will serve the younger" (Genesis 25:23). For it was the accepted custom that the younger son was subservient to the older. The Lord was saying of God's people that they were specially chosen, or elected, by him.

Facts 2

The exact crossing place of the Red Sea is specified as "directly opposite Baal Zephon" (Exodus 14:2). The Hebrew for "Red Sea" is the "Sea of Reeds." As reeds do not grow in salt water, the crossing is unlikely to have been in the north end of the Gulf of Suez. An Egyptian papyrus has placed Baal Zephon at the southern end of Lake Menzaleh.

We refer to the summary of God's law of Exodus 19:2-17 as the "Ten Commandments." Exodus 20:1 says, "God spake all these words." The Ten Commandments literally mean the "Ten Words." They are also known by the Greek term "Decalogue," which means "Ten Words."

For the Israelites, the tabernacle was God's royal tent. The Ten Commandments were placed inside the ark of the covenant. On top of the ark were two golden cherubim. Among the treasures found in King Tutankhaun's Egyptian tomb, are two winged guardians made to shield sacred places.

Rahab provided secret shelter for the spies who entered Jericho. Josephus says that Rahab was an innkeeper. Archeological evidence shows that houses were built into the walls of Jericho. Late Bronze Age fortifications at Jericho reveal casement (hollow) walls, which may have provided Rahab with her rooms.

When the Israelites attacked the city of Jericho, they were told to make a long blast on the trumpets. Such psychological warfare was meant to induce confusion, if not panic. In one of the Dead Sea Scrolls, "The War of the Sons of Light against the Sons of Darkness," the Levites were told to do this.

When Gideon was called by the Lord to lead the Israelites he was "threshing wheat in a winepress". Normally this would have been done in the open so the wind could blow the chaff away. But Gideon could stay hidden from the Midianites in a winepress.

Samson undertook the vows of a Nazirite (meaning "dedicated") and for him these lasted for his whole life. A Nazirite was never to cut his hair, so when Samson told Delilah the secret of his strength, he committed a great sin.

As seen in the book of Ruth, when a piece of land was sold, the seller took off his sandal as a way of showing, in public, that he renounced his rights to it.

When he anointed Saul, Samuel was following a custom that had applied to priests when they were appointed to serve God. But from this moment on in the Bible the phrase "the anointed of the Lord" usually referred to the king.

Facts 3

When Saul visited the medium at Endor, God may have allowed her to see the spirit of Samuel, or she may have had contact with an evil spirit, or she might have read Saul's thoughts through telepathy.

David was anointed by Samuel in the presence of his brothers. But when David became king over Judah he was anointed again in a public ceremony by his own tribe. This was to underline the fact that he had been chosen by God to be king.

The ancient Greeks, to whom the Philistines were probably related, developed a practice in which a war was decided by two champions fighting each other. It was called, "trial by battle ordeal".

As a sign of the friendship between them, Jonathan made a covenant with David. When Jonathan gave David not only his robe, but his belt, sword and bow he was ratifying this covenant and probably acknowledging that David would be king in his place.

When David conquered Jerusalem, he had a capital city of great strength. It was only 11 acres in extent and had no more than 3,500 inhabitants, it was almost impenetrable as it was surrounded on three sides by steep valleys.

The great value of Jerusalem to David was that it had never been conquered by the Israelites, so could be claimed by no tribe. It really was "David's city."

The floor plan of Solomon's temple had three divisions: a portico, main hall and inner sanctuary. This type of plan was often used in Semitic buildings. Sites at Syrian Ebla and at Tell Tainat in the Orontes basin reveal this tripartite division.

The Queen of Sheba probably came from the region of southwest Arabia. It was ideally situated to trade in the lucrative luxury goods which came by sea from India and east Africa. These goods were transported on caravan routes throughout the Arabian Desert.

Naaman was probably the commander-in-chief of the forces of Ben-Hadad II, who was king of Aram. Naaman's greatest victory came when the Arameans defeated the Assyrians in the Battle of Qarqar in 853 B.C.

Isaiah had his famous vision in the year that King Uzziah died, 740 B.C. During Uzziah's reign, 792 to 740 B.C., Uzziah had ruled in a godly way. But he was punished with leprosy because he burned incense in the temple—something which only the priests were permitted to do.

Facts 4

The only fact we know about Jesus' boyhood is that he went to the temple in Jerusalem when he was twelve years old. All Jewish adult males were supposed to go to three religious festivals every year: the Passover, Pentecost and the Feast of Tabernacles.

Luke records that John the Baptist began his preaching ministry in the fifteenth year of the reign of Tiberius Caesar, which was probably A.D. 25-26. Luke also notes that the Roman prefect of that time, who ruled Judea, Samaria and Idumea, was Pontius Pilate.

Herod the Great died in 4 B.C. His territory was then split up and ruled by his three sons: Archelaus, Herod Antipas and Herod Philip. Luke also notes (Luke 3:1) that Lysanias was tetrarch of Abilene, and a number of inscriptions bearing his name have been found.

Luke records that at Jesus' baptism, the Holy Spirit descended on him "in bodily form like a dove" (Luke 3:22). This was an important sign. John the Baptist had been told that the person on whom the Holy Spirit came would baptize people with the Holy Spirit (John 1:33).

John the Baptist was arrested and then beheaded because he publicly rebuked Herod the tetrarch for marrying his brother Philip's wife, while Philip was still alive! The woman was Herodias who was a granddaughter of Herod the Great.

Herodias married her uncle, Herod Philip. While Herod the tetrarch was their guest in Rome, Herodias left her uncle for the tetrarch.

There are four lists of Jesus' apostles: Matthew 10:2-4; Mark 3:16-19; Luke 6:14-16 and Acts 1:13. The order in which the names of the apostles are listed varies. But the list always starts with Peter, the leader of the Twelve, and always concludes with Judas Iscariot, who betrayed Jesus.

Nazareth is called Jesus' hometown, not because he was born there, but because he grew up there. When he revisited Nazareth, he infuriated the people by commending the faith of two non-Israelites, a widow in Zarephath and Naaman, a commander in the army of the king of Aram.

In Capernaum, Jesus healed a demon-possessed man. To pagans, a "demon" was a supernatural being which could be good or bad. To Jesus, demons were evil spirits.

Facts 5

On one occasion, Jesus fed 5,000 people at one time. This number refers only to the men; the women and children may have brought the numbers to over 10,000 people. The size of this crowd is quite staggering, as the closest towns, Capernaum and Bethsaida, probably only had a population of five thousand between them.

When Jesus was transfigured only his inner circle of three close disciples were with him: Peter, James and John. Two figures from the Old Testament appeared with Jesus. It is thought that Moses represents the old covenant and its promise of salvation, and Elijah represents the prophets.

Caesarea Philippi, a particularly pagan area, had been built by one of Herod the Great's sons, Philip, who named the town after himself and Tiberius Caesar. It had originally been called Paneas, after the Greek god Pan.

Jesus said, "I tell you that you are Peter, and on this rock I will build my church" (Matthew 16:18). This is a play on words. In Greek, "Peter" is *petros*, and "rock" is *petra*. Jesus would build his church on Peter's inspired confession.

When Jesus arrived at the tomb of his friend Lazarus, Lazarus had been dead for four days. Jews thought that the soul remained in the body for three days after death, hoping that the body might come alive again. But after three days all hope was gone. John says that many Jews put their faith in Jesus when he raised Lazarus.

When Jews saw Jesus entering Jerusalem on a donkey, their minds would have gone back the time when Solomon, David's son, rode on a donkey on his way to be publicly acclaimed as king. Jesus, the Son of David, was now arriving to claim his kingship, just as the prophets had said (Zechariah 9:9).

When Jesus washed his disciples' feet at the Last Supper, he was performing a most menial act of service. Disciples did most things for rabbis, but one thing that was specifically excluded was to undo the thongs of their sandals. Jesus gave his disciples a lesson in humility.

During the Last Supper, when Jesus gave his disciples the bread, he said "Do this in remembrance of me." The first Passover was always meant to be remembered by the Jews as the time when God delivered them from Egypt. Jesus wanted his followers to remember he was their Passover lamb, who was about to take away their sin.

Travel Itineraries

Quiz #1

1. Who planned to travel to Tarshish?

2. When Cain left Eden, where did he go?

3. Who was taken as a prisoner to the island of Patmos?

4. Who traveled to Dothan in search of his brothers?

5. True or false? Jesus was once caught in a storm on the Red Sea.

6. How many years did it take the Israelites to travel from Kadesh Barnea to the Zered Valley?

7. True or false? Moses crossed the Jordan into Canaan.

8. Following Paul's conversion, did he go to Jerusalem or Arabia first?

9. Fill in the gap from the testimony of Ezekiel: "The Spirit lifted me up between earth and heaven and in visions of God he took me to ____."

10. True or false? God promised that the Israelites would travel to a land rich in gold and jewels.

11. Which city did Joshua and the people travel around once for six days and seven times on the seventh day?

12. When Demas deserted Paul, where did he go?

13. Whose army marched to Jerusalem in the reign of King Jehoiachin?

14. Who went with Naomi from Moab to Bethlehem?

15. In which town did Samson fall in love with a young Philistine woman?

Answers

1. Jonah **2.** To the land of Nod **3.** John **4.** Joseph **5.** False. It was the Sea of Galilee (Mark 4:35-41)
6. 38 years **7.** False. It was Joshua (Joshua 3:1) **8.** Arabia **9.** Jerusalem
10. False. They were to go to a land flowing with milk and honey! (Exodus 3:8) **11.** Jericho
12. Thessalonica **13.** Nebuchadnezzar **14.** Ruth **15.** At Timnah

Quiz #2

1. Which town, less than two miles from Jerusalem, did Jesus travel to in order to visit the bereaved sisters Mary and Martha?

2. Put the following towns in the order in which Paul visited them during the course of his travels: Rome, Berea, Athens.

3. Name two of the people who traveled to the great tree of Moreh before pitching their tents on the hills east of Bethel.

4. In what book of the Bible is King Solomon described as "coming up from the desert like a column of smoke"?

5. According to Proverbs, whose "house leads down to death and her paths to the spirits of the dead"?

6. In John's vision of the woman and the dragon, where did the woman flee for 1,260 days—the mountains, the city or the desert?

7. From where did David set out when he was told by his father to visit his brothers?

8. According to Isaiah, whose fugitives "flee as far as Zoar, as far as Eglath Shelishiyah"?

9. Where was Moses told to go so he could view the land of Canaan?

10. Outside which town did Jesus bring back to life the only son of a widow?

11. To whom did Paul write, "I will go to Spain and visit you on the way"?

12. Fill in the missing word in this verse from Jeremiah: "Go up and down the streets of ___, look around and consider, search through her squares."

13. According to the book of Samuel, who went up every year from Ramathaim to Shiloh to worship God? (1 Samuel 1:1-3)

14. Where did the Babylonian army take Zedekiah after capturing him on the plains of Jericho?

15. When did David move to Hebron?

Answers

1. Bethany 2. Berea, Athens, Rome 3. Abram, Sarai, Lot and their servants 4. Song of Songs 5. The adulteress 6. The desert 7. Bethlehem 8. The fugitives of Moab 9. To Mount Nebo 10. Nain 11. The church at Rome 12. Jerusalem 13. Elkanah and his family 14. To Riblah, the Babylonian headquarters in Syro-Palestine 15. After the death of Saul

Quiz #3

1. From which direction did the wise men come?

2. Who welcomed three visitors when his tents were pitched near the great trees of Mamre?

3. How long did Paul stay in Corinth when he founded the church there?

4. True or false? In Jesus' parable about a mugging, the man was traveling up from Jericho to Jerusalem.

5. After Jesus walked on the water, where did the boat come ashore?

6. In what direction did Mary and Joseph go when they fled from Herod with the child Jesus?

7. When the Hebrew slaves left Egypt, what shorter route did God forbid them to take because it was more dangerous?

8. Who did the writer of Ephesians promise to send to Ephesus?

9. Name three places in mainland Italy that we know Paul visited.

10. When Paul set out from Macedonia, which was the only church to support him by sending aid?

11. Who, according to Isaiah, will travel on the Way of Holiness?

12. To which city did David eventually take Goliath's head?

13. According to Chronicles, people as far away as Issachar, Zebulun and Naphtali brought food to the celebrations at Hebron. Name two of the four beasts of burden mentioned.

14. What did Solomon's men bring him when they sailed back from Ophir?

15. Where were Joshua and the tribes when Joshua sent out two spies to Jericho?

Answers

1. The East 2. Abraham 3. 18 months
4. False. He was traveling down from Jerusalem to Jericho (Luke 10:30) 5. Gennesaret 6. South-west
7. The road through Philistine country 8. Tychicus 9. Rhegium, Puteoli, Rome, Forum of Appius, Three Taverns
10. The church at Philippi 11. The redeemed 12. Jerusalem 13. Donkeys, camels, mules and oxen
14. 420 talents of gold 15. Shittim, the last camp site before crossing over the Jordan into Canaan

Quiz #4

1. In his first letter to the Corinthians, Paul wrote that he intended to stay in what city until Pentecost?

2. Who accompanied Jesus on his final journey to Golgotha, carrying Jesus' cross?

3. After David took a census, plague swept through the land, but God stopped it when it reached what town?

4. At which port on the island of Sicily did the ship on which Paul was sailing put in for three days?

5. From where to where did Mary and Joseph have to travel to record their names in the census?

6. True or false? Philip was among Paul's companions when Paul traveled to Cyprus.

7. The judge Gideon led a surprise attack against Midianite raiders who came from what direction against the Israelites?

8. In what sea was Paul shipwrecked?

9. True or false? Jesus went by boat to the region of Dalmanutha.

10. Who was brought from the house of Makir in Lo Debar to live with David at Jerusalem?

11. Who traveled from Rome with Tychicus to Colosse?

12. According to the book of Ruth, which two brothers left their homes in Bethlehem for Moab but never returned?

13. Why did these two brothers go with their parents to Moab?

14. Where did Absalom flee after killing Amnon, David's son?

15. When Paul was transferred to Caesarea from Jerusalem how many armed men protected him?

Answers

1. Ephesus 2. Simon of Cyrene 3. Jerusalem 4. Syracuse 5. From Nazareth to Bethlehem
6. False. Philip never made a journey with Paul 7. The East 8. The Mediterranean Sea
9. True (Mark 8:10) 10. Mephibosheth, the crippled son of Jonathan 11. Onesimus
12. Mahlon and Kilion, sons of Elimelech and Naomi 13. Because of a famine 14. To Geshur
15. 470 (200 soldiers, 70 horsemen, 200 spearmen)

Quiz #5

1. To which city did Peter come only to find himself in open conflict with Paul?

2. Who fled to Seirah after he killed Eglon, King of Moab, with a double-edged sword?

3. On his third missionary journey, in what order did Paul visit Rhodes, Patara and Cos?

4. "Have you journeyed to the springs of the sea or walked in the recesses of the deep?" Who put this question to Job?

5. Who told the prophet Amos, "Go back to the land of Judah… Don't prophesy any more at Bethel"?

6. Which young man was sent by Paul to Thessalonica to encourage the church?

7. Why did Moses flee from Egypt to Midian?

8. Where did Ezra assemble the family heads and camp for three days before returning to Jerusalem?

9. Off which island was Paul shipwrecked?

10. Where was Jacob going when he had the dream about the ladder reaching up to heaven?

11. Did Paul tell Timothy that Crescens or Luke had left him to go to Galatia?

12. Fill in the missing word from Isaiah's prophecy about the restoration of Egypt: "In that day there will be a ____ from Egypt to Assyria."

13. Who escaped from Gath and hid in the cave of Adullam?

14. Who was on the road to Damascus when he was converted?

15. Mary, Joseph and baby Jesus traveled to which city, where they met the devout and holy man Simeon?

Answers

1. Antioch 2. Ehud 3. Cos, Rhodes, Patara 4. God 5. Amaziah, the priest of Bethel
6. Timothy 7. Because news that he had killed an Egyptian began to spread 8. Ahava Canal
9. The island of Malta (Melita) 10. On his way to Haran 11. Crescens 12. highway
13. David 14. Saul 15. Jerusalem

Quiz #6

1. Where was Paul when John Mark left him to return to Jerusalem?

2. True or false? Paul's intended destination was Corinth when he was shipwrecked.

3. To whom did God say, "Leave here, turn eastward and hide in the Kerith Ravine, east of the Jordan"?

4. True or false? Jesus visited Cana in Galilee to attend a wedding reception.

5. When Paul was surrounded by difficulties in Macedonia, who came to him with good news from Corinth?

6. When Jesus met Zacchaeus, he was passing through which town on his way to Jerusalem?

7. Who was instructed to go to Perath and hide his linen belt in the rocks there?

8. Which two men were sent with Paul and Barnabas to Antioch by the Council of Jerusalem?

9. Philip was on the road to which town when he met the Ethiopian eunuch?

10. In which town were Paul and Barnabas when they met the Jewish sorcerer, Elymas?

11. Where did Moses meet Zipporah who became his wife?

12. Which two towns on Cyprus does Luke say Paul visited?

13. Fill in the missing words: "You will receive power when the Holy Spirit comes on you; and you will be my witnesses in ___, and in all ___ and ___, and to the ends of the earth."

14. Where did Samuel take the people to confirm Saul as king?

15. Name two of the areas from where, according to Matthew, those baptized by John the Baptist came?

Quiz #7

1. When Abraham and his family left Ur, what city did they travel to?

2. Was it Haman himself or the king's couriers who went to all the provinces to distribute the edict concerning the annihilation of the Jews?

3. Which animal in Daniel's vision charged towards the west and the north and the south?

4. Were Paul and Barnabas in Lystra, Iconium, or Antioch when they were called Hermes and Zeus?

5. How many men did Moses send out from the Desert of Paran to explore the land of Canaan?

6. Why did Saul go to the Crags of the Wild Goats in the Desert of En Gedi?

7. What was by the sheep pens in the Desert of En Gedi?

8. Which king of Persia allowed God's people to leave Babylon and go up to Jerusalem to rebuild the temple?

9. From where was Jesus traveling when he saw the fruitless fig tree?

10. Where was Jesus going when he saw the fruitless fig tree?

11. After passing through Amphipolis and Apollonia Paul came to a town in which he established a Christian church. Which town?

12. From what country did King Ahab's wife Jezebel come?

13. Name two of the three women who, according to Mark, followed Jesus from Galilee to care for him.

14. Did Jesus' mother make a three-month visit to Elizabeth in a town near the Sea of Galilee or a town in the hill country of Judea?

15. Where, according to Matthew, did Jesus tell his eleven disciples to meet him after the resurrection?

Answers

1. Haran 2. The king's couriers 3. The ram 4. Lystra 5. 12 men 6. To look for David
7. A cave 8. Cyrus 9. Bethany 10. Jerusalem 11. Thessalonica 12. Sidon
13. Mary Magdelene, Mary the mother of James and Joses, and Salome
14. A town in the hill country of Judea 15. Galilee

Quiz #8

1. The prophet Elijah came from which city in Gilead?

2. On Paul's last missionary journey, why did he decide to sail past Ephesus?

3. Was the town which Elisha often visited Seir, Shunem or Sychar?

4. What animal accompanied Balaam on his early morning journey with the princes of Moab?

5. When Joshua was in Jericho, to what town did he send spies?

6. To which city did Elisha travel to see a sick king?

7. True or false? Nehemiah went to meet Sanballat and Geshem in the villages on the plain of Ono.

8. According to Luke, as Jesus approached Jerusalem for the last time, he came to two villages, at the Mount of Olives, and there he sent his disciples for the colt. One village was Bethany, what was the other village?

9. What town was Elijah's base, when he wasn't doing his circuit as a judge?

10. Who climbed to the top of Mount Gerizim to deliver a message to the citizens of Shechem about an olive tree, a fig tree, a vine and a thorn-bush?

11. True or false? As Paul was throwing wood on to a fire on the island of Malta, a tarantula fastened itself onto his hand.

12. Why did the islanders think Paul must be a god?

13. Which prophet wrote: "See, the Lord rides on a swift cloud and is coming to Egypt"?

14. When David was on the run from Saul, he moved down to the Desert of Maon, and from there he sent messengers to which very wealthy man who was shearing sheep?

15. Where was Jesus when Nicodemus came to see him secretly at night?

Answers

1. Tishbe 2. He was in a hurry to get to Jerusalem in time for Pentecost 3. Shunem 4. A donkey
5. Ai 6. Damascus 7. False. Nehemiah refused to meet them (Nehemiah 6:1-3) 8. Bethphage
9. Ramah 10. Jotham 11. False. It was a viper (Acts 28:3) 12. Because he had survived death for a second time
13. Isaiah 19:1 14. To Nabal 15. Jerusalem

Quiz #9

1. Who said to the Lord that he had been "roaming through the earth and going to and fro in it"?

2. Was Jeremiah instructed by the Lord to go down to a house of a carpenter, a potter or a tent-maker?

3. Did the Lord send Samuel on a journey to Socoh or Bethlehem to find Jesse and his sons?

4. According to Mark's Gospel, when Peter said, "You are the Christ," Jesus and the disciples were in the vicinity of which town?

5. In Jesus' Parable of the Good Samaritan, how many people traveled along the road?

6. After Jonathan shot his three warning arrows into the field where David was hiding, where did David go?

7. Following the first persecution of the church, the apostle Philip traveled to which city?

8. Which island was John exiled to when he wrote the book of Revelation?

9. In Paul's vision, was he invited to make a journey to Macedonia or Thessalonica?

10. From where, according to Isaiah, will people come to Zion, "Bearing gold and incense and proclaiming the praise of the Lord"?

11. When Saul searched the hill country of Ephraim and the districts of Shaalim and Zuph, what was he looking for?

12. Who traveled to Judah armed with letters for the governors of the Trans-Euphrates region asking them to ensure his safe journey?

13. Who would benefit from fleeing to a city of refuge?

14. Which Hittite did David summon to Jerusalem before sending him out to battle with Joab?

15. When Naomi went back to Bethlehem, which of her daughters-in-law stayed in Moab?

Answers

1. Satan **2.** To the house of a potter **3.** Bethlehem **4.** Caesarea Philippi **5.** 4: the priest, the Levite, the Good Samaritan and the traveler who was robbed **6.** To Nob, to see Ahimelech, the priest **7.** Samaria **8.** Patmos **9.** Macedonia **10.** From Sheba **11.** His father's lost donkeys **12.** Nehemiah **13.** Someone who had accidentally killed a person **14.** Uriah, the husband of Bathsheba **15.** Orpah

Quiz #10

1. Philip was on the road to which town when he met the Ethiopian eunuch?

2. Where did Saul go to find a medium?

3. According to Jeremiah, when Zedekiah and his soldiers fled from Jerusalem to escape from Nebuchadnezzar armies, which direction did they head?

4. As Zedekiah tried to escape, where was he caught?

5. To which city did Peter travel to meet the Roman centurion Cornelius?

6. True or false? Jesse sent David to the Valley of Elah with grain and bread for his brothers.

7. Who came down from Judah to visit Nehemiah in the citadel of Susa?

8. True or false? A queen came from Samaria to talk to Solomon.

9. Who moved from Canaan to live in Sodom?

10. Fill in the missing word from Isaiah's prophecy: "Who is this coming from ___, from Bozrah with his garments stained crimson?"

11. Where was Joseph taken by the Ishmaelite traders?

12. Fill in the missing words: "These things I remember as I pour out my soul: how I used to go with the multitude, leading the procession to ___ ___ ___ ___."

13. What journey did Moses ask Pharaoh to allow the Israelites to make?

14. Did Paul visit Cyprus on his first or second missionary journey?

15. To which city did Paul return, taking Barnabas with him, after fourteen years' absence?

Answers

1. Gaza **2.** To Endor (6 miles north-west of Shunem) **3.** Towards the Arabah
4. In the plains of Jericho **5.** Caesarea **6.** True (1 Samuel 17:17-19)
7. His brother, Hanani (Nehemiah 1:2) **8.** False. The queen came from Sheba (1 Kings 10:1)
9. Lot and his family **10.** Edom **11.** To Egypt **12.** The house of God
13. A 3 day journey into the desert to offer sacrifices **14.** Paul visited Cyprus on his first missionary journey
15. Jerusalem

Facts 1

Nearly all the events covered by the Bible took place in a part of the world known today as "the Near East."

Luke 9:51 tells us that "Jesus resolutely set out for Jerusalem". Luke's words emphasize that Jesus was determined to see his mission through to its end, that is, to his death in Jerusalem.

The Holy Land is given a number of names in the Bible. In the time of Abraham and the exodus it was known as Canaan, and the original inhabitants were known as the Canaanites.

Canaan became known as the Promised Land, because it was the land promised to Abraham and his descendants; and also Israel, because the descendants of Israel (another name for Jacob) settled there.

When the kingdom of Israel divided into two, the northern kingdom kept the name Israel, while the southern kingdom was called Judah. David was descended from the tribe of Judah, which had chosen him as their king from the beginning.

The kingdom of Israel and its capital city Samaria were conquered by the Assyrians who resettled the population in other parts of the empire. The northern kingdom was then repopulated by foreigners, who eventually became known as Samaritans.

Judah was all that was left of the original Israel. After the conquest by Babylon, the people of Judah were deported to Babylon, but were later allowed to return to Jerusalem. Judea was the name of this small district within the Persian Empire.

In 135 A.D., the Romans renamed the country Palestine, taking the name from the Philistines, who lived along the coast, and with whom the Romans were familiar. To them, the whole country was Philistine country!

When the Israelites first came to Canaan it was a cosmopolitan center of international trade, with strong fortified cities. The hill country, however, was relatively unpopulated.

The land of Moab, Ruth's home, was a strip of arable land in the Transjordan, lying between the Dead Sea and the desert, with the Arnon River to the north and the Zered River to the south.

Following successive conquests by many empires, from the Babylonian Empire to the Roman Empire, many Jews were "dispersed" to other lands. These Jews, known as Diasapora Jews, attempted to maintain their heritage in these foreign lands.

Facts 2

The Mount of Olives is a limestone ridge a little over a mile in length, running approximately north to south, just east of Jerusalem. It provides a beautiful panoramic view of the city.

Paul was largely responsible for the spread of Christianity to non-Jews. He came from Tarsus, a cosmopolitan center of trade. He was justly proud of being a Roman citizen.

Most of the events mentioned in the Old Testament are located between Dan in the north, and Beersheba in the south, and between the coast of the Mediterranean Sea in the west and the high plateau beyond the Jordan in the east.

Midway along the western shore of the Dead Sea and 35 miles south-east of Jerusalem are the hot water springs of En Gedi, ensuring rich vegetation all year round. En Gedi means "spring" or "fountain".

The word "Bethlehem" comes from the Hebrew words *beth* meaning "house", and *lehem*, meaning "bread."

Bethlehem is about six miles southwest of Jerusalem, on the edge of the desert of Judah. It is on a rocky spur of the mountains, just off the road to Hebron and Egypt.

The traditional site of Jesus' baptism is in the wide river valley of the lower Jordan River, about five miles to the east of Jericho.

A Sabbath day's journey (Acts 1:12) was about three quarters of a mile (2,000 paces). Jews who kept the Old Testament regulations carefully would not travel further than this on the Sabbath.

Some Jews, wanting to get round the Sabbath travel regulations, would send a servant the day before with possessions to be left along the route, perhaps at a friends' house. The possessions marking a "home" from which the Sabbath day's journey could start again.

The sea port of Caesarea became a focal point for the spread of the gospel. Here God led Peter to preach to the Roman centurion Cornelius and his family. Paul landed at Caesarea after both his second and third missionary journeys (Acts 18:22 ; 21:8).

Caesarea, 23 miles south of Mount Carmel, had been built by Herod the Great over a period of 12 years. During New Testament times, it was the seat of Roman power and Pontius Pilate had his headquarters there.

Facts 3

Caesarea Philippi was in northern Palestine, on the southern slopes of Mount Hermon. It was outside Galilee, and was the capital of the province ruled over by Herod Philip.

Nineveh was on the east bank of the Tigris River, more than 500 miles away from Israel. King Sennacherib made it the capital of Assyria in about 700 B.C.

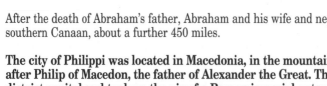

When commanded to go to Nineveh, Jonah headed for Tarshish, in the opposite direction. Tarshish was located in the south of Spain, two thousand miles away from Palestine.

Roman milestones were placed along the fine roads built by the Romans. A Roman soldier was permitted by law to force a civilian to carry his pack from one milestone to another.

At the time of Christ, large Jewish populations could be found in cities such as Rome, Alexandria, Antioch and Ephesus. Paul was a "diaspora" Jew from the city of Tarsus in Cilicia.

Romans chapter 16 bears witness to the extent to which people traveled about the Roman empire, very often for commercial reasons.

Archaeological excavations at Ur, the city from which Abraham came, show that 500 years before the time of Abraham Ur was a wealthy and important city. Intricate works of art in gold and other precious metals reveal a standard of workmanship rarely surpassed in later ages.

The citizens of Ur worshiped the moon, as did the people of Haran, 560 miles further north, where Abraham and his family settled.

After the death of Abraham's father, Abraham and his wife and nephew traveled to southern Canaan, about a further 450 miles.

The city of Philippi was located in Macedonia, in the mountains. It was named after Philip of Macedon, the father of Alexander the Great. The city was a district capital and took on the air of a Roman imperial outpost.

Facts 4

The wise men who came to see Jesus saw the star "at its rising." They seem to have deduced that they should therefore go to Jerusalem. They saw the star again when they left Jerusalem.

Throughout the history of the Jews, during peril, famine or tyranny, God's people fled to Egypt. The Bible writers are sympathetic towards Egypt. Though often condemned, a final restoration is promised.

To travel from Philippi to Thessalonica involved a hard trek of rather more than 100 miles.

The city of Thessalonica, was the main city on the Egnatian Way, the great Roman road from the Adriatic Sea to the Middle East. It was therefore in a key position for the spread of the gospel.

In Paul's day, Athens was an intellectual and tourist center. Its heyday, however, had long passed, and Athens was less important than Corinth.

Corinth was known as the "bridge of Greece" because all north and south traffic had to pass through this city. It has been called "the market place of Greece". The Isthmian Games, second only in importance to the Olympic Games, were held in Corinth.

The wealthy city of Corinth was notorious for its vice. In Greek theater, if a man from Corinth appeared on the stage, he appeared as a drunkard. The Greeks had a verb, "to play the Corinthian," which meant to lead a dissolute and depraved life.

Corinth had many religious groups. It was known as a center for the healing cult of Asklepios. Also prominent was the Egyptian Isis cult.

Standing at the mouth of the Cayster River, Ephesus, the Roman capital of the province of Asia, was known as the market of Asia and the treasure house of Asia. The temple of Diana in Ephesus had the right of asylum, so Ephesus became a base for the criminals of the ancient world.

People from all over the world came to Ephesus to admire the temple of the goddess Diana, which was one of the seven wonders of the world.

People also came to Ephesus to buy the charms and spells for which Ephesus was famous. Called "Ephesian Letters" these were supposed to give safety in travel and success in enterprises.

River Deep Mountain High

Quiz #1

1. Where were Adam and Eve first placed by God following their creation?

2. True or false? The garden where Adam and Eve lived was in Egypt.

3. How many rivers flowed through the Garden of Eden?

4. On which mountains did Noah's ark come to rest following the flood?

5. Give the names of two of the rivers in the Garden of Eden.

6. From what city on the River Euphrates did Abraham's family originate?

7. When Hagar left home for the first time, what was she next to when the angel found her in the desert?

8. Fill in the missing words: "He leads me beside quiet waters, he ___ ___ ___."

9. In Revelation 22, what flows from the throne of God?

10. What mountain-top citadel did David capture?

11. By what river did an Egyptian princess find a baby in a basket-boat?

12. On what day of creation did God separate the water and the dry land?

13. Supply the missing word from the Song of Moses: "In a ___ land he [God] found him, in a barren and howling waste."

14. When Joshua led the Israelites to the edge of the Jordan River, what miraculous event occurred?

15. True or false? The Gospels do not give the name of the mountain where Jesus was transfigured.

Answers

1. The Garden of Eden **2.** False. It was to the east, in Eden (Genesis 2:8) **3.** 4
4. The mountains of Ararat **5.** Pishon, Gihon, Tigris, Euphrates **6.** Ur **7.** A spring
8. restores my soul **9.** The river of life **10.** Jerusalem **11.** The Nile **12.** Day 3
13. desert **14.** The waters dried up and the people crossed over **15.** True (Mark 9:2)

Quiz #2

1. In Genesis 15, God promised to give Abraham and his descendants the land from the river of Egypt to the great river. What is the name of the great river?

2. Which large body of water did the Israelites cross after leaving Egypt on the exodus?

3. At the foot of which mountain did the Israelites sin by worshiping a golden calf?

4. How did Moses make the bitter water of Marah sweet?

5. What did Moses see for the first time from Mount Nebo?

6. What kind of people did Moses send into the Promised Land, from the wilderness at Kadesh?

7. True or false? Moses was buried in Jerusalem.

8. Which tribes of Israel did not settle in the Promised Land west of the Jordan River?

9. On what plains did Moses deliver his final speech to the Israelites before his death?

10. Supply the missing word from the Song of Miriam: "The horse and its rider he has hurled into the ___."

11. To whom were these words spoken: "Who cuts a channel for the torrents of rain... to water... a desert with no-one in it"?

12. Who said that in the day of the Lord's judgment, "The whole land will rise like the Nile; it will be stirred up and then sink"?

13. In Luke's Gospel, who did people try to hurl down a cliff?

14. In what valley did Goliath and David meet while the armies faced each other from opposite hills?

15. On the last night before his arrest, what valley did Jesus and the disciples cross over?

Answers

1. The Euphrates 2. The Red Sea (the Sea of Reeds) 3. Mount Sinai (Mount Horeb)
4. God showed Moses a piece of wood which he threw into the water 5. The Promised Land
6. Spies 7. False. He was buried in the valley opposite Beth Peor. (Deuteronomy 34:6)
8. The Reubenites, the Gadites and the half-tribe of Manasseh 9. The plains of Moab 10. sea 11. To Job
12. Amos 13. Jesus 14. The Valley of Elah 15. The Kidron Valley

Quiz #3

1. On which mountain did Joshua renew the covenant with the people of Israel following the defeat at Ai?

2. During the time of the judges, who uttered taunting parables from Mount Gerizim?

3. In which Old Testament book is the mount of assembly referred to?

4. In 2 Kings 23, what name is given to the hill where Solomon built shrines to false gods?

5. True or false? King David fled from his son Absalom to the Mount of Olives.

6. According to the prophet Zechariah, during the last days, upon which mountain will the feet of the Lord stand?

7. Which Old Testament book speaks about "a river whose streams make glad the city of God"?

8. True or false? Cities along the Euphrates River include Babylon, Ur, and Jerusalem.

9. Which river is mentioned the most in the Bible?

10. The judge Ehud fought the Moabites near what river?

11. In the book of Genesis, who took his son up a mountain?

12. Who told priests to take stones from a dry river bed?

13. Supply the missing word from John's vision in the book of Revelation: "The angel showed me the river of the water of life as clear as ____."

14. Where was Paul when Luke wrote, "On the Sabbath we went outside the city gate to the river, where we expected to find a place of prayer"?

15. Fill in the missing three words from Hosea's prophecy: "I will make the Valley of Achor a ____ ____ ____."

Answers

1. Mount Ebal 2. Jotham 3. Isaiah 4. Hill of Corruption 5. True 6. The Mount of Olives
7. Psalms 8. False, Jerusalem is nowhere near the Euphrates
9. The Jordan River which is mentioned in 211 verses 10. The Jordan
11. Abraham 12. Joshua 13. crystal 14. Philippi 15. door of hope

Quiz #4

1. On what mountain was King Saul killed at the battle between his forces and the Philistines?

2. Who, according to the Psalmist, is like a tree planted by streams of water?

3. In the desert of Ziph, David spared King Saul's life and to prove it he took a jug of water, and what else that was by Saul's head?

4. In the desert of En Gedi, David spared King Saul's life and did what instead of killing Saul?

5. In Moses' instructions to the people recorded in Deuteronomy 11, on what mountain were the people to proclaim God's blessings?

6. In Moses' instructions to the people recorded in Deuteronomy 11, on what mountain were the people to proclaim the curses?

7. When David was fleeing from King Saul, he fled to what coastal country and became a vassal there?

8. After Elijah announced a drought, where did God tell him to go for water?

9. In the book of Genesis, who chose to live in a fertile place, instead of in the desert or the mountains?

10. Supply the missing three words from Jesus' prophecy about the destruction of Jerusalem which he spoke to the weeping women of Jerusalem: "Then [in that day] they will say to the mountains ___ ___ ___."

11. What desert did the Queen of Sheba cross when she visited Solomon?

12. True or false? In the book of Revelation, John wrote that in the new Jerusalem there would no longer be any sea.

13. The Psalmist wrote that the Lord surrounds his people just as what surrounds Jerusalem?

14. In Exodus, who led his sheep to the far side of the desert and then came to Horeb?

15. True or false? Jesus and his disciples baptized people in the River Jordan.

Answers

1. Mount Gilboa 2. A man whose delight is in the law of the Lord 3. A spear
4. He cut a piece of material from Saul's robe 5. Mount Gerizim 6. Mount Ebal
7. Philistia (the land of the Philistines) 8. The Kerith Ravine where there was a brook
9. Lot 10. Fall on us 11. Arabian Desert 12. True (Revelation 21:1) 13. Mountains
14. Moses 15. False. Only Jesus' disciples and John the Baptist baptized people in the Jordan

Quiz #5

1. On what mountain did the prophet Elijah confront the prophets of Baal, challenging their god to send fire from heaven?

2. Where did the prophet Elijah flee to where he heard the still small voice of God?

3. Fill in the missing two words from the sufferings endured by men of faith described in Hebrews 11: "They wandered in ___ and ___, and in caves and holes in the ground."

4. Ezekiel had a vision in which he saw a valley full of what?

5. True or false? Amos said to the people that they should let justice roll on "like the sea."

6. Where did Jesus tell people to flee to when they saw the abomination standing where it did not belong?

7. In Paul's catalogue of his sufferings, how long had he spent on the open sea?

8. In Paul's sufferings described in 2 Corinthians 11, fill in the missing word: "I have been in danger from ___, in danger from bandits, in danger from my own countrymen."

9. True or false? The Psalmist said, "I lift up my eyes to the cedars of Lebanon."

10. When the spies explored the land for Joshua, from which desert did they set out?

11. According to John's Gospel, in what pool did Jesus tell the blind man to wash?

12. What was the first indication, after Noah's ark grounded on Mount Ararat, that the flood was going down?

13. What, according to Isaiah, would have been like a river if the people had listened to God?

14. In Isaiah's prophecy about obedience, what would have been like the waves of the sea?

15. On what mountain was Elijah when his servant saw a cloud as small as a man's hand?

Quiz #6

1. Where did Elisha direct Naaman to wash in order to rid himself of leprosy?

2. By the rivers of which city did the Psalmist say that he wept and remembered Zion?

3. According to the prophet Isaiah, what mountain will be established as chief among the mountains?

4. In what valley was Naboth's vineyard?

5. What is the name of the mountainous land to which Moses escaped after he had killed the Egyptian?

6. Fill in the name of the river from Deborah's victory song in Judges: "The river ____ swept them away, the age-old river, the river ____."

7. According to Matthew, Jesus left Nazareth and went to what lakeside town?

8. During the storm at sea described in Acts, the sailors thought the ship was going to break up against the rocks. How did the soldiers stop the sailors escaping?

9. Fill in the missing words from Jesus' words about faith: "If you have faith as small as a mustard seed, you can say to this ____, 'Move from here to there' and it will move."

10. True or false? In Genesis, when the four kings fought against the five kings, to the south of the Dead Sea, the Valley of Siddim was a swamp.

11. Balak took Balaam to the top of what hill for his second oracle?

12. Balak took Balaam to the top of what hill for his third oracle?

13. In Acts, the angel told Philip to go south to what road?

14. In Psalm 44, what does the deer pant for?

15. Supply the missing two words from this verse in Proverbs: "The fountain of wisdom is a ____ ____."

Answers

1. The Jordan **2.** By the rivers of Babylon **3.** The mountain of the Lord
4. The Valley of Jezreel **5.** Midian **6.** Kishon **7.** Capernaum
8. The soldiers cut the lifeboat's ropes and it fell away into the sea **9.** mountain
10. False. It was full of tar pits (Genesis 14:10) **11.** Pisgah **12.** Peor **13.** The desert road
14. Streams of water **15.** bubbling brook

Quiz #7

1. In the book of Obadiah, the prophet issues a judgment to those who are on a mountain named after Jacob's brother. What is that mountain's name?

2. The prophet Amos pronounced a woe on those who live on which mountain in the northern kingdom of Israel?

3. In the book of Joel, the prophet mentions a mountain that is holy. What is the name of that mountain?

4. Supply the missing name from Zechariah's prophecy: "What are you, O mighty mountain? Before ____ you will become level ground."

5. According to Isaiah, who has "measured the waters in the hollow of his hand... or weighed the mountains on the scales and the hills in a balance"?

6. In which desert did John the Baptist preach?

7. In which river did John the Baptist and his disciples baptize the repentant Jews?

8. After leaving Marah, where did the Israelites find twelve springs and seventy palm trees?

9. Fill in the missing word from Exodus: "The Lord descended to the top of Mount ____ and called Moses to the top of the mountain."

10. After leaving Elim, and before they came to Sinai, the Israelites traveled through which desert?

11. As the people of Israel wandered through the wilderness, they had two major problems. One was getting enough food. What was the other problem?

12. True or false? Abraham went to Mount Gerizim to sacrifice Isaac.

13. According to the Psalmist, who may ascend the hill of the Lord?

14. When God wanted to reduce the numbers in Gideon's army, he told Gideon to take his men to the water to drink. Which men did God not choose?

15. True or false? Jesus was tempted by the devil three times on the Sea of Galilee.

Answers

1. Mount Esau **2.** Mount Samaria **3.** Mount Zion **4.** Zerubbabel **5.** The Sovereign Lord
6. The desert of Judea **7.** The Jordan **8.** Elim **9.** Sinai
10. The Desert of Sin **11.** Getting water **12.** False. He went to Mount Moriah (Genesis 22:2)
13. "He who has clean hands and a pure heart" **14.** The men who got down on their knees to drink
15. False. He was tempted in the desert (Luke 4:2)

Quiz #8

1. For how many days did the Israelites wander in the desert without finding water, after they had crossed the Red Sea?

2. Where were Jesus and the disciples when Jesus told Simon to let down his nets into the water?

3. True or false? Before Jesus chose his twelve disciples, he prayed all night in the Garden of Gethsemane.

4. At what place did Peter suggest that he, James, and John should build booths for Elijah, Moses and Jesus?

5. True or false? Jesus did many healings at Gennesaret, near the Sea of Galilee.

6. True or false? Jesus walked on the surface of the Dead Sea.

7. According to the Psalmist, what is "as if the dew of Hermon were falling on Mount Zion"?

8. Who blew a trumpet in the hills, and with the tribal army that rallied to him, captured the fords of the Jordan?

9. On the Day of Atonement, where was the scapegoat sent?

10. Supply the missing word from the verse in the Song of Songs: "Many waters cannot quench ____; rivers cannot wash it away."

11. What food did John the Baptist eat in the desert?

12. True or false? Jesus was tempted by the devil in the land of the Philistines.

13. Jesus calmed a storm on which sea?

14. Jesus healed a lame man next to the pool of Bethesda. In which city was this pool found?

15. On which mountain did Jesus speak of the future of the temple and the last days?

Quiz #9

1. Supply the missing four words from Jeremiah's prophecy: "If you stumble in safe country, how will you manage in the ___ ___ ___ ___?"

2. The writer to the Hebrews says that Christians have not come to a mountain burning with fire. What have they come to? Give one of the three descriptions in Hebrews 12.

3. What did Elijah use instead of a stick to make the water in the Jordan move back?

4. Who proclaimed these words to the people left in Jerusalem: "The mountains of Israel will become desolate so that no-one will cross them"?

5. To whom did Jesus say: "The water I give him will become in him a spring of water welling up to eternal life"?

6. Supply the missing word from Isaiah's prophecy of the future restoration: "The desert and the parched land will be glad; the ___ will rejoice and blossom."

7. Who said to the people, "The land you are crossing the Jordan to take possession of is a land of mountains and valleys that drinks rain from heaven"?

8. Who, at the command of Deborah, gathered his forces on Mount Tabor?

9. To what river did Deborah lure the king of Canaan?

10. Why did the people say to Jesus, "Our forefathers ate the manna in the desert"?

11. In what desert were the people when they said to Moses, "Why did you bring us out of Egypt to die in this terrible place?"?

12. Ezekiel was by which river when he saw visions of God?

13. What mountain was David speaking to when he said in his lament: "How the mighty have fallen in battle! Jonathan lies slain on your heights."

14. Supply the missing word from the Psalmist's song of praise: "He lifted me out of the slimy pit, out of the mud and mire; he set my feet on a ___."

15. When Jesus said, "What did you go out into the desert to see?", what was the answer?

Answers

1. thickets of the Jordan 2. Mount Zion, the heavenly Jerusalem, the city of the living God 3. His rolled up cloak 4. Ezekiel 5. The Samaritan woman at the well 6. "wilderness" 7. Moses 8. Barak 9. River Kishon 10. They wanted Jesus to perform a miraculous sign to enable them to believe in him 11. Desert of Zin 12. Kebar River 13. Mount Gilboa 14. rock 15. A prophet (John the Baptist)

Facts 1

The land of Palestine is divided into five main geographical areas running roughly north to south parallel to the Mediterranean coast. There is also an area of desert in the south.

Moving from west to east the traveler passes through: the coastal plains; the low-lying hill country (called the Shephelah); the central highlands; the Jordan Valley; the high Trans-Jordan plateau.

The Negev (meaning "south") is the barren wilderness stretching south from Beersheba and the Dead Sea to the Gulf of Aqabah. The Desert of Zin is in the Negev.

In biblical times, the northern mountains of Carmel, Upper Galilee and northern Samaria were covered with dense woodland.

Mount Ebal is just north of Shechem and opposite Mount Gerizim, overlooking the Nablus Valley, the main east-west route into the central hill country. Mount Ebal rises 3077 feet above sea level.

A large altar, recently discovered on Mount Ebal, may be the altar built by Joshua (Joshua 8:30-35).

Mount Gerizim is 2,849 feet above sea level. Here, the Samaritans built a temple to rival the temple at Jerusalem. Though this was destroyed in 128 B.C., the Samaritans continued to worship on Mount Gerizim (John 4:20).

The Mount of Olives, a ridge of hills just east of Jerusalem across the Kidron Valley, was once covered with olive groves. It rises to a height of 2,660 feet.

One of the summits on the Mount of Olives is traditionally identified as the site of Christ's ascension.

The Mount of Olives is as important to Jews and Muslims as it is to Christians. In addition to the Old Testament references to the Mount, there is a vast Jewish burial ground there.

The Euphrates River, "the Great River," flows in a southeasterly direction for 1,780 miles. It is the longest river in western Asia. Cities of biblical importance along this river include Babylon and Ur.

Facts 2

The Tigris River originates in the melting snows of the Taurus Mountains in Turkey and flows southeast for 1,150 miles, joining the Euphrates 40 miles north of the Persian Gulf.

Nineveh, Asshur and Baghdad are on the banks of the Tigris.

The fortress of Masada became the last refuge of the Jewish people in their revolt against Rome in 70 AD. The fortress is near the Dead Sea and is situated on a rock surrounded by ravines.

Dew was a very important characteristic of the Palestinian climate. An abundance of dew was seen as a blessing from the Lord (Deuteronomy 33:28), and its absence was seen as a curse (Haggai 1:10).

Hail is uncommon. When it occurred in the land it was seen as a punishment from the Lord (Ezekiel 13:11, 13). On one occasion it was seen as intervention for God's people during a battle (Joshua 10:11).

The patriarchs wandered in the central hill country of Palestine. They are portrayed as a pastoral people who avoided the urban life of Canaan.

A number of sites have been proposed for Mount Sinai (Mount Horeb). Deuteronomy 1:2 states that the journey from Horeb by way of Mount Seir to Kadesh-barnea takes eleven days. This points to a location in the south of the Sinai peninsula.

The route that the Israelites took from Egypt to the Promised Land is under debate. The best biblical description for the journey is found in Numbers 33.

The exact location of the Sermon on the Mount is in doubt. One possibility is near the town of Chorazin in Galilee, just north of the Sea of Galilee.

Snow-capped Mount Hermon marked the extreme north of the territory occupied by Joshua in the conquest. It is a range of mountains, covering about 18 miles, the highest peak rising to 9,232 feet above sea level.

Because Mount Hermon is close to Caesarea Philippi, it has been suggested as the probable site of the transfiguration.

Facts 3

It is thought that the Dead Sea Scrolls formed the library of a Jewish sect called the Essenes. The scrolls are more than 1,000 years older than any other known biblical manuscript.

"Dead Sea" is a name coined in the second century A.D. for the large salt lake at the southern end of the River Jordan. In the Bible it is called the Salt Sea and the Sea of Arabah.

The Dead Sea is the lowest point on the earth's surface, about 1,294 feet below sea level. At its deepest point it is more than 1,300 feet lower than sea level.

The water of the Dead Sea is 25 to 30 per cent salt. It is the most saline natural body of water in the earth, and nothing can live in it. Earthquakes are frequent in this area.

The Jordan River, beginning at Lake Huleh in the north, is the lowest river in the world. From Lake Galilee the Jordan twists down for some 65 miles to the Dead Sea in the south.

The Jordan River is from 90 to 100 feet wide and is rapid and muddy: General Naaman scorned the unappealing Jordan (2 Kings 5:12).

From early spring to late autumn, the Jordan Valley is hot. The heat and luxuriant vegetation turn the valley into a jungle. In ancient times, lions and other wild beasts roamed "the thickets of the Jordan."

In Old Testament times, the Jordan formed a boundary and military frontier. Many battles were fought in the fords of the Jordan.

Jericho is in the southern part of the Jordan Valley, nearly ten miles north-west of the Dead Sea. Old Testament Jericho was at an oasis fed by a perennial spring, and was sometimes called "The City of Palms."

The Jericho of the Old Testament was one of the oldest cities in the world. It was, however, a ruin in New Testament times. New Testament Jericho was a little to the south of the original site having been built by King Herod as a winter residence.

The Mediterranean Sea is frequently called "the Sea" in the Old Testament. It is also called "The Great Sea." In some Bibles it is sometimes called "the sea behind," "the western sea" or "the uttermost sea."

Rich Man, Poor Man

Quiz #1

1. Who was the first son of Adam and Eve?

2. Name one of Noah's three sons.

3. Who lived for the longest according to the Bible?

4. In the book of Genesis what was the name of the man who never died?

5. Which ruler's house in Egypt did the Lord punish because Abraham's wife told the people that she was Abraham's sister?

6. What was the name of Abraham's rich relative who lived in Sodom?

7. What was the name of Sarah's Egyptian maid?

8. What was the name of Hagar's son?

9. Who was Rachel's father?

10. Who became Jacob's first wife?

11. How were Jacob's two wives related to each other?

12. Who was the mother of Reuben?

13. Who was the mother of Judah?

14. Who was the mother of Joseph?

15. Who was the mother of Benjamin?

Quiz #2

1. What was the name of the Egyptian officer who bought Joseph from the Ishmaelites?

2. Which of Jacob's twelve sons was the father of Er and Onan?

3. Who was Manasseh and Ephraim's father?

4. Who drew Moses out of the River Nile when he was in a basket?

5. What was the name of Moses' father-in-law?

6. What was the name of Moses' wife?

7. How were Moses and Aaron related?

8. Who was the son of Nun who succeeded Moses as the leader of Israel?

9. What was the name of the man who owned a talking donkey?

10. What was the name of the left-handed judge who fought the Moabites?

11. Who was the female judge who led the Israelites against the Canaanites?

12. Which Israelite judge laid a fleece out over night to see if the Lord wanted him to lead Israel against the Midianites?

13. Which Israelite judge confronted the Philistines and slew many of them with a jawbone of a donkey?

14. Luke wrote his Gospel and the Acts of the Apostles for a person whose name is found in the first few verses of both books. Who is he?

15. What was Matthew's occupation before he was called to be Jesus' disciple?

Answers

1. Potiphar 2. Judah 3. Joseph 4. Pharaoh's daughter 5. Jethro 6. Zipporah 7. They were brothers 8. Joshua 9. Balaam 10. Ehud 11. Deborah 12. Gideon 13. Samson 14. Theophilus 15. Tax collector

Quiz #3

1. What did Jesus say must be done to a strong man before anyone can enter his house and carry off his possessions?

2. Who said this to a Syro-Phonecian woman: "First let the children eat all they want, for it is not right to take the children's bread and toss it to their dogs"?

3. What righteous man, who was born before Jesus, acknowledged that Jesus surpassed him because he was "before" him?

4. What type of person did Jesus allow to cast the first stone at the woman caught in adultery?

5. Who was the eldest son of Gideon?

6. As a result of the death of which king did David compose a famous lament?

7. In the first chapter of 1 Kings, which of David's sons was trying to take possession of the throne of Israel?

8. Which king's decree is recorded in the first chapter of Ezra?

9. Which captured Jewish king received a regular allowance from the king of Babylon?

10. Which Jewish prophet who lived in the time of Ahab is mentioned in the last chapter of the book of Malachi?

11. According to the last verse of the book of Deuteronomy, who did the most powerful and awesome deeds in the sight of all Israel?

12. Who was the righteous and most famous king of Israel descended from Ruth?

13. Which rich and powerful man did Ruth marry?

14. How was Ruth related to Naomi?

15. From which people was Ruth descended?

Answers

1. He must be tied up 2. Jesus 3. John the Baptist 4. The one without sin
5. Jether 6. King Saul 7. Adonijah 8. King Cyrus' decree 9. King Jehoiachin
10. Elijah 11. Moses 12. King David 13. Boaz
14. She was her daughter-in-law 15. The Moabites

Quiz #4

1. Who was Israel's first king?

2. Who was Saul's son who befriended David?

3. Who defeated Goliath?

4. Who was king over Israel when the confrontation with Goliath occurred?

5. What was the name of Saul's daughter whom he gave to David as a wife?

6. Ahimilech the priest, Samuel the judge, Jonathan the son of Saul, and Achish the king of Gath, protected which future king of Israel?

7. Which king of Israel slaughtered priests while chasing after David?

8. Which of David's wives had once been married to Nabal?

9. Which Philistine king did David serve under?

10. Who did the medium at Endor say she saw after she had "brought him up"?

11. Who was the commander of David's army?

12. How old was David when he became king over all of Israel?

13. True or false? Mephibosheth was related to David.

14. What was the name of the prophet who confronted David after his adulterous affair?

15. Absalom led a revolt against his father who was king of Israel. Who was Absalom's father?

Answers

1. Saul 2. Jonathan 3. David 4. Saul 5. Michal 6. David 7. Saul 8. Abigail
9. Achish 10. Samuel 11. Joab 12. 30 years old 13. False. He was related to Saul (2 Samuel 9:1-13)
14. Nathan 15. David

Quiz #5

I. Who succeeded David?

2. Who was Solomon's mother?

3. Which king of Israel asked the Lord if he could build a temple for the Lord?

4. During the reign of which king of Israel was the temple built?

5. True or false? King David was known as the wisest man in all of Israel.

6. True or false? King Solomon was known for his skills in constructing Psalms.

7. Which royal dignitary came to King Solomon with spices, precious stones, and 120 talents of gold?

8. Which group of people were responsible for King Solomon's spiritual decline?

9. Which prophet tore a new cloak into twelve pieces in front of Jeroboam as he told him that the nation of Israel would be divided into two kingdoms?

10. Who was the first king of the southern kingdom of Judah?

11. Who was the first king of the northern kingdom of Israel?

12. True or false? King Jeroboam gave special respect to the Levites, assuring them that they alone would be priests in his kingdom.

13. Which king, who came from Egypt, attacked Jerusalem and carried off the treasures of the temple during King Rehoboam's reign?

14. True or false? King Abijah was King Rehoboam's son.

15. Who was the son of King Jeroboam who succeeded him in Israel?

Answers

1. Solomon **2.** Bathsheba **3.** King David **4.** King Solomon
5. False. King Solomon was known for his wisdom (1 Kings 3:10-12)
6. False. It was Solomon's father, David **7.** The Queen of Sheba **8.** The foreign women whom he loved
9. Ahijah **10.** King Rehoboam **11.** King Jeroboam **12.** False. King Jeroboam was disobedient and placed anyone as priest over Israel (1 Kings 13:33-34) **13.** King Shishak **14.** True **15.** Nadab

Quiz #6

1. What was the name of the last king of the northern kingdom of Israel?

2. True or false? King Hezekiah was known as being one of Judah's worst kings.

3. Who was the king of Assyria who conquered the northern kingdom of Israel when Hoshea was king?

4. Who was King Hezekiah's son who became a wicked king in Judah?

5. Who was the king of Judah who rediscovered the law?

6. Who was the Babylonian king who conquered the southern kingdom of Judah?

7. Who was the first king from Judah who was taken prisoner to Babylon?

8. Which king of Judah was blinded immediately after seeing his sons put to death and was then deported to Babylon?

9. What was the name of the king of Persia who decreed that the temple should be rebuilt in Jerusalem?

10. Who led the people of Israel from Babylon back to Jerusalem during the reign of King Artaxerxes?

11. Who was a cupbearer to King Artaxerxes who petitioned this king so that he could return to Jerusalem to rebuild the city's walls?

12. Which Israelite renewed the covenant with the Lord following the rebuilding of the temple and the rebuilding of the walls of Jerusalem?

13. Who did King Xerxes divorce before he married Esther?

14. Who influenced King Xerxes to decree that all of the Jews throughout his entire kingdom should be killed?

15. Who persuaded King Xerxes to permit all of the Jews within his kingdom to defend themselves against their enemies?

Answers

1. Hoshea **2.** False. King Hezekiah was known as one of Israel's best kings (2 Kings 18:1-12) **3.** Shalmaneser **4.** Manasseh **5.** King Josiah **6.** King Nebuchadnezzar **7.** King Jehoiachin **8.** King Zedekiah **9.** King Cyrus **10.** Ezra **11.** Nehemiah **12.** Ezra **13.** Vashti **14.** Haman **15.** Esther

Quiz #7

1. Who was known to be a righteous and blameless man but lost seven sons and three daughters and was afflicted with terrible sores?

2. True or false? Satan appears before the Lord at the beginning of the book of Job.

3. Who appeared to Job out of a storm leaving Job speechless?

4. Who wrote the book of Proverbs according to its first verse?

5. Who was the author of the book of Ecclesiastes according to its first verse?

6. Who saw the Lord in his temple in the year that King Uzziah died and as a result was commissioned to prophesy?

7. What name did the Babylonians give to Daniel?

8. Who interpreted King Nebuchadnezzar's dream about a statue which had many different metals?

9. Who set up a gold statue on the plain of Dura and commanded his subjects to bow down to it?

10. Who were the three Israelites King Nebuchadnezzar threw into the fiery furnace?

11. Which king of Babylon ate grass like the wild animals?

12. Which king of Babylon saw handwriting appear on the wall?

13. What Israelite was thrown into the lions' den?

14. Who was the king at the time that Daniel was thrown in the lions' den?

15. Who was the king who overthrew Babylon on the night that the Babylonian king saw the handwriting on the wall?

Answers

1. Job 2. True (Job 1:6-11; 2:1-6) 3. The Lord 4. Solomon 5. Solomon
6. Isaiah 7. Belteshazzar 8. Daniel 9. King Nebuchadnezzar
10. Shadrach, Meshach, and Abednego 11. King Nebuchadnezzar
12. King Belshazzar 13. Daniel 14. King Darius 15. King Darius

Quiz #8

1. Who was Mary's husband?

2. Who met Jesus in the wilderness where Jesus had fasted for 40 days and 40 nights?

3. Who baptized Jesus?

4. Who were the first two disciples that Jesus called who were fishing in the Sea of Galilee at the time?

5. Who were the sons of Zebedee, called "sons of Thunder," whom Jesus called to follow him?

6. Who was the first disciple who confessed that Jesus was the Son of God?

7. Which disciple's mother-in-law did Jesus heal?

8. Who criticized the disciples when they were picking grain on the Sabbath?

9. Jesus called two disciples named James to follow him. One was the son of Zebedee, the other was the son of whom?

10. What was the other name of the woman called Magdalene?

11. What was the name of the demon-possessed man who lived in the land of the Gerasenes?

12. What was the name of the synagogue official who came to Jesus to ask for his daughter to be healed?

13. What did the woman with a hemorrhage do to be healed by Jesus when she was in a large crowd with him?

14. In one of Jesus' parables, who came to the aid of the man who was attacked on the road to Jericho from Jerusalem?

15. What was the name of the woman whom Jesus said was worried and bothered by so many things that she was too busy to simply be with Jesus?

Answers

1. Joseph **2.** The devil **3.** John the Baptist **4.** Simon who was called Peter and Andrew **5.** James and John **6.** Peter **7.** Peter's **8.** The Pharisees **9.** Alphaeus **10.** Mary **11.** Legion **12.** Jairus **13.** She touched the edge of Jesus' cloak **14.** The Good Samaritan **15.** Martha

Quiz #9

1. To whom did Jesus teach the prayer we now know as the Lord's Prayer?

2. Who did Jesus say were like whitewashed tombs, who appear beautiful on the outside but inside are filled with dead men's bones?

3. Who said he was the "good shepherd" who lays down his life for the sheep?

4. What was the nationality of the healed leper who returned to give thanks to Jesus?

5. What was Zacchaeus' occupation?

6. Why did Zacchaeus climb a sycamore tree in order to see Jesus?

7. What was the name of the blind man whom Jesus healed as he traveled to Jerusalem?

8. Whose image was on the coin that the Pharisees showed to Jesus when they asked him a trick question about paying taxes?

9. Who was the brother of Mary and Martha who Jesus raised from the dead?

10. True or false? The Pharisees brought Jesus a donkey so that he could ride into Jerusalem.

11. Which two disciples asked Jesus if he would grant them the favor of sitting on his right and left hand when he came into his glory?

12. Which of Jesus' disciples did Satan enter?

13. Which disciple denied Jesus three times on the night that Jesus was betrayed?

14. Whose ear was cut off on the night that Jesus was betrayed?

15. To whose house did Jesus' captors first take him on the night he was betrayed?

Answers

1. The disciples **2.** The Pharisees **3.** Jesus **4.** He was a Samaritan
5. He was a tax collector **6.** Because he was short **7.** Bartimaeus **8.** Caesar's image **9.** Lazarus
10. False. Two of Jesus' disciples brought the donkey to Jesus (Luke 19:28-35)
11. James and John the sons of Zebedee **12.** Judas **13.** Peter **14.** Malchus, the high priest's slave
15. The high priest's house

Quiz # 10

1. To whom did Pilate send Jesus?

2. Who was the Roman ruler who handed Jesus over to be crucified?

3. Who did the crowd demand to be freed from prison when Jesus was on trial?

4. Who carried Jesus' cross?

5. What type of people were crucified on the crosses to the right and left of Jesus?

6. Who asked Pilate for Jesus' body?

7. True or false? John was the first person to come to the tomb on the day that Jesus rose from the dead.

8. True or false? A man named Cleopas was one of the people walking with Jesus on the road to a village named Emmaus.

9. When the wine ran out at the wedding in Cana of Galilee, who told Jesus?

10. What was the nationality of the woman who Jesus met at a well?

11. Which disciple said that eight months' wages would not be enough to feed 5,000 people?

12. What group of Jewish people are described as those "who say there is no resurrection"?

13. Who was the high priest when Jesus was crucified?

14. Who was the father-in-law of the high priest when Jesus was crucified?

15. What was the name of Simon Peter's father?

Quiz #11

1. True or false? Joseph of Barsabbas is mentioned as one of the people present at Jesus' crucifixion.

2. Who preached the sermon on the Day of Pentecost?

3. Which apostle was with Peter when he healed a lame man at the temple gate called Beautiful?

4. Who, according to Peter, was the stone which was rejected by the builders?

5. What were the names of the two people who lied to the Holy Spirit and then dropped dead?

6. Who was the Pharisee who defended Peter after the Jewish leaders had told him not to preach in the name of Jesus?

7. Who was the first Christian martyr?

8. Who was the first Christian to preach in Samaria?

9. Who helped to restore Saul's sight?

10. Philip preached to an Ethiopian eunuch on the road to Gaza. What was this Ethiopian's employment?

11. What was Saul of Tarsus' other name?

12. What was the name of the centurion to whom Peter preached?

13. What is the name of the person whom Peter raised from the dead in Joppa whose name is translated as Dorcas?

14. Who was the leader of the church in Jerusalem?

15. Who killed James?

Answers

1. False. He was one of the men put forward to be an apostle (Ac 1:23)

2. Peter 3. John 4. Jesus 5. Ananias and Sapphira 6. Gamaliel 7. Stephen
8. Philip 9. Ananias 10. He was treasurer to the Queen of Ethiopia 11. Paul
12. Cornelius 13. Tabitha 14. James 15. Herod Agrippa I

Facts 1

When King Herod died his three sons ruled over his divided kingdom. From 4 BC-AD 37 Herod Antipas ruled as tetrarch of Galilee and Peraea. The region of Gaulanitus, Ituraea, and Trachonitis was ruled by Herod Philip from 4 BC to AD 34. Archelaus ruled Judea, Samaria and Idumea until from 4 BC-AD 6.

The person who lived the longest in the Bible is Methuselah. He lived 969 years. Other people in Genesis 5 also lived long lives. For example, Mahalalel lived 895 years.

Noah is the son of Lamech. About his son Noah, Lamech says, "He will comfort us in the labor and painful toil of our hands caused by the ground the Lord has cursed" (Genesis 5:29). He comforts humankind by building the ark and so became the means of rescuing humankind.

Although the book of Lamentations does not name its author, the consensus of Jewish tradition attributes it to Jeremiah. A superscription to the Vulgate, the Latin Bible, reads "Jeremiah sat weeping and lamented with this lamentation over Jerusalem."

The prophet Jeremiah is described in a variety of ways. He has been called "the weeping prophet" (Jeremiah 9:1; 13:17), the "prophet of loneliness" (Jeremiah 16:2), and the "reluctant prophet" (Jeremiah 1:6).

The prophet Isaiah was born into an influential, upper-class family. He lived most of his life in Jerusalem. Tradition has it that he was martyred during the reign of Manasseh (696-642 BC) by being sawn in two inside a large hollow log.

Timothy was the son of a Greek father and a Jewish mother named Eunice. Paul referred to him as his "true son in the faith." Timothy received two letters from Paul now known as 1 Timothy and 2 Timothy.

Titus was a convert from Paul's ministry and was later an emissary to the church at Corinth. When Paul writes to him, in the letter we now call "Paul's letter to Titus," Titus has been left in Crete to lead the work there.

The name Beelzebul mean "lord of flies." It is the Greek form of the Hebrew word *"Baal-Zebul"* who was a deity of the Ekronites (2 Kings 1:2). It is used in the Gospels as a name for Satan.

Moses was timid about speaking. The Lord provided Aaron, his brother, to be his mouthpiece (Exodus 4:10-17).

Facts 2

Job's friends who spoke to him in the midst of his calamity-Eliphaz, Bildad, Zophar and Elihu-gave poor comfort to Job since they tried to find some reason in Job's life for his acute suffering.

Many significant women of the Bible were infertile or "barren" at some point in their lives. Such women include Sarah, Rebekah, Rachel, Samson's mother, and Hannah, Samuel's mother.

The name James is the English equivalent of the Hebrew name Jacob.

Of the 41 times James appears in the Bible, it refers 19 times to James the son of Zebedee and brother of John, 4 times to James the son of Alphaeus and 3 times to a son of Mary.

In the New Testament a "pillar of the church," was a recognised leader of the church, like James, Peter, and John (Galatians 2:9).

Jesus is not only mentioned in the New Testament. The Jewish historian Josephus mentions Jesus in his writings known as *The Antiquities of the Jews*.

Jesus is called by many different names. For example, he is called "Immanuel" (which means "God with us"); "Root of David"; "The Lion of the tribe of Judah"; "The Bright and Morning Star" and "the shoot from the stump of Jesse."

John the Baptist was known as "the Baptist" since his ministry involved preaching repentance and performing baptisms in the Jordan River.

The name Moses is derived from the verb, "to draw out". It was a suitable name for a man who was drawn out of the River Nile .

Jacob's name came from the fact that he grasped the heel of his twin brother Esau during their birth.

Facts 3

Titus, a fellow worker of Paul, was left in Crete to oversee the work there (Titus 1:5). The Jewish Christians in Jerusalem wanted Titus, a Gentile, to be circumcised. Paul, however, did not circumcise him (Galatians 2:3).

Joseph, the husband of Mary, appears only in the narratives of Jesus' infancy and boyhood. This has led many to speculate that he had died before Jesus' public ministry began.

The man who stepped forward to bury Jesus was Joseph of Arimathea. He was a rich man and a member of the Sanhedrin.

The name Isaac is related to the verb "to laugh". Isaac was the promised son of Abraham who was born to Sarah when Abraham was 100 years old.

Isaiah's name means "Yahweh is salvation." His name is similar in meaning to the names Joshua, Elisha and Jesus.

Matthew's Gospel has an extensive genealogy of Jesus (Matthew 1:1-17). One of its unusual features is that it includes four non-Jewish women: Tamar and Rahab, (both prostitutes), Bathsheba, (an adulteress) and Ruth (a Moabitess).

Ancient Near Eastern genealogies sometimes omit people from the lines of descent for a variety of reasons. Genealogies were used to authenticate hereditary succession, and inheritance rights, to confirm biological descent, and to establish geographical and ethnological relationships.

Old Testament genealogies appear in many places in Genesis. For example, in Genesis 4 Cain's lineage is given. In Genesis 5:1-32, Adam's lineage is traced through Noah. In Genesis 10 Noah's descendants are listed.

The most comprehensive genealogical list in the Bible is found in 1 Chronicles chapters 1-9. It covers people from Adam to Saul.

Paul had a number of traveling partners with him on his missionary journeys. Such companions included Barnabas, Silas, Luke, Titus and Timothy.

Facts 4

The angel Gabriel is mentioned twice in the New Testament. He appears to Zechariah the priest announcing the birth of his son (Luke 1:11-20) and announces the impending conception and birth of Jesus to Mary (Luke 1: 26-38).

The angel Gabriel appears twice in the Old Testament. In Daniel 8:16 he is the one "who looked like a man." In Daniel 9:21 he appears to Daniel when he is praying at the time of the evening sacrifice.

The very short New Testament letter, 3 John, is written to a man named Gaius. This man was beloved by John and is commended for the truth of his life and his hospitality.

The name Gideon means "cutter down," "feller" or "hewer." He and his followers cut down many Midianite oppressors in the time of the judges (Judges 7-8).

Gamaliel, the Jewish rabbi who taught Paul, was a member of the Sanhedrin and a teacher of Paul. He was the first of seven successive leaders of the school of Hillel to be honored with the title Rabban ("Our Rabbi/Master").

The great Old Testament prophet Jeremiah dictated his prophecies to his scribe Baruch who in turn read them to the people (Jeremiah 36).

In the days of Jesus, tax collectors were viewed with contempt because they collected money for the Romans who occupied the Jewish land. They were often corrupt. Two prominent tax collectors became followers of Jesus: Matthew and Zacchaeus.

Famous slaves in the Old Testament include Hagar, Joseph, and the nation of Israel during their time in Egypt.

Famous slaves in the New Testament include Onesimus who belonged to Philemon, and Malchus who had his ear cut off on the night of Jesus' betrayal. Malchus was the slave of the high priest.

Famous rich people in the Old Testament include Abraham, Pharaoh, Boaz, King David, King Solomon and King Nebuchadnezzar.

Names and Nicknames

Quiz #1

1. According to Genesis who gave names to the animals?

2. In the Old Testament who named her son Ben-Oni as she lay dying?

3. How many Old Testament books bear the names of men?

4. According to Genesis who was given a name which meant that he would provide comfort for his father?

5. Which son of the patriarch Jacob bears the name meaning "good fortune"?

6. Which Old Testament character named his first born Manasseh to help him forget his family and his troubles?

7. What does the name Ebenezer, which Samuel gave to a stone, mean?

8. According to Psalm 49, who had land named after themselves?

9. In the account of creation what does God call the light?

10. According to Isaiah 60, what name will be given to the gates of the city of Zion?

11. What does the name Abram mean?

12. In Genesis a heap of stones left by Laban and Jacob was called Mizpah. What does it mean?

13. According to Numbers 32, what did Nobah rename Keneth?

14. In Malachi what will be called the "Wicked Land"?

15. At Lystra what name did the enthusiastic citizens give the apostle Paul?

Answers

1. Adam 2. Rachel 3. 23 4. Noah 5. Gad 6. Joseph 7. Stone of help
8. The dead 9. Day 10. Praise 11. Exalted father 12. Watchtower 13. Nobah
14. Edom 15. Hermes

Quiz #2

1. What is the meaning of the name Salome?

2. When was Adam's wife first called "Eve"?

3. Who renamed his son Benjamin after the death of the boy's mother?

4. What is the appropriate meaning of the Old Testament name Nabal?

5. Which Old Testament character's name means "hairy"?

6. One of Jacob's sons had a name which sounds like the Hebrew for "reward." Which one was it?

7. What name meaning "twice fruitful" did Joseph give to his second child?

8. According to 2 Samuel what does the name Baal Perazim mean?

9. According to Ecclesiastes what has already been named?

10. In the account of the creation what does God call the darkness?

11. According to Isaiah 62 what names will no longer be used to describe Zion?

12. What is the meaning of the name Abraham?

13. In the Old Testament why did Jacob name a place Peniel?

14. According to Deuteronomy what name did the Ammonites give to the Rephaites?

15. Of whom was it said "He will be called a Nazarene"?

Answers

1. Peace 2. After the Fall 3. Jacob 4. Fool 5. Esau 6. Issachar 7. Ephraim
8. The Lord who breaks out 9. Everything that exists 10. Night 11. Deserted and Desolate
12. Father of many 13. He saw God's face and survived there 14. Zamzummites 15. Jesus

Quiz #3

1. By what name is the Mediterranean island, once named Alashiya, known today?

2. True or false? The name Saul means "answered".

3. What is the most confusing name in the Bible?

4. What Aramaic name did Jesus give to Peter?

5. Which New Testament place name means "skull"?

6. According to Genesis which patriarch's name means deceiver?

7. True or false? The name Zebulun given to a son of Jacob means "brave".

8. Who named his first son saying, "I have become an alien in a foreign land"?

9. According to 2 Samuel what was Solomon's other name?

10. What is the ironic meaning of the name of the runaway slave Onesimus?

11. According to Genesis what did God call the expanse that separated the waters?

12. In chapter 62 of Isaiah which name meaning "my delight is in her" will be given to Zion?

13. In Genesis, what name did Abraham give to the place where he swore an oath with Abimelech?

14. Which wicked man was buried at a place named the Valley of Achor?

15. What name was given to the place where Joshua had the Israelites circumcised?

Answers

1. Cyprus 2. False. It means "asked" 3. Babel 4. Cephas 5. Golgotha
6. Jacob 7. False. It probably means "honor" (Genesis 30:20)
8. Moses 9. Jedidiah 10. Useful 11. Sky
12. Hephzibah 13. Beersheba 14. Achan 15. Gilgal

Quiz #4

1. What does the Old Testament name Hannah mean?

2. What name is given to the first five books of the Old Testament?

3. In the Old Testament what was the name given to the places where a person who had accidentally killed another could flee?

4. According to Genesis 10 why was Peleg, the son of Eber, so named?

5. Which of Jesus' disciples was called the Zealot?

6. Which Old Testament name means "God is my judge"?

7. Who named a well Esek because his herdsmen quarreled with those of Gerar?

8. True or false? The name of the patriarch Joseph means "may he add".

9. What name, meaning "my God is helper," did Moses give to his second son?

10. In the Old Testament which prophet told King David to give his son Solomon the name Jedidiah?

11. According to Ezekiel 48 what will be named after the tribes of Israel?

12. As recorded in Genesis, what did God call the ground at creation?

13. According to Isaiah 62 which new name, meaning "married," will be given to Zion?

14. What name did Abraham give to the place where he nearly sacrificed Isaac?

15. According to Genesis why is Succoth so named?

Answers

1. Grace 2. Pentateuch 3. Cities of Refuge 4. The earth was divided and his name means division
5. Simon 6. Daniel 7. Isaac 8. True 9. Eliezer 10. Nathan 11. The gates of the city of God
12. Land 13. Beulah 14. The Lord will provide 15. Because Jacob built shelters there

Quiz #5

1. What Aramaic name does John use for the Sheep Gate in Jerusalem?

2. What name was given to non-Greeks who nevertheless spoke Greek themselves?

3. How many letters in the New Testament are named after their author?

4. By what name does the writer of Ecclesiastes refer to himself?

5. Why was Isaac given his name?

6. What does the nickname Boanerges mean?

7. The name Deborah is derived from the name of an insect. Which one?

8. As recorded in Joshua by what name was Hebron formerly known?

9. On his way to meet Esau, Jacob saw two angels and exclaimed "This is the camp of God." What name did he give to the place?

10. According to Numbers 11, what name was given to the place where the Israelites buried people who had craved other food?

11. What does Jedidiah, the name God gave to Solomon, mean?

12. Who in the Old Testament named his daughters Jemimah, Keziah and Keren Happuch?

13. What did God call the waters during the week of creation?

14. According to Jeremiah 3, what will Jerusalem be called in the future?

15. In the Old Testament by what name was Esau also known?

Answers

1. Bethesda 2. Hellenists 3. 7. Those of James, Peter (2), John (3) and Jude
4. Qoheleth 5. Isaac means "he laughs" Sarah laughed when she heard that she was to have a son in her old age
6. Sons of Thunder 7. Bee 8. Kiriath Arba 9. Mahanaim 10. Kibroth Hattaavah
11. Loved by the Lord 12. Job 13. Seas 14. The Throne of the Lord 15. Edom

Quiz #6

1. According to the book of Joshua by what new name was Kiriath Sepher known?

2. Which disciple of Jesus, also called Barsabbas and Justus, failed to be selected to replace Judas Iscariot?

3. What does the Hebrew name "Hermon" mean?

4. How many New Testament letters bear the names of people?

5. What is the uncomplimentary meaning of the name Leah?

6. In the Old Testament why did Hannah name her son Samuel?

7. When did God first reveal his name as Yahweh?

8. According to Genesis, Jacob named an altar El Elohe Israel within sight of which city?

9. According to Genesis 26, how many wells did Isaac name?

10. In the Old Testament what name was given to the place where Rebekah's nurse, Deborah, died?

11. According to Numbers 21 what name did Israel give to the region belonging to the King of Arad after they had destroyed it?

12. In the Old Testament who named a pillar after himself because he had no son?

13. What is the meaning of the name Edom?

14. Who in Old Testament wanted to be called Mara instead of her real name?

15. As recorded in Jeremiah 7 what new name will be given to Topheth?

Answers

1. Debir **2.** Joseph **3.** Sanctuary

4. 11. 1 Timothy, 2 Timothy, Titus, Philemon, James, 1 Peter, 2 Peter, 1 John, 2 John, 3 John, Jude

5. Weak eyes or wild cow **6.** Samuel sounds like the Hebrew for "heard of God". He was an answer to Hannah's prayer

7. To Moses at the burning bush **8.** Shechem **9.** Three **10.** Allon Bacuth **11.** Hormah **12.** Absalom

13. Red **14.** Naomi **15.** Valley of Slaughter

Quiz #7

1. According to Exodus 15 why did the Israelites call a place Marah?

2. In the book of Judges why did the Israelites rename Gilgal, Bokim?

3. In the New Testament what was the name of the temple gate where Peter and John healed a beggar?

4. According to Numbers by what name was Joshua originally known?

5. As recorded in 1 Samuel 23 what name was given to the place where Saul stopped pursuing David?

6. According to Acts 13 what was the name of the false prophet who met Paul and Barnabas?

7. What does the name Moses mean?

8. In the book of Daniel who was renamed Abednego?

9. What is the meaning of the common Old Testament name Eliab?

10. In the Old Testament who named her child Reuben thinking that her husband would now love her?

11. Who gave the patriarch Jacob the name Israel?

12. According to Deuteronomy, what name was given to Bashan in honor of its owner Jair?

13. Where did Absalom erect the pillar he named after himself?

14. What is the meaning of the name Tabitha?

15. According to the book of Ruth why did Naomi wish to be called Mara?

Answers

1. Because of the bitter water 2. Because they met an angel there who made them weep
3. Beautiful 4. Hosea 5. Sela Hammahlekoth 6. Bar-Jesus 7. Drew out 8. Azariah
9. God is father 10. Leah 11. God 12. Havvoth Jair 13. The King's Valley 14. Gazelle
15. It means bitter and she felt the Lord had made her life bitter

Quiz #8

1. According to Jeremiah, why will Topheth be named the Valley of Slaughter?

2. In the Old Testament by what name was Bethel formerly known?

3. What name did the Israelites give to the bread from heaven?

4. What name did the judge Gideon give to the altar where he met an angel of the Lord?

5. According to Acts what was Mark's other name?

6. What does the name "Israel" mean?

7. True or false? The Old Testament name Rachel means "calf."

8. What does the name Ichabod mean?

9. According to Acts who bought a field named Akeldama?

10. What does Akeldama mean?

11. According to Genesis 4:26 what did men begin to do for the first time?

12. Which child of Leah has a name meaning "attached"?

13. Where was Jacob given the name Israel?

14. By what name is Yam Suph better known?

15. In the Old Testament who named the temple pillars Jakin and Boaz?

Answers

1. Because the dead will be buried there until there is no more room **2.** Luz **3.** Manna
4. The Lord is Peace **5.** John **6.** God strives **7.** False. Rachel means ewe **8.** "The glory has departed"
9. Judas Iscariot **10.** Field of Blood **11.** Call on the name of the Lord **12.** Levi
13. Bethel **14.** Sea of Reeds **15.** Hiram

Quiz #9

1. According to Jesus who loved to have men call them "Rabbi"?

2. Which patriarch renamed Luz, calling it Bethel?

3. According to Exodus why did Moses build an altar called the Lord is My Banner?

4. Which Old Testament hero was known as Jerub-Baal?

5. According to the book of Acts, where were the disciples first called Christians?

6. In the New Testament what title was given to the son of Zechariah and Elizabeth in later life?

7. Which of Jesus' disciples was known as Didymus?

8. In the Old Testament who did not drink alcohol, shave or approach dead bodies?

9. What does the name of the Old Testament patriarch Jacob mean?

10. According to the book of Revelation what does the names Alpha and Omega mean?

11. Why did Adam call his wife Eve?

12. True or false? Bilhah, the slave of Rachel, named her child Dan.

13. According to Genesis 35 what name did Jacob give to the place where God spoke with him?

14. As recorded in Joshua what name did the Danites give to the captured city of Leshem?

15. True or false? The name Jabez sounds like the Hebrew for "pleasure".

Answers

1. Teachers of the Law and the Pharisees 2. Jacob 3. To commemorate victory over the Amalekites 4. Gideon 5. Antioch 6. The Baptist 7. Thomas 8. Nazarites 9. He deceives 10. First and last 11. Because she would become the mother of all living things 12. False. Rachel gave the child her name (Genesis 30:6) 13. Bethel 14. Dan 15. False. Jabez sounds like the Hebrew for "pain" (1 Chronicles 4:9)

Quiz #10

1. What was the name of the companion of Cleopas who met Jesus on the road to Emmaus?

2. According to Isaiah what name will the virgin give to her son?

3. Why did the disciples of Jesus call him "Teacher" and "Lord"?

4. In the Old Testament Laban called it Jegar Sahadutha. What did Jacob call it?

5. According to Numbers 11 what place was given its name because fire from the Lord burned among the Israelites?

6. As recorded by the prophet Zechariah, who took two staffs calling one "Favor" and the other "Union?"

7. By what name was Simon, one of the leaders of the Antioch Church also known?

8. What does the name of the Old Testament prophet Jonah mean?

9. True or false? Rhoda, the name of the servant girl who opened the door to Peter after his escape from prison, means "orchid."

10. What was Abraham called before God changed his name?

11. What does the name of the prophetess Anna mean?

12. What name did Cain give to the city he built in Genesis 4?

13. Why did Cain name the city he built in Genesis 4, Enoch?

14. Which name, meaning "my struggle" did Rachel give to one of her servants children?

15. In the Old Testament who named one of her children Zerah because he was born with a scarlet thread on his wrist?

Answers

1. His name is not recorded 2. Immanuel 3. Because he was their Teacher and Lord
4. Galeed 5. Taberah 6. God 7. Niger 8. Dove 9. False. It means rose 10. Abram 11. Grace
12. Enoch 13. It was the name of his son 14. Naphtali 15. Tamar

115

Quiz #11

1. But for the intervention of his mother what name would have been given to John the Baptist?

2. According to Isaiah 60 what name is to be given to the walls of the city of Zion?

3. In Genesis, why was the town Lot fled to named Zoar?

4. Which location in the Promised Land was so named because the spies found clusters of grapes there?

5. At Lystra what name did the citizens give Barnabas?

6. How many of Jesus' disciples names are replicated?

7. According to Zechariah 8, Jerusalem will be called the city of what?

8. How many Old Testament books bear the names of women?

9. In 1 Corinthians 1, Paul mockingly asks if his readers were baptized into whose name?

10. According to Genesis, by what name was Jegar Sahadutha, or Galeed also known?

11. What was Sarah called before her name was changed by God?

12. In the New Testament whose name means "Son of Encouragement"?

13. What name did Adam give to the son who replaced the murdered Abel?

14. Which name, meaning "happy" did Leah give to the child of her servant Zilpah?

15. What name was given to the twin of Zerah who "broke out" of the womb before his brother?

Answers

1. Zechariah 2. Salvation 3. Because it was a small town
4. Valley of Eschol 5. Zeus 6. 2, Simon and James 7. Truth
8. Two, Ruth and Esther 9. Paul's 10. Mizpah 11. Sarai
12. Barnabas 13. Seth 14. Asher 15. Perez

Facts 1

Eve is the first person in the Bible to have two names: Eve and woman.

The word "abba" meaning "father" occurs only three times in the New Testament.

Jonah was the first Hebrew prophet to be sent into a pagan country. Jonah hated the idea that he should tell the wicked people of Nineveh to repent. Through Jonah, the Jewish people learned that God cared for all the nations.

The place name Bethlehem means "house of bread."

The name "David" is mentioned 58 times in the New Testament. Despite some spectacular failures, David was "a man after God's own heart," and he became a model for Israel's future Messiah.

El, a basic name used for God or gods, occurs widely in Semitic literature and can also mean an image revered as a god.

Jerusalem is called by its shortened form "Salem" in Genesis 14:18. "Salem" is related to the Hebrew word for "peace" (Hebrews 7:2).

The name "Teacher" given to Jesus (Mark 4:38) was often conferred upon people who passed on teaching to a group of disciples.

In the Gospels, Jesus' often referred to himself as "Son of Man."

The name Lucifer means "light bearer" in Latin.

Ruah, the Hebrew name for the Spirit of God, occurs 378 times in the Old Testament and eleven times in its Aramaic form in Daniel.

When the Lord called people to fulfil his Divine purposes. For this new role he often gave them new names. Such people were Abraham (Abram), Sarah (Sarai), Israel (Jacob) and Peter (Simon) to name just a few.

Facts 2

The tetragrammaton, YHWH, was considered too sacred to be pronounced so the Hebrew "adonai" (my Lord) was substituted when it was read out loud.

In the Bible children are named 28 times by their mothers.

The name "Adam" means "mankind" and is used over 500 times in that sense in the Bible.

"Baal," the name commonly used of foreign gods, means "master," "possessor," "Lord" or "husband."

The Hebrew word "beth" means simply "house" or "building" and is often used as the first part of a place name, for example: Bethlehem; Bethesda and Beth-Gilgal.

The Greek name Eutychus, belonging to the young man Paul raised from the dead, appropriately means "lucky" (Acts 20:7-12).

"Pneuma," the Greek word used for the Holy Spirit, occurs 379 times in the New Testament.

The name Jesus means "The Lord saves."

The title "Rabbi" means "my great one" or "my master" or "my teacher." It was a commonplace term of respect.

Two people in the Bible were called Jonah: the Old Testament prophet and the father of Simon Peter (Matthew 16:17).

Four people in the New Testament are named Philip: two sons of Herod the Great, the apostle, and one of the seven chosen in Acts to serve the Church.

The naming of "woman" by Adam is an example of the conferring of a name conveying status.

Facts 3

"Mary" is the Greek form of the Hebrew name "Miriam".

The name Zechariah or Zacharias is given to 28 men in the Bible.

The name prefix "Bar" which occurs frequently in the Bible means "son of".

"Shaddai" translated Almighty is used 48 times in the Old Testament for God.

The title "Lamb of God" appears only twice in the New Testament, both in John's Gospel (John 1:29, 36).

Two towns are named Bethlehem in the Old Testament, Bethlehem in Judah where Jesus was born, and Bethlehem in the territory of Zebulun (Joshua 19:15).

Jacob's children born to his wives' maidservants were named by Jacob's wives rather than by their biological mothers.

Nicodemus, the name of the man who came to see Jesus at night, means "conqueror of the people."

Jesus was a fairly common name in the first half of the first century A.D.

Peter's confession of Jesus as Messiah appears only in the Synoptic gospels.

The New Testament name Simon is a later form of the Old Testament name Simeon.

The name "The Holy One of Israel" occurs 29 times in the book of Isaiah.

Paul uses the expression "Son of God" 15 times in the New Testament.

Children are named 18 times in the Bible by their fathers.

"Shaddai", meaning "Almighty" occurs 31 times alone in the book of Job.

Who Said That?

WHO SAID THAT?

Quiz #1

1. Which Old Testament prophet responded to the Lord's call with the words, "Here am I. Send me"?

2. Who instructed some servants, "Fill the jars with water"?

3. "O man of God, there is death in the pot!" Who said this to Elisha?

4. Who was afraid and said, "What I did must have become known"?

5. "Rabbi, we know you are a teacher who has come from God." Who said this?

6. Who promised, "I will come back and take you to be with me"?

7. True or false? Adam said to Eve, "You will not surely die."

8. Which group of people declared, "Saul has slain his thousands, and David his tens of thousands"?

9. Who said to Elijah, "let me kiss my father and mother goodbye"?

10. Which disciple said, "Unless I see the nail marks in his hands... I will not believe it"?

11. Who said, "Please test your servants for ten days. Give us nothing but vegetables to eat and water to drink"?

12. "It would not be right for us to neglect the ministry of the word of God in order to wait on tables." Who said this?

13. Which three men agreed, "If we are thrown into the blazing furnace, the God we serve is able to save us from it"?

14. Who explained to the crowd at Pentecost, "These men are not drunk, as you suppose"?

15. "The donkeys are for the king's household to ride on, the bread and fruit are for the men to eat, and the wine is to refresh those who become exhausted in the desert." Who said this to king David?

Quiz #2

1. Did Solomon, Job, or David say "In you, O Lord, I have taken refuge; let me never be put to shame"?

2. Who requested, "Lord teach us to pray"?

3. Who presented the Israelites with a choice when he said, "Choose for yourselves this day whom you will serve"?

4. Who said, "You are the God who sees me"?

5. Who swore, "I don't know the man"?

6. Whose address on Mars Hill began, "Men of Athens! I see that in every way you are very religious"?

7. Who said, "I am the good shepherd"?

8. Which Old Testament prophet cried out, "Ah, sovereign Lord! Are you going to destroy the entire remnant of Israel in this outpouring of your wrath of Jerusalem?"

9. Was it Joseph, Isaac or Abraham who said, "The voice is the voice of Jacob, but the hands are the hands of Esau"?

10. "Do whatever he tells you." Who gave this instruction to servants at a wedding?

11. Which mother cried, "I cannot watch the boy die"?

12. Who offered these words of comfort, "Do not be afraid, Mary, you have found favor with God"?

13. Who called out, "Treason! Treason!"?

14. Which king said, "As I was lying in my bed, the images and visions that passed through my mind terrified me"?

15. Did Saul, David or Jonathan ask "Do you think it is a small matter to become the king's son-in-law?"?

Answers

1. David 2. The disciples 3. Joshua 4. Hagar 5. Peter 6. Paul's address 7. Jesus 8. Ezekiel 9. Isaac 10. Jesus' mother, Mary 11. Hagar 12. The angel Gabriel 13. Athaliah 14. Nebuchadnezzar 15. David

Quiz #3

1. Who made this claim, "All the prophets testify about him that everyone who believes in him receives forgiveness of sins through his name"?

2. Which disciple responded to the risen Christ with the words, "My Lord and my God"?

3. Which young boy said to a frightened king, "Let no-one lose heart on account of this Philistine; your servant will go and fight him"?

4. Who spoke these words, "Let the little children come to me, and do not hinder them"?

5. "The boy has not awakened." Who said this to Elisha?

6. True or false? Jesus said, "I lay down my life for the sheep."

7. Which priest said to the men of Judah and Benjamin, "You have been unfaithful; you have married foreign women, adding to Israel's guilt. Now make consecration to the Lord, the God of your fathers"?

8. Who prayed and restored life to a young girl with the instruction, "Tabitha arise"?

9. Which mighty warrior said, "If the Lord is with us, why has all this happened to us?"?

10. Was it Mary or Martha who said, "The teacher is here and is asking for you"?

11. Who said to Elisha, "When I bow down in the temple of Rimmon, may the Lord forgive your servant for this"?

12. "The battle is the Lord's, and he will give all of you into our hands." Who believed this?

13. True or false? It was the high priest who said to Peter, "Didn't I see you with him in the olive grove?"

14. Did Elijah or Elisha say to a widow, "How can I help you? Tell me, what do you have in your house?"?

15. Who gave the excuse, "I have just got married, so I can't come"?

Answers

1. Peter **2.** Thomas **3.** David **4.** Jesus **5.** Gehazi **6.** True (John 10:15)

7. Ezra **8.** Peter **9.** Gideon **10.** Martha

11. Naaman **12.** David **13.** False, the high priest's servant (John 18:26)

14. Elisha **15.** An invited guest in the Parable of the Great Banquet

Quiz #4

1. Who said, "With a donkey's jaw-bone I have killed a thousand men"?

2. Which blind man called out, "Jesus, Son of David, have mercy on me"?

3. Who cried out to the Lord, "What am I to do with these people? They are almost ready to stone me"?

4. Which great friend of David said, "My father Saul is looking for a chance to kill you"?

5. Which man used this line in his preaching, "Cast your bread upon the waters, for after many days you will find it again"?

6. "I am a woman who is deeply troubled. I have not been drinking wine or beer; I was pouring out my soul to the Lord." Who protested her innocence to Eli with these words?

7. Who spoke these words of praise around the throne in heaven: "You are worthy, our Lord and God, to receive glory and honor and power, for you created all things"?

8. "Is it nothing to you, all you who pass by? Look around and see. Is any suffering like my suffering?" Which weeping prophet said this?

9. Which man in authority said to Paul, "You have permission to speak for yourself"?

10. Who, described as a devout believer in the Lord, asked, "Is it really you, my lord Elijah?'"?

11. True or false? Martha said to Jesus, "Lord, if you had been here, my brother would not have died."

12. Which lady sang these words, "Sing to the Lord, for he is highly exalted. The horse and its rider he has hurled into the sea"?

13. Was it Naomi, Martha or Esther who said to her daughters-in-law, "Go back each of you to your mother's home"?

14. Who asked his friends, "Why are you so afraid? Do you still have no faith?"?

15. Who said to Job, "Are you the first man ever born? Were you bought forth before the hills?'"?

Answers

1. Samson 2. Bartimaeus 3. Moses 4. Jonathan 5. The preacher, Ecclesiastes
6. Hannah 7. The four living creatures 8. Jeremiah 9. Agrippa
10. Obadiah 11. False, Mary (John 11:21) 12. Miriam 13. Naomi 14. Jesus 15. Eliphaz

WHO SAID THAT?

Quiz #5

1. Did men from Gilgal, Beth Shemesh or Ashdod say, "Who can stand in the presence of the Lord, this holy God? To whom will the ark go up from here?"?

2. Which Old Testament prophet instructed his servant, "Get some flour"?

3. Who said to Jesus, "but even the dogs eat the crumbs that fall from the masters' table"?

4. Which Old Testament prophet advised his travelling companions, "Pick me up and throw me into the sea"?

5. Who advised Isaiah, "Go out, you and your son Shear-Jashub to meet Ahaz at the end of the aqueduct of the Upper Pool"?

6. Did Solomon, Hezekiah or Ahab say, "I intend, therefore, to build a temple for the Name of the Lord my God"?

7. "Come, be our commander, so we can fight the Ammonites." Who made this request of Jephthah?

8. Who said, "Draw your sword and run me through"?

9. "Talitha Koum!" Who gave this instruction?

10. Who said, "My silver has been returned. Here it is in my sack"?

11. Which old man on an island said, "On the Lord's day I was in the Spirit, and I heard behind me a loud voice like a trumpet"?

12. Who asked his wife, "Don't I mean more to you than ten sons?"?

13. Who made the request of Philip, "Sir, we would like to see Jesus"?

14. Who flattered Solomon, "How happy your men must be! How happy your officials who continually stand before you and hear your wisdom"?

15. Who said to God, "Stretch out your hand and strike his flesh and bones, and he will surely curse you to his face"?

Quiz #6

1. Which major prophet said, "I was among the exiles by the Kebar River"?

2. Who said to Peter and John, "Go and make preparations for us to eat the Passover"?

3. Was it Micaiah or Micah who prophesied against Ahab, "I saw all Israel scattered on the hills like sheep without a shepherd"?

4. Whose final words of blessing included the words, "May the angel who has delivered me from all harm bless these boys"?

5. "Are you only a visitor to Jerusalem and do you not know the things that have happened there in these days?" Who asked this question of a travelling companion?

6. Who warned Asahal, "Stop chasing me! Why should I strike you down? How could I look your brother Joab in the face?"?

7. True or false? Peter protested, "Although I have done nothing against our people or against the customs of our ancestors, I was arrested in Jerusalem and handed over to the Romans."

8. Who instructed Joseph, "Get up, take the child and his mother and escape to Egypt"?

9. Which queen said, "How can I bear to see disaster fall on my people? How can I bear to see the destruction of my family?"?

10. Who prayed, "Father, forgive them, for they do not know what they are doing"?

11. "I'm convinced! My son Joseph is still alive. I will go and see him before I die." Who said this before setting out for Egypt?

12. Who asked Rebekah, "Please give me a little water from your jar"?

13. In Jesus' parable, who said, "Give us some of your oil; our lamps are going out"?

14. "If you are the Son of God, throw yourself down." Who tempted Jesus in this way?

15. Did Joab, Joram, or Joash send this message to Jehoshaphat, "Will you go with me to fight against Moab?"?

Answers

1. Ezekiel **2.** Jesus **3.** Micaiah **4.** Jacob **5.** Cleopas **6.** Abner, the commander of Saul's army
7. False, Paul (Acts 28:17) **8.** An angel of the Lord
9. Esther **10.** Jesus **11.** Israel/Jacob **12.** Isaac's servant who met her at a well outside Nahor
13. The foolish five virgins **14.** The devil **15.** Joram

WHO SAID THAT?

Quiz #7

1. Who told Jeroboam, king of Israel, "Amos is raising a conspiracy against you in the very heart of Israel. The land cannot bear all his words"?

2. Who prayed, "Lord, do not let this sin be held against them"?

3. Which prophet said to a king, "Prepare a poultice of figs"?

4. Who said to David, "May my lord pay no attention to that wicked man Nabal. He is just like his name—his name is Fool and folly goes with him"?

5. Was it the Pharisee or the tax collector in Jesus' parable who prayed, "I thank you that I am not like other men—robbers, evildoers, adulterers"?

6. Who asked the Lord, "How can I save Israel? My clan is the weakest in Manasseh, and I am the least in my family"?

7. "Where is the one who has been born king of the Jews? We saw his star in the east and have come to worship him." Who said this?

8. Who said to Jonah, "How can you sleep? Get up and call on your god! Maybe he will take notice of us, and we will not perish"?

9. True or false? The men of Athens said to the apostles, "We want to hear you again on this subject."

10. Who said to Eli, "Here I am; you called me"?

11. "The Lord's name for you is not Pashhur, but Magor-Missabib." Which prophet said this after being released from stocks?

12. Whose parents said, "Ask him. He is of age; he will speak for himself"?

13. Who lamented, "Utterly meaningless! Everything is meaningless"?

14. Who challenged the Pharisees, "What do you think about the Christ?"?

15. Which prophetic figure claimed, "After me will come one more powerful than I, whose sandals I am not fit to carry"?

WHO SAID THAT?

Quiz #8

1. Who tempted Jesus by saying, "If you are the Son of God, tell this stone to become bread"?

2. Which wife cynically commented, "How the king of Israel has distinguished himself today, disrobing in the sight of the slave girls of his servants as any vulgar fellow would"?

3. Who protested against God's call with the words, "Who am I that I should go to Pharaoh and bring the Israelites out of Egypt?"?

4. Which New Testament writer claimed, "I have fought the good fight, I have finished the race, I have kept the faith"?

5. Was it Peter, Andrew or Matthew who said, "Here is a boy with five small barley loaves and two small fish, but how far will they go among so many?"?

6. True or false? John the Baptist said, "You brood of vipers. Who warned you to flee from the coming wrath?"?

7. "The God of heaven will give us success. We his servants will start rebuilding, but as for you, you have no share in Jerusalem or any claim or historic right to it." Who said this to Sanballat, Tobiah and Geshem?

8. Who announced Jesus to the crowds with the words, "Here is the man"?

9. "Didn't I tell you not to sin against the boy? But you wouldn't listen! Now we must give an accounting for his blood." Which of Joseph's brothers said this?

10. Who said to Jesus, "Here and now I give half of my possessions to the poor, and if I have cheated anybody out of anything, I will pay back four times the amount"?

11. Which king said to Paul, "Do you think that in such a short time you can persuade me to be a Christian?"?

12. Who posed this question to Jesus, "Are you the one who was to come or shall we expect someone else?"?

13. Which teacher explained, "It is not the healthy who need a doctor, but the sick"?

14. Who said to Elisha about an ax, "O my Lord, it was borrowed"?

15. Which Moabite woman said to Naomi, "Let me go to the fields and pick up the leftover grain"?

Answers

13. Jesus **14.** One of the company of the prophets **15.** Ruth

11. King Agrippa **12.** The disciples of John the Baptist

6. True (Luke 3:7) **7.** Nehemiah **8.** Pilate **9.** Reuben **10.** Zacchaeus

1. The devil **2.** Michal, David's wife **3.** Moses **4.** Paul to Timothy **5.** Andrew

129

Quiz #9

1. Did Balaam or Barak say, "Build me seven altars here, and prepare seven bulls and seven rams"?

2. Which brother saw his sister inflicted with leprosy and pleaded with Moses, "Please, my lord, do not hold against us the sin we have so foolishly committed"?

3. Was it Moses, Manasseh or Manoah who said to his wife, "We are doomed to die! We have seen God"?

4. Who protested, "Should a man like me run away? Or should one like me go to the temple to save his life? I will not go"?

5. Did Jesus say to his disciples, "Come and have breakfast"?

6. Who said to Zedekiah the king "They (the Babylonians) will not hand you over"?

7. "Here I am today, eighty-five years old. I am still as strong today as the day Moses sent me out." Who said this to Joshua at Gilgal?

8. Which son said to Jacob, "If you will send our brother along with us, we will go down and buy food for you"?

9. Which king protested about the Lord's instruction to him by saying, "But what about the hundred talents I paid for these Israelite troops?"?

10. Which disciple declared to Jesus, "You are the Christ, the son of the living God"?

11. Who spoke up on behalf of the poor saying to nobles and officials, "You are exacting usury from your own countrymen"?

12. Was it a poor man, a rich man, a Jewish man or a Samaritan who asked Jesus, "Teacher, what good thing must I do to get eternal life?"?

13. Which king instructed his messengers, "Go and consult Baal-Zebub, the god of Ekron, to see if I will recover from this injury"?

14. Who expressed his generosity with the words "Come over here. Have some bread and dip it in wine vinegar"? Was it Boaz or Hosea?

15. Who said to Jesus, "Lord, if you are willing you can make me clean"?

Answers

1. Balaam said this to Barak. 2. Aaron, regarding Miriam 3. Manoah
4. Nehemiah 5. Yes, after his resurrection 6. Jeremiah 7. Caleb 8. Judah
9. Amaziah 10. Peter 11. Nehemiah 12. A rich man
13. Ahaziah 14. Boaz 15. A man with leprosy

Quiz #10

1. Who made the excuse, "The serpent deceived me, and I ate"?

2. Who reassured some women, "Do not be afraid, for I know that you are looking for Jesus, who was crucified. He is not here; he has risen"?

3. Who said to Isaac, "This is from the Lord. We can say nothing to you one way or the other. Here is Rebekah; take her and go"?

4. True or false? Martha said about Lazarus' tomb, "By this time there is a bad odor, for he has been there four days."

5. This Old Testament prophet said, "Ah, Sovereign Lord, I do not know how to speak; I am only a child."

6. Who identified Jesus with the words, "Behold the lamb of God"?

7. Was it Jews or Jesus' disciples who responded to Jesus' teaching saying, "This is a hard teaching. Who can accept it?"?

8. Who promised Solomon, "I will give you what you have not asked for—both riches and honor—so that in your lifetime you will have no equal among kings"?

9. "This is my body, which is for you; do this in remembrance of me." Who said this on the night he was betrayed?

10. What was the surprising source of this comment, "What have I done to you to make you beat me these three times?"?

11. Who told David, "Your servant Uriah the Hittite is dead"?

12. True or false? Jesus said to his disciples, "Not one stone here will be left on another."

13. Who said to a horseman, "What do you have to do with peace?"?

14. Was it Joseph's brothers or Nebuchadnezzar's advisers that said, "Here comes that dreamer! Come now, let's kill him"?

15. Who said, "Now I know without a doubt that the Lord sent his angel and rescued me from Herod's clutches"?

Quiz #11

1. Who said, "My father has made trouble for the country. See how my eyes brightened when I tasted a little of this honey?"?

2. Whose daughter demanded, "I want you to give me right now the head of John the Baptist on a platter"?

3. "Is the Lord's arm too short? You will now see whether or not what I say will come true for you." Who said this to Moses reassuring him about the promise of quail?

4. Was it the chief priests or the disciples who asked Jesus "Who is the greatest in the kingdom of heaven?"?

5. "I am the most ignorant of men; I do not have a man's understanding." Who made this confession?

6. Who declared, "Even if all fall away on account of you, I never will"?

7. Was it Adam or Eve who said to God, "I heard you in the garden, and I was afraid because I was naked, so I hid"?

8. True or false? Jesus said, "Saul, Saul, why do you persecute me?"?

9. Which concerned mother said, "If Jacob takes a wife from among the women of this land, from Hittite women like these, my life will not be worth living"?

10. Who said to Araunah when he was buying a threshing-floor, "I insist on paying the full price. I will not take for the Lord what is yours, or sacrifice a burnt offering that costs me nothing"?

11. Who asked the crowd, "Which one do you want me to release to you: Barabbas, or Jesus who is called Christ?"?

12. Which patriarch said to God, "If only Ishmael might live under your blessing"?

13. Who lied when she claimed, "Yes, the men came to me but I did not know where they had come from. At dusk...the men left. I don't know which way they went"?

14. True or false? Jesus' family said about him, "He is out of his mind."

15. Who said to Joseph, "I too had a dream: on my head were three baskets of bread"?

Answers

1. Jonathan 2. Herodias' daughter 3. The Lord 4. The disciples 5. Agur, son of Jakeh (Proverbs 30:2) 6. Peter 7. Adam 8. True (Acts 9:4) 9. Rebekah 10. King David 11. Pilate 12. Abraham 13. Rahab 14. True (Mark 3:21) 15. The chief baker

Quiz # 12

1. Which prophet cried out, "Woe to me! I am ruined! For I am a man of unclean lips and I live among a people of unclean lips"?

2. Who asked Philip, "Why shouldn't I be baptized?"?

3. Who said to his brothers, "I am about to die. But God will surely come to your aid and take you up out of this land"?

4. "Go make the tomb as secure as you know how." Who gave this instruction?

5. Who told the Israelites, "I am now a hundred and twenty years old and I am no longer able to lead you"?

6. Who said to Jesus, "I have no one to help me into the pool when the water is stirred"?

7. Which prophet answered the Lord, "I see a boiling pot, tilting away from the north"?

8. Who said while being stoned, "Look, I see heaven open and the Son of Man standing at the right hand of God"?

9. Which king of Moab said, "A people has come out of Egypt, they cover the face of the land and have settled next to me"?

10. Which disciple asked Jesus, "Lord, how many times shall I forgive my brother when he sins against me? Up to seven times?"?

11. Who said to Paul, "The magistrates have ordered that you and Silas be released. Now you can leave"?

12. Was it Job, Joel or Joseph who declared, "I know that my redeemer lives"?

13. True or false? The Pharisees said about Jesus, "See this is getting us nowhere. Look how the whole world has gone after him."

14. Who was the speaker in Revelation who stood in the sun and cried out with a loud voice, "Come, gather together for the great supper of God"?

15. Who said to his traveling companions, "Now I urge you to take some food. You need it to survive. Not one of you will lose a single hair from your head"?

Answers

1. Isaiah 2. The Ethiopian eunuch 3. Joseph 4. Pilate 5. Moses
6. The invalid at the pool of Bethesda
7. Jeremiah 8. Stephen 9. Balak 10. Peter 11. The jailer 12. Job
13. True (John 12:19) 14. An angel 15. Paul

WHO SAID THAT?

Quiz #13

1. Who said, "Arise, Balak, and listen; hear me son of Zippor. God is not man, that he should lie"?

2. Who asked Pharaoh's daughter, "Shall I go and get one of the Hebrew women to nurse the baby for you?"?

3. "I cannot redeem it because I might endanger my own estate." Who said this to Boaz?

4. Who asked Paul and Silas, "What must I do to be saved?"?

5. True or false? David said to Saul, "I cut off the corner of your robe but did not kill you."

6. Who advised Jesus, "Send the crowd away so they can go to the surrounding villages and countryside and find food and lodging"?

7. Did David or Delilah say, "The Philistines are upon you"?

8. Who encouraged Hobab the Midianite, "Come with us and we will treat you well, for the Lord has promised good things to Israel"?

9. Which disciple said to Jesus, "Show us the father"?

10. Who said, "I am a Jew born in Tarsus of Cilicia"?

11. Which woman said, "If I just touch his clothes, I will be healed"?

12. "If only my master would see the prophet who is in Samaria! He would cure him of his leprosy." Who gave this advice concerning Naaman?

13. Who pleaded with Ishmael, son of Nethaniah, "Don't kill us! We have wheat and barley, oil and honey, hidden in a field"?

14. True or false? Caiaphas said, "I am innocent of this man's blood. It is your responsibility."

15. "Go into the prostitute's house and bring her out and all who belong to her." Who gave this instruction to his two spies?

Quiz # 14

1. Who gave this verdict on Jesus, "Surely this was a righteous man"?

2. Which king said about Ahimaaz, "He's a good man. He comes with good news"?

3. Was it two men dressed in white or three strangers who asked the apostles, "Men of Galilee, why do you stand here looking into the sky?"?

4. Who turned down favors from a king with the words, "You may keep your gifts for yourself and give your rewards to someone else"?

5. "I do believe; help me overcome my unbelief." Were these the words of a father whose son was healed or a Pharisee who asked Jesus about the kingdom of heaven?

6. Was it Crispus, Gallio, or Felix who said, "Since it involves questions about words and names and your own law—settle the matter yourselves"?

7. "Every boy that is born you must throw into the Nile." Who gave this instruction?

8. Which prophet gave this instruction concerning Joshua the high priest: "Put a clean turban on his head"?

9. Who told Simon Peter, "They have taken the Lord out of the tomb, and we do not know where they have put him"?

10. "The virgin will be with child and will give birth to a son, and will call him Immanuel." Which prophet gave these details about a sign from God for Ahaz?

11. Which king gave the order, "Cut the living child in two and give half to one and half to the other"?

12. "Let us put up three shelters—one for you, one for Moses and one for Elijah." Which disciple who witnessed the transfiguration made this suggestion?

13. Who offered the apostles money saying, "Give me also this ability so that everyone on whom I lay my hands may receive the Holy Spirit"?

14. Who tested her husband with the words, "How can you say I love you, when you won't confide in me?"?

15. True or false? Felix said to Paul, "I will hear your case when your accusers get here."

Answers

1. The centurion at the cross **2.** David **3.** 2 men dressed in white
4. Daniel **5.** A father whose son was healed from spirit possession
6. Gallio **7.** Pharaoh **8.** Zechariah **9.** Mary Magdalene **10.** Isaiah
11. Solomon **12.** Peter **13.** Simon **14.** Delilah **15.** True (Acts 23:25)

Facts 1

The Hebrew title for the book of Deuteronomy is simply "these are the words". This reflects its main content: God's words to his people.

The first question in the New Testament is that of the wise men, "Where is the one who has been born king of the Jews?" (Matthew 2:2).

The Ten Commandments are collectively known as the Decalogue, meaning literally "the ten words". Throughout the centuries Jewish people have understood these ten words as the basis of all Jewish law, and the benchmark of all religious life and conduct.

Jesus himself shows us that quoting from the Bible is a useful thing to do. This is how he deals with the devil before the start of his public ministry when he was tempted in the desert (Luke 4:1-13).

The most famous example of Jesus' teaching is to be found in the Sermon on the Mount (Matthew 5-7). This may be a summary of what Jesus taught on one occasion or a compilation of various sermons.

The Bible can be read aloud in about 70 hours.

The book of Psalms contains many examples of the psalmist talking and reasoning with himself. Perhaps the best example is Psalm 42-43 (originally one psalm) with the refrain "Why are you downcast, O my soul? Why so disturbed within me?"

John 14-16 contain Jesus' words of comfort and instruction to his disciples. Unique to John's Gospel these chapters have become known as "the farewell discourses."

Deborah is the only woman in the Bible identified as a judge. Her instructions to Barak were that he should lead the Israelite army against Sisera. She gave thanks to God for the ensuing victory in a great poem (Judges 4-5).

Jesus is frequently addressed as "Rabbi". This is simply a title of distinction given to those who teach and its nearest equivalent is "master" or "sir."

Facts 2

Moses undertakes a very special role as mediator between God and man. He has direct access to God and is portrayed as an obedient servant who mediates the covenant to the people. The writer to the Hebrews understands Moses as one who foreshadows the ministry of Jesus, the mediator of the new covenant.

The first recorded words of Jesus' public ministry are, "Repent, for the kingdom of heaven is near" (Matthew 4:17).

Peter's ministry becomes very significant after the resurrection. He is the first to address the crowds on the Day of Pentecost.

Angels perform a special role as God's messengers making known his word to human beings. Their messages frequently bring the opportunity of salvation (see Acts 11:13-14).

The phrase "I am coming soon" punctuates the text of the final chapter of the Bible occurring three times (Revelation 22:7, 12, 20).

Moses and Aaron suffered a great deal because the people of Israel "grumbled" at them (see Exodus 15:24; Numbers 14:1, 29).

The first speech recorded in the New Testament belongs to the angel of the Lord who appeared to Joseph in a dream predicting Jesus' birth (see Matthew 1:20-21).

The New Testament word "parable" is a broad term, which can be used of practical sayings and stories, and can be used of quite short metaphorical phrases and similes. Literature throughout the centuries has made use of parabolic phrases and stories.

Isaiah 13-23 contain a series of prophetic oracles of judgment against 13 nations who stand in opposition to God and his people. Ezekiel 25-32 contains a similar series of oracles against seven nations.

James 3:1-12 discusses the evil power of the tongue. The tongue is described as "a restless evil, full of deadly poison" (verse 8), which "corrupts the whole person" (verse 6).

The first words God spoke to man and woman were words of blessing (see Genesis 1:27-30).

Facts 3

Jesus' first recorded words are, "Why were you searching for me? Didn't you know I had to be in my father's house?" (Luke 2:49).

The judges were responsible for making impartial judgments but also became important political and military figures. Othniel was the first judge of Israel; Deborah was the first woman judge.

When Jesus is asked, "Which is the greatest command in the Law?" he responds with two quotations from the Old Testament taken from Deuteronomy 6:5 and Leviticus 19:18.

Zechariah was struck with temporary dumbness because he didn't believe Gabriel's message (see Luke 1:11-22).

The address "son of man" is used over one hundred times in the book of Ezekiel.

Some of the Psalms are best described as conversations with God. Many of these contain the vocative address "O God" or "O Lord". They are honest and often urgent pleas to God. Psalm 38 is a good example.

Hagar was found by the angel of the Lord by a fountain (Genesis 16:7). This is the first angel visitation recorded in the Bible.

Jesus emphasizes the importance of keeping oaths in Matthew 5:33-37. His point is that his followers should have a scrupulous regard for the truth and be known as people of their word.

In the entire book of Esther, God is not mentioned once. But his guidance and presence is assumed throughout.

The word "disciple" simply means "learner". Being a disciple includes listening to the words of your teacher.

There are many poems and songs in the book of Psalms that express praise to God for his work, his goodness and his love. Of particular importance is the "hallelujah" collection (Psalms 146-150).

Facts 4

Prophets existed in Old Testament times from the time of Moses. Moses is described as a prophet of special status because God spoke to him face to face and he was able to perform miracles (Deuteronomy 34:10-12).

Conversation and debate is key to the content of the book of Job. Job, his three friends, and God, speak together in this gripping story that is told through speeches, replies and monologues.

In every day conversations we use phrases from the Bible all the time. Here are a few: weighed and found wanting, the root of all evil, a word in season, casting pearls before swine, an eye for an eye.

Binding agreements in the Bible are called covenants. There are 7 covenants in the Bible between God and his people.

Rachel died in childbirth and her final words were to name her son Ben-Oni (son of my trouble). Jacob renamed him Benjamin (son of my right hand).

Jesus' use of parables is quite surprising. He chose to speak to the crowds almost exclusively in parables.

Psalm 119, the longest chapter in the Bible, is a celebration of God's word emphasizing its eternal worth and value (verses 89, 105).

Every chapter of the Book of Hebrews either contains a quotation from the Old Testament or mentions an Old Testament character by name.

The Gospels give us over one hundred examples of Jesus using parabolic language.

It has been suggested that 1 Peter is largely made up of a sermon that was delivered to first century baptismal candidates. This would explain the dominant imperatives (commands and exhortations) throughout its chapters.

In Luke 4:31-37 Jesus drives out an evil spirit from a man who was shouting out and taunting him. Jesus' command "Be quiet" achieves its desired effect and underlines his amazing authority.

Eat, Drink and Be Merry

Quiz #1

1. What tasted "like something made with olive oil" when it was ground and baked? It also tasted like wafers made with honey.

2. What does the word "manna" mean?

3. In which Old Testament book do your find the words, "A man can do nothing better than to eat and drink and find satisfaction in his work"?

4. In which New Testament letter is it written, "It is better not to eat meat or drink wine or do anything else that will cause your brother to fall"?

5. Who were critical of Jesus eating with tax collectors and "sinners"?

6. Jesus enjoyed receiving hospitality more than once in the home of two sisters and a brother. What were their names?

7. Who in the New Testament was blind for three days during which time he did not eat or drink anything?

8. What advice does the book of Proverbs give to its readers about, "those who drink too much wine or gorge themselves on meat"?

9. Which group of Christians did Paul accuse of misbehaving at the Lord's Supper, because some people remained hungry while others got drunk?

10. What did God forbid concerning an animal that had died by itself?

11. When Jesus' disciples urged him, "Rabbi, eat something," how did Jesus reply?

12. Olive oil had many purposes in Bible times. What did James' letter say oil should be used for?

13. Who plotted to get Lot drunk?

14. What was a favorite food for Isaac?

15. Which queen agreed that she and her maids should fast for three days and nights?

Answers

1. Manna **2.** "What?" Or, "What is it?" **3.** Ecclesiastes 2:24 **4.** Romans
5. The Pharisees **6.** Mary, Martha and Lazarus **7.** Saul, who became Paul
8. Do not join them **9.** The Corinthians **10.** You were not allowed to eat it
11. "I have food to eat that you know nothing about" **12.** Anointing a sick person **13.** His two daughters
14. Wild game **15.** Queen Esther

Quiz #2

1. According to Paul what must the man who eats everything not do in connection with the person who only eats vegetables?

2. Which two Old Testament books record a governor giving this order: "Do not eat any of the most sacred food until there is a priest ministering with Urim and Thummin"?

3. How many people were in the crowd when Jesus said, "They have already been with me three days and have nothing to eat"?

4. Who wrote, "We give you this rule: 'If a man will not work, he shall not eat' "?

5. What food and drink did Melchizedek bring when he blessed Abram?

6. When Abraham invited his three visitors to stay for a meal, what did he give them to eat?

7. Who gave a boy a drink of water from a well?

8. True or false? Breakfast is never mentioned in the Old Testament.

9. What was the nationality of the man brought to David who was given to eat "part of a cake of pressed figs and two cakes of raisins"?

10. Who wrote, "No priest is to drink wine when he enters the inner court"?

11. In the Bible, what is God's second recorded question?

12. Who was commanded to eat bread while he lay for 390 days on his side?

13. As the Israelites prepared to leave Egypt what were they told must be eaten inside the house?

14. Which Bible book asks, "Is tasteless food eaten without salt?"?

15. What does the book of Proverbs tell us not to do with a stingy man's food?

Answers

1. Not look down on him **2.** Ezra 2:63; Nehemiah 7:65 **3.** 4,000 **4.** Paul

5. Bread and wine **6.** Veal, freshly baked bread, milk curds and milk **7.** Hagar **8.** True

9. Egyptian **10.** Ezekiel **11.** "Have you eaten from the tree which I commanded you not to eat?"

12. Ezekiel **13.** Their Passover meal of roast lamb **14.** Job **15.** Do not eat it

Quiz #3

1. Which Old Testament prophet had a vision of two baskets of figs?

2. True or false? Babies were not given special food in the Old Testament as they were breast-fed until they were two or three years old.

3. Which book of the Bible records ten banquets?

4. Who described Israel's misery in the following way? "I am like one who gathers summer fruit at the gleaning of the vineyard; there is no cluster of grapes to eat, none of the early figs I crave."

5. About which type of tree did Jesus say, "May no one ever eat fruit from you again"?

6. One of the most famous Bible verses has the words, "I will come in and eat with him." Which verse?

7. Which prophet recorded this warning from God, "I will make this people eat bitter food and drink poisoned water"?

8. Who became a bride because she said, "I'll draw water for your camels too"?

9. Who did Absalom order his men to kill when he "is in high spirits from drinking wine"?

10. According to Jesus, John the Baptist "came neither eating nor drinking", but what was John accused of?

11. Jesus said, "The Son of Man came eating and drinking." What was Jesus accused of being?

12. What fruit woven in blue, purple and scarlet yarn decorated the edge of the priests' robes in the book of Exodus?

13. What accusation did Isaiah bring against "those who are heroes at drinking wine and champions at mixing drinks"?

14. Which Old Testament prophet accused the Israelites of unfaithfulness by asking, "Now why go to Egypt to drink water from the Shihor?"?

15. What fruit-bearing plant did Jesus liken himself to?

Answers

1. Jeremiah 2. True 3. Esther 4. Micah 5. A fig tree 6. Revelation 3:20 7. Jeremiah 8. Rebekah 9. Amnon 10. John was accused of having a demon 11. Jesus was accused of being a drunkard and a glutton 12. Pomegranates 13. They acquitted the guilty for a bribe and denied justice to the innocent 14. Jeremiah 15. The vine

Quiz #4

1. To whom was the following request made, "Sell us food to eat and water to drink for their price in silver"?

2. Jesus reminded the Pharisees of the following incident from the Old Testament. "He entered the house of God and ate the consecrated bread, which is lawful only for priests to eat." About whom was Jesus speaking?

3. True or false? When God told Noah to build the ark, he told him to take animals on board, and also lots of food.

4. What does a person have to do to have the right to eat from the tree of life?

5. When were the Egyptians not able to drink water from the river Nile?

6. Who was told to, "Eat this scroll; then go and speak to the house of Israel"?

7. Three men risked their lives to fetch water for David from the well near the gate of Bethlehem. What did David do with the water?

8. Who said, "Stay in that house, eating and drinking whatever they give you, for the worker deserves his wages"?

9. According to the apostle Paul, what are the fruits of the Spirit?

10. Who, in the New Testament, said, "Do not worry about your life, what you will eat or drink"?

11. In which book of the Bible are we told that honey is good for us and that we should eat it?

12. Which Old Testament prophet said that God's people would "eat but not have enough" because they had deserted the Lord?

13. Which Old Testament prophet said that God's people would "have plenty to eat" until they were full?

14. What was the answer to Samson's riddle "Out of the eater, something to eat; out of the strong, something sweet"?

15. The men who explored Canaan returned with a single cluster of what hanging on a pole carried by two men?

Answers

1. Sihon, King of Heshbon 2. David and his companions 3. True (Genesis 6:20-21)

4. Overcome 5. When the fish in the river Nile died 6. Ezekiel

7. David refused to drink the water and he poured it on to the ground before the Lord

8. Jesus 9. Love, joy, peace, patience, kindness, goodness, faithfulness, gentleness and self-control 10. Jesus

11. Proverbs 12. Hosea 13. Joel 14. "What is sweeter than honey? What is stronger than a lion?" 15. Grapes

Quiz #5

1. Who gave the following order, "Collect all the food of these good years that are coming and store up the grain under the authority of Pharaoh"?

2. In what unusual place did Samson find a beehive?

3. Who is in no danger of eating "the bread of idleness"?

4. Who said to Jesus, "even the dogs eat the crumbs that fall from their masters' table"?

5. Who asked the following question, "Do people pick grapes from thorn-bushes, or figs from thistles?"?

6. Who in the Old Testament told a king, "Even if you were to give me half your possessions, I would not go with you, nor would I eat bread or drink water here"?

7. Which judge regained his strength when he drank water from the hollow place in Lehi?

8. True or false? Every year at the Passover meal the Israelites ate roast beef with bitter herbs.

9. Which prophet prophesied that the Edomites would have a trap set for them by those who ate their bread?

10. Why did Jesus and his disciples not even have time to eat?

11. In which of Jesus' parables does a farmer say to himself, "Take life easy; eat, drink and be merry"?

12. What did David prepare for Abner when he came to David at Hebron?

13. Who in the Old Testament allowed each guest to drink whatever they liked?

14. After Solomon had asked the Lord for wisdom he sacrificed some offerings in front of the ark of the Lord's covenant. What did he do next?

15. When Hagar was sent away who gave her some food and a skin of water before she left?

Answers

1. Joseph 2. A lion's carcass. 3. The wife of noble character (Proverbs 31:10, 27) 4. A Canaanite mother who had a daughter suffering from demon-possession. (Matthew 15:27) 5. Jesus 6. An unidentified "man of God" 7. Samson 8. False. They ate roast lamb (Exodus 12:3-14) 9. Obadiah 10. Because crowds of people demanded their attention 11. The Parable of the Rich Fool 12. A feast 13. King Xerxes 14. He gave a feast for all his court 15. Abraham

Quiz #6

1. With what food did Jonathan refresh himself when he was in a wood during a battle?

2. Which book of the Bible states, "They eat the bread of wickedness and drink the wine of violence"?

3. Who quoted this famous proverb, "The fathers eat sour grapes, and the children's teeth are set on edge"?

4. True or false? Fasting had become an act of hypocrisy for some religious leaders in New Testament times.

5. True or false? There is no record that Jesus ever fasted.

6. In which of Jesus' parables do the following words appear, "For I was hungry and you gave me nothing to eat, I was thirsty and you gave me nothing to drink"?

7. Where were the Israelites when they complained to Moses, "Why did you bring us out of Egypt to this terrible place? It has no grain or figs, grapevines or pomegranates. And there is no water to drink"?

8. Who gave "clothes and sandals, food and drink, and healing balm" to whom?

9. Who said, "I give you every seed-bearing plant on the face of the whole earth and every tree that has fruit with seed in it. They will be yours for food"?

10. Who vowed, "If God will be with me and will watch over me on this journey I am taking and will give me food to eat and clothes to wear so that I return safely to my father's house, then the Lord will be my God"?

11. Who ordered his children, "Go back and buy us a little more food"?

12. What did Joseph say he would take in exchange for food from the Egyptians when they first came to him during the famine?

13. Who "seized all the goods of Sodom and Gomorrah and all their food"?

14. Who was given this instruction, "Fill the men's sacks with as much food as they can carry, and put each man's silver in the mouth of his sack"?

15. When the king of Israel saw that Elisha had trapped the blinded Arameans he asked the prophet, "Shall I kill them, my father? Shall I kill them?" How did Elisha reply?

---

15. Elisha ordered that a great feast should be prepared for the prisoners

9. God **10.** Jacob **11.** Jacob **12.** Israel/Jacob **13.** The four kings **14.** The steward of Joseph's house

6. The Parable of the Sheep and Goats **7.** Kadesh, in the Desert of Zin **8.** Soldiers to prisoners

5. False. Jesus fasted for forty days and forty nights in the desert (Matthew 4:2)

1. Honey **2.** Proverbs **3.** Ezekiel **4.** True (Matthew 6:16-18)

Answers

147

Quiz #7

1. Who was the Psalmist referring to when he declared, "Let me not eat of their delicacies"?

2. True or false? In the desert, Jesus was tempted to turn stones into biscuits.

3. What tasted as sweet as honey in Ezekiel's mouth?

4. "You will plant vineyards and cultivate them but you will not drink the wine or gather the grapes." What happened to these grapes?

5. Who told the Israelites not to listen to Hezekiah and made the following false promise: "Then every one of you will eat from his own vine and fig-tree and drink water from his own cistern"?

6. "After Gaal son of Ebed and his brothers had gone out into the fields and gathered grapes and trodden them they held a festival in the temple of their god." While they were eating and drinking who did they curse?

7. Which Old Testament book states, "you have eaten the fruit of deception"?

8. What kind of heart, according to Proverbs, has a continual feast?

9. Who said to Joseph, "Give us food. Why should we die before your eyes? Our money is used up"?

10. What were the Israelites told to do so that God's blessing would be on their food and water?

11. Who was meant to benefit from fields left unplowed and unused every seven years, and from vineyards and olive groves left untended every seven years?

12. To whom were the Israelites not allowed to lend money at interest or sell food at a profit?

13. What kind of first fruits from their soil did God say the Israelites should bring to the house of the Lord at the Feast of Ingathering?

14. Who was promised that his food would be rich and that he would "provide delicacies fit for a king"?

15. According to the opening chapter of Acts what command did the risen Jesus give to his disciples while he was eating with them?

---

15. "Do not leave Jerusalem, but wait for the gift my Father promised, which you have heard me speak about"

. 13. The best of their first fruits 14. Asher

12. One of their countrymen who had become poor and could not support himself

9. All Egypt 10. Worship the Lord God, not foreign gods 11. Poor people and animals

4. They were eaten by worms 5. The king of Assyria 6. Abimelech 7. Hosea 8. A cheerful heart

1. Evildoers 2. False. Jesus was tempted to turn stones into bread (Matthew 4:3) 3. A scroll

Answers

148

Quiz #8

1. To whom did David say, "You will always eat at my table"?

2. Where in the Bible does wisdom say, "Come, eat my food and drink the wine I have mixed"?

3. Which Old Testament prophet prophesied that a siege would become so severe that people would "eat the flesh of their sons and daughters... [and] eat one another's flesh"?

4. In which of Jesus' parables does a servant beat the menservants and maidservants and eat and drink and get drunk?

5. According to Proverbs 25:21 what should you do if your enemy is hungry?

6. If a priest bought a slave or if a slave was born in his house what might the slave expect to receive?

7. Who "grew fat and wicked; filled with food, he became heavy and sleek. He abandoned the God who made him"?

8. Which queen was provided with beauty treatments and special food?

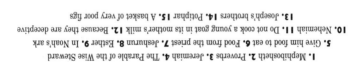

9. Where was the food mentioned in the following verse to be stored, "You are to take every kind of food that is to be eaten and store it away as food for you and for them"?

10. As 150 Jews and officials ate at his table, who had prepared for him each day one

11. What instruction did God give the Israelites about eating a young goat?

12. If you sit down to eat with a ruler, why should you not "crave his delicacies"?

13. In reply to Joseph's question, "Where do you come from?", who said, "From the land of Canaan . ... to buy food"?

14. Which army officer had such a good steward that he did not have to concern himself with anything except the food he ate?

15. What, according to one of Jeremiah's visions, was so bad that they could not be eaten?

Answers

1. Mephibosheth **2.** Proverbs **3.** Jeremiah **4.** The Parable of the Wise Steward
5. Give him food to eat **6.** Food from the priest **7.** Jeshurun **8.** Esther **9.** In Noah's ark
10. Nehemiah **11.** Do not cook a young goat in its mother's milk **12.** Because they are deceptive
13. Joseph's brothers **14.** Potiphar **15.** A basket of very poor figs

Quiz #9

1. Who is the first person in the Bible who is recorded as becoming drunk?

2. True or false? In the desert John the Baptist used to eat wild honey and locusts.

3. Who appeased David's anger with 200 loaves of bread, two skins of wine, five dressed sheep, five seahs of roasted grain, 100 cakes of raisins and 200 cakes of pressed figs?

4. In which Old Testament book does someone long to give the one she loves spiced wine to drink?

5. Food was set before this visitor, but he said, "I will not eat until I have told you what I have to say." Who was the visitor?

6. When Joseph's brothers went back to Egypt they took some nuts with them, which are only mentioned once in the Bible. What sort of nuts were they?

7. What no longer appeared the day after the Israelites ate food for the first time from the land in Canaan?

8. Who told the widow of Zarephath, "The jar of flour will not be used up and the jug of oil will not run dry until the day the Lord gives rain on the land"?

9. In a time of acute famine who prophesied, "About this time tomorrow, a seah of flour will sell for a shekel and two seahs of barley for a shekel at the gate of Samaria"?

10. Who did Paul remind were once greedy, drunkards, slanderers and swindlers?

11. Who was told, "By the sweat of your brow you will eat your food"?

12. Who had seven sons who took turns holding feasts in their homes, and invited their three sisters to eat and drink with them?

13. To whom did Paul write, "All food is clean"?

14. Who used the following ruse, "The men put worn and patched sandals on their feet and wore old clothes. All the bread of their food supply was dry and moldy"?

15. In which Old Testament book is it said, "Food gained by fraud tastes sweet to a man, but he ends up with a mouth full of gravel"?

Answers

1. Noah **2.** True (Matthew 3:4) **3.** Abigail **4.** Song of Songs **5.** Abraham's servant **6.** Pistachio **7.** The manna stopped coming **8.** Elijah **9.** Elisha **10.** The Corinthians **11.** Adam **12.** Job **13.** The Romans **14.** The people of Gibeon **15.** Proverbs

Quiz # 10

1. What is compared in the book of Proverbs to "apples of gold in pictures of silver"?

2. Who were told that they would never hunger again?

3. About which group of people did Paul write that they should "not be given to drunkenness"?

4. In which book of the Bible is it stated that "evildoers are those who devour my people as men eat bread"?

5. How many Jews formed a conspiracy and bound themselves with an oath not to eat or drink until they had killed Paul?

6. Which Old Testament prophet records these words about Israel's faithless watchmen, "'Come,' each one cries, 'let us get wine! Let us drink our fill of beer!'"?

7. Which Old Testament book states that, "Stolen water is sweet; food eaten in secret is delicious"?

8. Who spent three days with David, eating and drinking, as their families had supplied provisions for them?

9. True or false? Jesus fed 5,000 people with five bread rolls and two small fish.

10. Identify two sorts of people mentioned in the Old Testament who were forbidden to consume alcohol.

11. Who wrote, "Do not let anyone judge you by what you eat or drink"?

12. Who said, "When you enter a town and are welcomed, eat what is set before you"?

13. What is Nathan describing to David here: "It shared his food, drank from his cup and even slept in his arms"?

14. True or false? 200 ornamental pomegranates decorated each of the two free standing pillars in Solomon's temple.

15. Joseph was joined in prison by two people who knew a great deal about food and wine. Who were they?

Answers

1. Words fitly spoken (Proverbs 25:11 KJV) **2.** People in heaven who were wearing white robes **3.** Overseers **4.** Psalm **5.** More than 40 people **6.** Isaiah **7.** Proverbs **8.** David's fighting men **9.** True (John 6:9) **10.** Nazarites and the priests when they were on duty in the temple **11.** Paul **12.** Jesus **13.** A little ewe lamb **14.** True (1 Kings 7:20) **15.** A baker and a cupbearer

Quiz #11

1. After Jesus rose from the dead, he ate some food to prove he was not a ghost. What did he eat?

2. Who was using goblets brought from the temple when the inscription, MENE, MENE, TEKEL, PARSIN suddenly appeared on the wall?

3. In what town was David given, wheat and barley, flour and roasted grain, beans and lentils, honey and curds, sheep, and cheese from cows' milk?

4. Who, according to the book of Proverbs, "become poor and find that drowsiness clothes them in rags"?

5. Who prophesied of God's people that they would drink the milk of nations and be nursed at royal breasts?

6. Which Bible book says "A generous man will himself be blessed, for he shares his food with the poor"?

7. About whom did a priest of Midian say "Invite him to have something to eat"?

8. Which prophet said that he ate God's words in the following way: "When your words came, I ate them; they were my joy and my heart's delight"?

9. Where in the Bible are Christians told, "Do not get drunk on wine, which leads to debauchery"?

10. Who wrote that "He [God] makes... wine that gladdens the heart of man"?

11. What food did an angel tell Elijah to eat after he had slept under a broom tree after fleeing from Jezebel?

12. Who wrote, "those who get drunk, get drunk at night"?

13. Who was concerned that, "The food in our sacks is gone. We have no gift to take to the man of God"?

14. Which Old Testament prophet wrote: "On this mountain the Lord Almighty will prepare a feast of rich food for all peoples, a banquet of aged wine, the best of meats and the finest of wines"?

15. In the book of Revelation what does the tree of life produce?

Facts 1

In New Testament times two women worked together using a hand mill to grind grain. One poured the grain into the mill, while the other turned the wheel of the top millstone. This sheds light on Jesus' saying in Matthew 24:41.

In times of famine bread could be made with not only grain, but could have "beans and lentils, millet and spelt" (Ezekiel 4:9) mixed with it.

Showbread (KJV), "Bread of Presence", means bread set before the presence, or, face of God. It consisted of a dozen loaves of unleavened bread arranged in two rows of six. It was set out on a low table in the tabernacle.

During the seven days following Passover the Israelites ate unleavened bread to remind them of their hasty departure from Egypt in the days of the Exodus.

In the days of Jesus a blessing or short prayer was offered before eating. Jesus did this when he blessed the bread before feeding the 5,000 in Matthew 14:19. The traditional Jewish blessing is, "Blessed art Thou, Jehovah our God, King of the world, who causes to come forth bread from the earth."

In Bible times quantities of food were measured more by volume than by weight. So a "homer", the largest measure for cereals, was equivalent to an "ass-load."

In Corinth, archaeologists have dug up two temples which contain rooms apparently used by pagans for their feasts in which meat that had been offered to idols was eaten. Hence Paul wrote his warning in 1 Corinthians 8:10.

In the Old Testament, blood shed for sacrifices was considered to be sacred. It stood for the life of the sacrificed animal. As life was sacred, so blood become sacred and had to be treated with respect. So the Israelites were told not to drink blood (Leviticus 17:11; 7:26-27).

The *tilapa*, also known as "St. Peter's fish," is a type of fish which carries its eggs and young fish within its mouth. When the mother fish wants to keep the young fish out of her mouth she picks up an object, preferably a bright one. This is the likely background to the unusual account in Matthew 17:24-27 where Peter finds a 4 drachma coin in the mouth of a fish.

One helpful way to study the book of Esther is to note how its numerous banquets set the scene for important developments in the plot (Esther 1:3-4; 5-8; 9; 2:18; 3:15; 5:1-8; 7:1-10; 8:17; 9:17; 9:18-32).

Facts 2

In New Testament times washing one's hands before a meal was the common practice and was observed as a religious duty, especially by the Pharisees (Mark 7:3).

Gnosticism, a dangerous heresy, taught that the spirit was good and the body was evil. So the body had to be treated harshly and this led to asceticism. This is the apparent background for Paul's words in 1 Timothy 4:3, "They [the Gnostics]... order them to abstain from certain foods."

The food which Nebuchadnezzar ate would have had its first portion offered to idols and some of his wine would have been poured out on a pagan altar. This explains why Daniel "resolved not to defile himself with the royal food and wine" (Daniel 1:8).

Cannibalism, due to severe sieges, is recorded in the Old Testament more than once (2 Kings 6:28-29; Ezekiel 5:10). Josephus records in his Jewish War, 6.3.4 that this also happened when Jerusalem was besieged in AD 70, "A woman... who... had fled to Jerusalem... killed her son, roasted him, and ate one half, concealing and saving the rest."

The Israelites were promised by the Lord that they would enter "a land flowing with milk and honey" (Joshua 5:6 KJV). This indicated abundant prosperity.

Israelites love pomegranates. The juice of pomegranates was highly prized (Song of Solomon 8:2). In the Promised Land, pomegranates were one of the fruits which were grown.

Double invitations were issued for formal meals in the New Testament. The first invitation was refused. "I cannot come. I am not worthy." But the guests were then sent a second invitation urging them to come and accept the invitation (Luke 14:16, 23).

In New Testament times, the nearer a guest sat to the host the more highly he was honored. In Jesus' parable, the beggar, Lazarus, sat at "Abraham's side" (Luke 16:22).

In the Bible, eating with someone was a sign of participation. So when Paul ordered that Christians in Corinth should "not even eat" (1 Corinthians 5:11) with an immoral Christian he was ordering complete isolation from such a sinning brother.

Israelites were used to eating insects. Skewered locusts were considered a delicacy. Grasshoppers were mixed with honey to take away their bitterness and were then cooked and eaten.

The importance of hospitality is often mentioned in the Bible and nomadic peoples welcomed strangers. But they had a tradition that the stranger was only welcome for 3 days and 4 hours, the length of time they thought their food sustained their guest.

Facts 3

The Egyptians cultivated barley to feed their cattle. But bread made from barley was used by poor Jews. John notes that the five small loaves which Jesus used to feed 5,000 were barley loaves (John 6:9).

In the New Testament, the morning meal was a light one and usually consisted of bread, fruits, and cheese.

Grain makes bread and bread sustains nations. Millstones were so important to the Jews that their Law stated that no one could take the millstone as a pledge, as that would be like taking a man's life as a pledge (Deuteronomy 24:6).

Jesus used many everyday words in a figurative sense. Leaven, a ferment used in baking to make the bread rise, was likened to God's kingdom because it has power to change the whole (Matthew 13:33).

Jewish people loved feasts. They would often have music and dancing, as in the case when Herodias' daughter danced for Herod and his guests (Mark 6:32).

Feasts were very much part of the following Jewish religious festivals: The Sabbath, the Feast of the New Moons, the Year of Jubilee, Passover, Pentecost, the Feast of the Tabernacles and the Feast of Purim.

At the Passover meal Jesus shared with his disciples, everyone reclined on couches, around a table. The traditional way to recline was to lean on the table with one elbow and eat food with the other hand.

In Bible times the Jews did not eat with cutlery. They took a sop, a piece of bread, and dipped it into the soup or dip that was in the center of the table. The host of a feast might show his favor to a guest by offering a dipped sop to that guest (John 13:26-27).

In the Bible the word "bread" often stands for food in general. This is so in the Lord's Prayer and when Jesus said of himself, "I am the bread of life" (John 6:48).

Fish were often dried or salted and so preserved. This industry centered on Magdala, on the Sea of Galilee. Dried fish and bread were often eaten together, as in the case of Jesus feeding the 5,000.

The Dead Sea gives an endless supply of salt. But the outer layer of its rock salt was often hard and impure. It was used to spread on the temple courtyards in wet weather.

Facts 4

Paul stated that deacons should "not indulge in much wine" (1 Timothy 3:8).

Paul urged Timothy to drink a little wine because of his frequent illnesses. It seems that Timothy suffered from some kind of stomach ailment (1 Timothy 5:23).

Sheep were bred by the Jews for their meat and milk. The fat in a sheep's tail was also prized.

The Jews did not usually cut bread with a knife. They broke or tore a piece of bread from the loaf. Acts 20:7 describes the Lord's Supper as a time when they came "together to break bread."

In the Old Testament meat was a luxury food. King Solomon's wealth was described in terms of how much meat was provided daily, "Solomon's daily provision were… ten head of stall-fed cattle, twenty of pasture-fed cattle and a hundred sheep and goats, as well as deer, gazelles, roebucks and choice fowl" (1 Kings 4:23).

It is not surprising that John the Baptist found enough honey for his daily diet of locusts and honey in the desert since swarms of bees settled not only in hollow trees (1 Samuel 14:25-27), but also in holes in rocks (Psalm 81:16; Deuteronomy 32:13).

To the Jews, the calf was considered a delicacy reserved for their special festivals. Hence the detail in Jesus' Parable of the Prodigal Son in which the father had the "fatted calf" killed (Luke 15:23 KJV).

Wine was stored in goatskins, but they had to be new ones, because wine gives off gas as it ferments and only a new skin was supple and strong enough to expand. Jesus referred to this in his saying recorded in Matthew 9:17.

The Hebrews usually ate only twice a day. The light morning meal, between 9 a.m. and noon, and the main meal of the day in the evening, in the cool of the day.

The Psalmist says that the sweetness of milk and honey is surpassed by that of the words of the Law (Psalm 19:10).

There are four accounts of the Lord's Supper in the New Testament (Matthew 26:26-28; Mark 14:22-24; Luke 22:19-22; 1 Corinthians 11:23-25). Each account includes the words "This is my body", emphasizing that the bread represents the body of Jesus which was given for his followers.

Facts 5

When Jesus said, "Blessed is the man who will eat at the feast in the kingdom of God" (Luke 14:15), he was referring to the coming great Messianic banquet. The Bible often pictures the future kingdom as a feast (Isaiah 25:6; Matthew 8:11; 25:1-10; 26:29; Luke 13:29; Revelation 19:9).

The day Jesus instituted the Lord's Supper is a matter of great debate. From Scripture we know that it took place on the first day of the Feast of Unleavened Bread, or the day of preparation for the Passover, which was the 14th of Nisan. After sunset on the 14th of Nisan the Passover meal was eaten. As the Jewish day ended at sunset, this day was, technically, the 15th of Nisan, hence the debate.

In Bible times food was bartered for and paid for in markets. The traders sometimes had two sets of scales: one set they used for buying things and another set they used for selling things. (See Deuteronomy 25:13).

The six stone water jars mentioned in John 2:6 each held "twenty to thirty gallons" according to the translation. If each jar held fifteen gallons, and were each filled to the brim, Jesus' miracle produced up to 3,000 glasses of wine!

The Israelites were forbidden to eat animals classified as "unclean" such as camels, rabbits and pigs (Leviticus 11). This sheds light of Peter's problem about being told to eat "all kinds of four-footed animals" (Acts 10:12) which he saw in his vision.

After water, which was often impure, wine was the most common drink in Bible times. But it was used for more than just drinking. When mixed with olive oil it was used to clean and heal wounds, as the Good Samaritan knew (Luke 10:34).

Some women of Jerusalem were reputed to provide some local wine, laced with myrrh for condemned criminals as an anaesthetic. When Jesus was offered such a drink he refused it (Mark 15:23).

In New Testament days the most wealthy homes had wine cellars. They imported bottled wine from many Mediterranean countries. These bottles had pointed ends so they could be easily pushed into the ground and kept cool.

Fish was a common food in Jerusalem. One of its gates is called the "Fish Gate" and it is probable that this was the site of an ancient open-air fish market.

Medicines were made from fruit in the Old Testament. Isaiah told King Hezekiah to make a paste from figs and to apply it as a poultice to his painful boil (Isaiah 38:21).

Family Ties

Quiz #1

1. Which Bible characters had no mother?

2. Ishvi, Malki-Shua, and Jonathan were sons of which Israelite king?

3. Which Old Testament prophet was the son of Iddo?

4. True or false? Noah had four sons.

5. What family occasion does the book the Song of Solomon celebrate?

6. Who replaced Queen Vashti when she displeased her husband Xerxes?

7. Name the prophet Hosea's wife.

8. What was the name of Isaac's grandfather?

9. In Acts, which greedy couple tried to deceive the apostles?

10. What was the name of King David's third son?

11. Whose father was struck dumb by an angel before his son's birth?

12. How many daughters did Lot have?

13. What was the name of King Ahab's wicked wife?

14. Who captured the servants of the Old Testament character Job?

15. In Genesis, who hid her child under a bush expecting him to die?

Quiz #2

1. What was the name of Saul's daughter who married King David?

2. How many wives did the patriarch Jacob have?

3. What was the name of Moses' mother?

4. How many women are named in Matthew's genealogy of Jesus?

5. Which Old Testament prophet was the son of Beeri?

6. What was the name of the apostle Peter's brother?

7. How many daughters-in-law went on to the ark?

8. What was the name of the synagogue leader whose daughter Jesus healed?

9. Who was King Saul's lame grandson?

10. Who was Adam and Eve's third son?

11. In Genesis, Lamech was the son of which long-lived character?

12. Alphaeus was the father of which apostle?

13. Whose wife was turned into a pillar of salt when Sodom was destroyed?

14. How many more sons did Job have after his time of testing had finished?

15. In which chapter of Proverbs is there a description of a noble wife?

Answers

1. Michal **2.** 4 **3.** Amram **4.** 4 **5.** Hosea
6. Andrew **7.** 3 **8.** Jairus **9.** Mephibosheth **10.** Seth **11.** Methuselah
12. James **13.** Lot's wife **14.** 7 **15.** Chapter 31

Quiz #3

1. How many of David's brothers are named at their meeting with Saul?

2. Name Naomi's two daughters-in-law.

3. How old was Adam when his son Seth was born?

4. In Matthew 1:1 Jesus is referred to as the son of which two Old Testament characters?

5. Which Old Testament prophet was the son of Pethuel?

6. In Genesis which couple pretended to be brother and sister rather than husband and wife?

7. Which of Noah's sons was older, Shem or Japheth?

8. Who was the youngest of Jacob's sons?

9. Which Old Testament figure buried his wife in the field of Machpelah near Mamre?

10. In the New Testament, Elizabeth was the wife of which priest?

11. Jesus healed the mother-in-law of which apostle?

12. True or false? Abel killed Cain.

13. Whose son was told by God to build an ark?

14. Hosea called one of his children Lo-Ruhamah. What does this name mean?

15. How many sisters did King David have?

Answers

1. 3 **2.** Ruth and Orpah **3.** 130 years old **4.** David and Abraham
5. Joel **6.** Abraham and Sarah **7.** Japheth **8.** Benjamin **9.** Abraham **10.** Zechariah
11. Peter **12.** False. Cain killed Abel (Genesis 4:8) **13.** Lamech's son **14.** Not loved **15.** 2

Quiz #4

1. Who was born first, Esau or Jacob?

2. Who was the sister of Jesus' friends Lazarus and Mary?

3. True or false? Reuben was the son of Leah and Jacob.

4. In the Old Testament what was the name of the widow who married Boaz?

5. Who was King Saul's father-in-law?

6. What was unusual about Jacob's wedding day?

7. In the Old Testament, who was the son of Haran?

8. Whose husband left Israel because of famine and then died in Moab?

9. What was the occupation of Moses' father-in-law?

10. Who was the mother of King Solomon?

11. According to Matthew's genealogy, who was the grandfather of Joseph, the husband of Mary?

12. Who rebuked King David when he killed Uriah in order to take his wife?

13. Which Old Testament builder was the son of Hacaliah?

14. Which patriarch gave his brother lentil stew?

15. Whose baby "leapt in the womb" when her cousin Mary came to visit her?

Answers

1. Esau 2. Martha 3. True (Genesis 29:32) 4. Ruth 5. Ahimaaz
6. He married Leah instead of Rachel 7. Lot 8. Naomi's 9. Priest 10. Bathsheba 11. Matthan
12. Nathan 13. Nehemiah 14. Jacob 15. Elizabeth's

Quiz #5

1. Who was the patriarch Isaac's favorite son?

2. Jemimah, Keziah and Keren-Happuch were daughters of which Old Testament character?

3. Which son of David killed his half-brother Amnon?

4. True or false? The prophet Isaiah was the son of Hilkiah.

5. Whose mother asked Jesus to place her sons next to him in heaven?

6. Whose son-in-law was the first king of Israel?

7. In Matthew's genealogy of Jesus how many generations are there from Abraham to David?

8. Name Hosea the prophet's unloved daughter.

9. How long did King David and Bathsheba's first child live?

10. How did King Solomon propose to resolve the case of two mothers claiming the same baby?

11. In the Old Testament who was the mother of Jacob's son Joseph?

12. In the book of Ruth what was the name of Naomi's daughter-in-law who remained in Moab?

13. Which Old Testament character was both father and grandfather to his children?

14. Whose brother died only to be brought back to life by Jesus several days later?

15. Who was the elder, Aaron or Moses?

Quiz #6

1. Who is the father of all mankind?

2. In Genesis, what was the name of Isaac's brother-in-law?

3. What was Obed's famous grandson's first occupation?

4. Who was the favorite child of Isaac's wife, Rebekah?

5. In the Old Testament which royal prince got his head caught in the branches of a tree?

6. What was the name of Jacob's only daughter?

7. What prize did Caleb the spy offer to the person who captured Kiriath Sepher?

8. How many son's did Zilpah, the wife of Jacob have?

9. What was the name of Abraham's first-born son?

10. What was the name of the first child ever born?

11. How old was Jesus when his parents left him behind in Jerusalem?

12. Which Old Testament prophet was the son of Amittai?

13. What was the name of Queen Esther's cousin who raised her from childhood?

14. What family arrangements of King Solomon angered God?

15. Who was Jacob the patriarch's second son?

Quiz #7

1. How did Zechariah the priest inform the crowd of his son's name?

2. Which son of King David wished to marry his father's nurse Abishag?

3. True or false? The prophet Hosea's first child was called Jezreel.

4. Which of Jacob's sons was born immediately before Joseph?

5. In the Old Testament how many brothers did David's father Jesse have?

6. How many years did Jacob have to work for his bride, Rachel?

7. True or false? Methuselah was the father of Enoch.

8. Which relative watched the baby Moses as he was set adrift on the Nile?

9. What was the name of Jesus' mother?

10. Which brother of Joseph tried to rescue him from his other brothers?

11. King David's wife Abigail was the widow of which foolish man?

12. In the Old Testament who was the father of Gershom and Eliezer?

13. When they questioned Jesus about marriage at the resurrection, the Sadducees challenged him with a story about how many brothers?

14. According to Luke, who was the father of Mary's husband Joseph?

15. After his fortunes were restored, how many daughters did the Old Testament character Job have?

Answers

1. He wrote it down **2.** Adonijah **3.** True (Hosea 1:4) **4.** Zebulun
5. 6 **6.** 14 **7.** False, Enoch was the father of Methuselah (Genesis 5:21)
8. His sister **9.** Mary **10.** Reuben **11.** Nabal
12. Moses **13.** 7 **14.** Heli **15.** 3

Quiz #8

1. Whose husband sold a field and pretended to give all the proceeds to the apostles?

2. Who was the mother of Abraham's son Ishmael?

3. How many sons did Bilhah bear to her husband Jacob?

4. True or false? Moses married Miriam.

5. How many months pregnant was Elizabeth when the angel Gabriel visited Mary?

6. Who asked, "Am I my brother's keeper?"?

7. Which Old Testament couple both changed their names?

8. What was the name of Jeremiah the prophet's father?

9. Who was the mother of Jacob's last child Benjamin?

10. Amnon and Absalom were sons of which famous king?

11. Which Old Testament woman is mentioned but not named in Matthew's genealogy of Jesus?

12. What had Peter's mother-in-law been suffering from when Jesus healed her?

13. Rehoboam was the son of which Old Testament king?

14. Which woman had no mother or father?

15. At the wedding at Cana who told Jesus the wine had run out?

Answers

1. Sapphira's 2. Hagar 3. 2 4. False, he married Zipporah (Exodus 2:21)
5. 6. 6 Cain 7. Abraham and Sarah from Abram and Sarai 8. Hilkiah
9. Rachel 10. David 11. Bathsheba
12. A fever 13. Solomon 14. Eve 15. Mary, his mother

Quiz #9

1. When Jesus met her, how many husbands had the woman of Samaria had?

2. Gad and Asher were Jacob's sons by which wife?

3. True or false? Eliab was the first of Jesse's sons.

4. George Eliot's Mill on the Floss concludes with the words "In their death they were not divided." Of which two Old Testament characters was this originally said?

5. Which Old Testament priest fell off his chair and died when he heard his sons had been killed in battle?

6. In the Old Testament what was the name of Isaac's wife?

7. In Genesis who was the father of the twins Perez and Zerah?

8. According to Matthew's genealogy of Jesus, how many generations were there from Abraham to the exile?

9. Who fled from the attentions of Potiphar's wife?

10. What Hebrew word, used by Jesus, means "Father"?

11. In the New Testament , what was the name of Timothy's grandmother?

12. Which relative of Moses suffered from leprosy when she grumbled against God in the desert?

13. Which prophet was the son of Amoz?

14. Who was the patriarch Jacob's third son?

15. In Genesis, who was the husband of Keturah?

Answers

1. 5 2. Zilpah 3. True (1 Samuel 17:13) 4. Saul and Jonathan
5. Eli 6. Rebekah 7. Judah 8. 28 9. Joseph 10. Abba 11. Eunice
12. Miriam 13. Isaiah 14. Levi 15. Abram

Quiz # 10

1. True or false? Esau and Jacob were twins.

2. According to Luke 8, who were Jesus' true brothers and sisters?

3. In the Old Testament who ate some honey not knowing it had been forbidden by his father?

4. What were the names of Aaron's sons who were killed by the Lord for offering unauthorized fire?

5. Who was the firstborn child of the Old Testament hero Joseph?

6. What was the relationship between King Saul and Abner, the commander of his army?

7. What nationality was Boaz's wife, Ruth?

8. In the Old Testament, who was the father of Enoch?

9. In the book of Numbers, whose daughters claimed property from Moses?

10. According to Judges, who found bees in the carcass of a lion while going to his wedding?

11. In Genesis, which brother guaranteed the safety of Benjamin as they traveled to Egypt for food?

12. Which Hebrew child was adopted by a daughter of Pharaoh?

13. What was the name of Samuel's father?

14. Name the son of Herod who was reigning in Judea when Jesus, Mary and Joseph returned to Nazareth.

15. Which king of Judah was the son of Josiah?

Answers

1. True (Genesis 25:26) 2. Those who hear God's word and put it into practice
3. Jonathan 4. Nadab and Abihu 5. Manasseh 6. They were cousins
7. Moabite 8. Cain 9. Zelophehad 10. Samson
11. Judah 12. Moses 13. Elkanah 14. Archelaus 15. Zedekiah

Quiz #11

1. What was the name of Abraham's nephew and traveling companion?

2. What was the profession of the apostles Andrew and Peter?

3. Who was King Saul's son and a great friend of David?

4. What name, meaning "Not my people", did God tell Hosea to give to his child?

5. Who was the grandfather of the first king of Israel?

6. True or false? Jephunneh was the father of Caleb, one of the spies who entered Canaan.

7. In the Old Testament, who took her son to serve in the temple alongside the priest Eli?

8. Manasseh was the first-born of which Old Testament character?

9. Whose wife warned him to have nothing to do with Jesus?

10. What is the name of the inhabitant of Jericho whose family Joshua spared when he captured the city?

11. What was the name of the woman from Moab who is mentioned in Matthew's record of Jesus' family tree?

12. Whose husband danced naked before the ark of the Lord?

13. In Judges, who sacrificed his daughter in return for victory over the Ammonites?

14. Cushi was the father of which Old Testament prophet?

15. According to Matthew, who was the father of Mary's husband Joseph?

Quiz # 12

1. What was the name of King Saul's wife?

2. True or false? Dan was the last son of Jacob's wife, Leah.

3. How old was Amon's son Josiah when he became king of Judah?

4. What was the name of Mordecai's cousin who married King Xerxes?

5. Who is the first woman mentioned in Matthew's genealogy of Jesus?

6. In the book of Judges, what was the name of the prophetess wife of Lappidoth?

7. In the Old Testament, what was the name of Nun's son?

8. Which son of Alphaeus became one of Jesus' apostles?

9. What was the name of Shealtiel's son who helped rebuild the walls of Jerusalem with Nehemiah?

10. What was the name of Moses' sister?

11. Iddo was the grandfather of which Old Testament prophet?

12. According to the book of 1 Samuel, which wife did Elkanah especially love?

13. To which of his sons did Jacob give a multi-colored coat?

14. In which Old Testament book do we read of the death of two brothers, Mahlon and Kilion?

15. Who named her son Ichabod when she heard of the death of her husband and father-in-law?

Answers

1. Ahinoam 2. False, he was Bilhah's first child (Genesis 30:6)
3. 8 4. Esther 5. Tamar 6. Deborah 7. Joshua 8. James
9. Zerubbabel 10. Miriam 11. Zechariah 12. Hannah
13. Joseph 14. Ruth 15. The wife of Phineas, son of Eli

Quiz #13

1. True or false? According to Luke, Elizabeth was a descendant of Aaron.

2. Who warned her husband not to act offensively towards King David?

3. What was the name of the child born to Gideon by a Shechemite concubine?

4. Whose name means "the father of many nations"?

5. In the Old Testament, what is the collective name given to the sons of Shem?

6. Which of Noah's sons discovered his father lying drunk?

7. Who did the apostle Paul think of as his son?

8. Which Old Testament prophet married an Ethiopian and a Cushite?

9. Where did Noah and his family come to rest in the ark?

10. What was the name of the father-in-law of Ruth the Moabitess?

11. Which survivor of Jericho married Salmon the ancestor of King David?

12. True or false? Abraham had a son called Medan.

13. Jesus gave the name Boanerges to which brothers?

14. Which Old Testament character defiled Jacob's daughter Dinah?

15. Which king of Israel was the youngest of eight brothers?

Quiz #14

1. As recorded in Genesis, how old was Abraham when his father died?

2. In the New Testament, what was the name of the tent maker, Aquila's wife?

3. Who was the mother of Timothy?

4. How many sons did Ishmael, the son of Abraham, have?

5. Abigail and Zaruiah were sisters of which king of Israel?

6. Who was King Saul's eldest son?

7. What are the names of Laban's two daughters?

8. Who was the father of the apostle Matthew?

9. Buzi was the father of which Old Testament prophet?

10. Which of Noah's sons had children named Elam, Asshur, Arphaxad, Lud and Aram?

11. Who is referred to as "Great David's greater son"?

12. What was the name of Judas Iscariot's father?

13. Who was the servant of Isaac's wife, Rivkah?

14. In the Old Testament, who cooked a meal for her son so he could pretend to be his brother?

15. True or false? Timothy's mother Eunice was Greek.

Answers

1. 75 years old 2. Priscilla 3. Lois 4. 12 5. David
6. Jonathan 7. Leah and Rachel 8. Alphaeus 9. Ezekiel
10. Shem 11. Jesus 12. Simon 13. Deborah
14. Rebekah 15. False, she was a Jew (2 Timothy 1:5)

Quiz #15

1. Which nephew of David was killed by Joab at the stone of Gibeon?

2. In Genesis, Nahor was the brother of which patriarch?

3. In the Old Testament what was the name of Judah's son, the twin of Perez?

4. What did Abraham's wife do when she heard she was to have a son in her old age?

5. Which daughter of an Egyptian priest married Joseph?

6. Whose wife organized the murder of Naboth so her husband could claim his vineyard?

7. Who did the patriarch Abraham commission to find a wife for his son Isaac?

8. Whose mother sang a song known as the Magnificat?

9. In the New Testament who was the "Son of Man"?

10. Which two sons covered up Noah's nakedness after he became drunk?

11. In the Old Testament, which son of Judah refused to marry his brother's widow?

12. What was the name of the second of King David's brothers?

13. Which daughter of Jacob was raped by Shechem?

14. Which Persian ruler married Esther the Jewess?

15. In which chapter of his Gospel does Luke recount the Parable of the Prodigal Son?

---

1. Amasa **2.** Abraham **3.** Zarah **4.** She laughed
5. Asenath **6.** Ahab's **7.** His servant
8. Jesus' mother **9.** Jesus **10.** Shem and Japheth **11.** Onan
12. Abinadab **13.** Dinah **14.** Ahasuerus (King Xerxes) **15.** Chapter 15

Answers

Quiz #16

1. What was the name of Jacob's only daughter?

2. Which brother and sister sang a duet in Exodus 15?

3. Did the apostle Peter have a wife?

4. What was the name of Shallum's wife, consulted by Hilkiah, following the discovery of the book of the law in the temple?

5. What was the name of Jacob's eighth son by his wife Zilpah?

6. In Exodus, which of his relations advised Moses to delegate some of his decisions to others?

7. Which son of Solomon was the last king of a united Israel?

8. Which of Lazarus' two sisters was busy preparing a meal while the other listened to Jesus?

9. Who is the first mother mentioned in the New Testament?

10. According to 2 Samuel which relative of King Saul cursed David, accusing him of being a man of blood?

11. Ahaziah, Jehoram and Athaliah were children of which evil King of Israel?

12. Dinah was Jacob's daughter by which wife?

13. The brothers Eschol, Mamre and Aner joined forces with whom in order to rescue Lot?

14. Which grandson of Zabdi sinned by taking some of the devoted spoil at Jericho?

15. What was the occupation of the man whose family Paul baptized at Philippi after an earthquake?

Answers

1. Dinah 2. Moses and Miriam 3. Yes 4. Huldah
5. Asher 6. Jethro, his father-in-law 7. Rehoboam 8. Martha
9. Tamar 10. Shimei 11. Ahab
12. Leah 13. Abraham 14. Achan 15. Jailer

Quiz #17

1. What were the names of Lot's grandchildren?

2. As recorded in Proverbs 31 who instructed King Lemuel?

3. Whose mother wanted the head of John the Baptist?

4. Who was the father of Hoshea, the last king of Israel?

5. Which member of the family did the last plague of Egypt kill?

6. Which son of Nebat was the first king of the separated state of Israel after Solomon?

7. Which of Jacob's sons slept with his concubine Bilhah?

8. Who was the elder of Joseph's sons, Manasseh or Ephraim?

9. Which sons of Zeus and Leda were carved as figureheads on a ship in which Paul sailed?

10. True or false? Jesus had a half-brother named Simon.

11. Jezebel, the wicked wife of Ahab, was the daughter of which king?

12. In the Old Testament, which grandson of Shem became father of Peleg?

13. Who wore the skin of a goat in order to trick his blind father?

14. Which son of Ahitub was David's most famous priest?

15. How many genealogies of Jesus are recorded in the New Testament?

Quiz #18

1. Who was the mother of Absalom, King David's son?

2. According to 2 Samuel, which son of Zadok was renowned for his running?

3. Which New Testament deacon had four daughters who were prophetesses?

4. Which good king of Judah was the son of Ahaz?

5. Who was the father of John the Baptist?

6. True or false? Jesus had four half-brothers.

7. After his escape from prison the apostle Peter went to the house of whose mother?

8. Who was the daughter of Lois mentioned by Paul in his letter to Timothy?

9. In the Old Testament who was the father of the hunter Nimrod?

10. Which son of King David was named Jeddiah by the prophet Nathan?

11. In Genesis, which son of Cush was a famous warrior?

12. In the Old Testament which son of Gera was renowned for being left-handed?

13. According to Romans which twin was loved by God whilst the other one was hated?

14. Who was the father of the apostles James and John, and the husband of Salome?

15. Which son of Jacob's name means "Good Fortune"?

Answers

1. Maacah 2. Ahimaaz 3. Philip 4. Hezekiah
5. Zechariah 6. True (Mark 6:3) 7. Mark's 8. Eunice 9. Cush
10. Solomon 11. Nimrod 12. Ehud
13. Jacob 14. Zebedee 15. Gad

Quiz #19

1. Which chapter of Genesis highlights the first disagreement between a husband and wife?

2. What name means "My brother is king"?

3. Who was the father of Isaac's wife, Rachel?

4. In the Old Testament what was the name of Lot's father?

5. What disgrace was suffered by Sarah and Rachel in the Old Testament and Elizabeth in the New Testament?

6. What was the name of the wife of Heber, who, according to the book of Judges, killed Sisera with a tent peg?

7. How many sons did King Saul have?

8. Whose wife was a "helper fit for him"?

9. True or false? King David had a son called Daniel.

10. Moses' father-in-law, Jethro, had another name. What was it?

11. Who was the father of Abram; Nahor and Haran?

12. According to Genesis, Nebaioth was the eldest son of which character?

13. Eleazer was the son of which Old Testament priest?

14. Who was the father of the patriarch Joseph's wife, Asenath?

15. In Acts, which relative of the apostle Paul informed him of a plot to take his life?

Answers

1. Chapter 3 2. Abimelech 3. Bethuel 4. Haran
5. They were barren 6. Jael 7. 5 8. Eve 9. True (1 Chronicles 3:1)
10. Reuel 11. Terah 12. Ishmael
13. Aaron 14. Potiphera 15. Nephew

Quiz #20

1. Adonijah was King David's son by which wife?

2. What was the name of Ahab's son who clashed with the prophet Elijah?

3. How many children did the patriarch Jacob have?

4. How many children did Hannah, wife of Elkanah, have?

5. In Genesis, what did Joseph order to be hidden in his brother Benjamin's sack?

6. According to the Old Testament, who was born clutching his brother's heel?

7. According to Jesus, which son of Barachiah was murdered in the temple of God?

8. Which son of the patriarch Jacob gave his name to the family of priests?

9. According to Daniel, who was the father of Xerxes?

10. Who was King Saul's elder daughter?

11. Which close friend of the apostle Paul had a Jewish mother and a Greek father?

12. What was the name of Jacob's second son by Bilhah?

13. Before the birth of his natural sons who was due to receive the inheritance of Abraham?

14. True or false? Elizabeth, the wife of Zechariah the priest, was herself from a priestly family.

15. According to Genesis, who was the son of Seth and the father of Kenan?

Answers

1. Haggith 2. Ahaziah 3. 13 4. 6
5. A silver cup 6. Jacob 7. Zechariah 8. Levi
9. Darius the Mede 10. Merab
11. Timothy 12. Naphtali 13. Eliezer the Damascene 14. True (Luke 1:5) 15. Enosh

Quiz #21

1. Whose son was Ahab, seventh king of Israel?

2. According to the writer of James, which woman was justified by her works?

3. Which child did his father Jacob rename when his mother died in childbirth?

4. What was the name of Jacob the patriarch's ninth child?

5. True or false? Seth was the third son of Adam and Eve.

6. According to Genesis which of Jacob's sons was a dreamer?

7. In the Old Testament, Abiram and his brother Dathan rebelled against which character?

8. Which woman did Jesus inform that her brother would rise again?

9. Whose husband was ordered to be killed by King David to cover up his adultery?

10. Which of Jesus' apostles was a twin?

11. In the Old Testament which son of Jared "walked with God"?

12. What was the name of the servant of Jonathan's son Mephibosheth?

13. In Genesis, who did Leah give to her husband Jacob as a concubine?

14. True or false? The apostle Paul testified before King Agrippa.

15. In the New Testament, what was the name of the mother of John Mark?

Answers

1. Omri 2. Rahab 3. Benjamin 4. Issachar
5. True (Genesis 4:25) 6. Joseph 7. Moses
8. Martha 9. Bathsheba's 10. Thomas 11. Enoch
12. Ziba 13. Zilpah 14. True (Acts 25:13) 15. Mary

Facts 1

The Old Testament has no word that corresponds exactly to the English word "family."

In the Old Testament, cursing one's father or mother carried the death penalty (Exodus 21:15).

The nation of Israel was regarded as God's adopted son (Jeremiah 3:19).

Abel and Cain are the first recorded brothers in the Bible.

Five of the ten commandments mention family relationships, either implicitly or explicitly.

In the Bible it was usual for the man's parents to choose a wife for him.

When Boaz bought land that had once belonged to Elimelech he also acquired a wife called Ruth.

The patriarch Jacob had four wives, twelve sons and one daughter.

Paul devotes a whole chapter of 1 Corinthians to marriage-related issues (1 Corinthians 7).

Luke's genealogy of Jesus traces his ancestors directly back to God whilst Matthew's goes back to Abraham.

When she was told that God was going to fulfil his promise of giving Abraham and herself a child, Sarah laughed. Later she called the boy Isaac which means "he laughs."

Facts 2

Paul tells fathers not to embitter their children or they will become discouraged.

In Bible times betrothal to be married was as binding as marriage itself.

Naomi is the first person to be called a mother-in-law in the Bible (Ruth 1:14).

Naamah is the first sister mentioned in the Bible (Genesis 4:22).

Adam, Eve and Jesus are the only people in the Bible who did not have human fathers.

In the Old Testament, wives would sometimes allow their husbands to have children by their servants in order to carry on the family line.

If a husband died, his brother was obliged to marry his widow in order to continue the family line.

A genealogy is a list of names linking ancestors or descendants of particular individuals.

Jesus had four half-brothers and an unknown number of half-sisters (Mark 6:3).

Jesus was born in Bethlehem because Joseph had returned to his family home for a census (Luke 2:1-3).

Great Love Stories

Quiz #1

1. What was Bathsheba doing when David first saw her?

2. In 2 Samuel, why did David contrive to have Uriah the Hittite killed?

3. How many children did David and Bathsheba have, and what were their names?

4. How did God punish David for his adultery with Bathsheba?

5. Which Old Testament prophet admonished David for taking Bathsheba as his wife?

6. In the account of the creation of the world, on which day were Adam and Eve made?

7. In Genesis 2, what reasons did God give for creating woman?

8. What did Adam and Eve do right after eating the fruit of the tree of knowledge of good and evil?

9. In Genesis 4, what are the names of Adam and Eve's children?

10. What do the names Adam and Eve mean?

11. In the book of Ruth, whose fields did Ruth glean barley from?

12. Ruth and Boaz were the great grandparents of which Old Testament king?

13. In the book of Ruth, how was Naomi related to Boaz?

14. In the Old Testament, God said, "Be fruitful and increase in number; fill the earth" first to Adam and Eve and then again to whom?

15. In Judges, who fell in love with a woman from the Valley of Sorek?

Answers

1. Bathing. **2.** Because David wanted Uriah's wife for himself. **3.** They had 5 children in all: Shammua (or Shimea), Shobab, Nathan, Solomon (Jedidiah), and the first child, who died. **4.** David and Bathsheba's first child became ill and died; and God also said that the sword would never depart from his house. **5.** Nathan. **6.** The sixth day. **7.** It was not good for man to be alone, and he needed a helper suitable for him. **8.** They sewed fig leaves together and made coverings for themselves. **9.** Cain, Abel, and Seth. **10.** Adam means "man" and Eve "living." **11.** Boaz. **12.** King David. **13.** Boaz was a relative of Naomi's dead husband, Elimelech. **14.** To Noah and his family. **15.** Samson.

Quiz #2

1. When Samson's first wife was given away to another man, what revenge did Samson take on the Philistines?

2. According to the book of Judges, where did Samson meet his first wife?

3. In Judges, who did Samson send to Timnah to get a Philistine woman as his wife?

4. What payment did the rulers of the Philistines promise Delilah in return for help in capturing Samson?

5. Which animal did Samson encounter on his way to meet his first wife?

6. To whom did Samson give the riddle, "Out of the eater, something to eat; out of the strong, something sweet"?

7. Which New Testament couple traveled with Paul and were mentioned by him in some of his letters?

8. Who disagreed with Samson over his choice of a bride?

9. Can you name the three different methods that Delilah used unsuccessfully when trying to subdue Samson?

10. Who went searching for a wife for Isaac?

11. In Genesis, what lie did Isaac tell to the men of Gerar?

12. Whose sister did Abraham's son Isaac marry?

13. In the book of Genesis, who was "a source of grief to Isaac and Rebekah"?

14. How did King Abimelech find out that Rebekah was Isaac's wife?

15. True or false? Peter took his wife with him when he went on his preaching missions.

Answers

1. He tied torches to the tails of foxes and set them loose among the corn belonging to the Philistines **2.** Timnah **3.** His father and mother **4.** Each ruler promised to give her 1100 shekels of silver **5.** A lion **6.** His wedding companions **7.** Priscilla and Aquila **8.** His parents **9.** She tied him with fresh thongs (bowstrings); new ropes and wove his hair into the fabric on the loom **10.** The chief servant of Abraham's household **11.** He said that Rebekah was his sister, not his wife **12.** Laban **13.** Esau and his wives, Olibhama (Judith), and Adah (Basemath) **14.** He saw Isaac caressing Rebekah **15.** True (1 Corinthians 9:5)

Quiz #3

1. What was the name of Abraham's second wife?

2. Who was the mother of Ishmael, Abraham's oldest son?

3. Why did Sarah laugh when a stranger promised her a son?

4. In Genesis, what happened to Lot's wife when she looked back at Sodom?

5. Where were Abraham and Sarah buried?

6. Who does the Lord describe in the Old Testament as "the mother of nations"?

7. When Abraham sent his servant to find a wife for Isaac, what did he give to Rebekah at the well?

8. Where did Rebekah first set eyes on Isaac?

9. Name Isaac and Rebekah's children in the order that they were born.

10. When Abraham's servant arrived at Haran to find a wife for Isaac, what prayer did he make at the well, that was subsequently answered?

11. True or false? Jacob loved Leah more than Rachel.

12. When Jacob married Leah, how many years had he worked for Laban?

13. How did Laban trick Jacob on his wedding night?

14. What were the names of Jacob and Rachel's children?

15. In the Old Testament, who was married to a prophetess and had a son called Maher Shalal-Hash-Baz?

Answers

1. Keturah 2. Hagar 3. She thought that she was too old to have a child 4. She turned into a pillar of salt 5. In the cave of Machpelah near Mamre, in a field Abraham bought from Ephron the Hittite 6. Sarah 7. He gave her a gold nose ring and two gold bracelets 8. In the fields near his home as she was traveling there by camel 9. Esau and Jacob 10. "When I say to a girl, 'Please let down your jar that I may have a drink,' and she says, 'Drink,' and I'll water your camels too,' let her be the one you have chosen." 11. False. He loved Rachel more (Genesis 29:16-28) 12. 7 years 13. He gave Jacob Leah instead of Rachel 14. Joseph and Benjamin 15. Isaiah

Quiz #4

1. How many children did Jacob and Leah have?

2. In the book of Genesis, what was Rachel's response to the problem of being barren?

3. Name the four women who had children with Jacob.

4. True or false? When Hagar was pregnant, she despised Sarah who mistreated her till she ran away.

5. How did Jacob's wife Rachel die?

6. When Joseph was a servant in Egypt, who fell in love with him?

7. Why was Joseph thrown into prison?

8. True or false? David married Abigail, wife of Nabal.

9. Which of the Ten Commandments refers to sexual relationships?

10. Who is reputed to be the author of the Old Testament book Song of Songs?

11. In 1 Samuel, which of Saul's daughters fell in love with David?

12. Which of Saul's daughters was offered first to David in marriage?

13. Who helped David to escape from Saul's men through a window?

14. How does an idol with goats' hair feature in 1 Samuel 19?

15. Complete these words spoken by the Beloved in the Song of Songs: "He has taken me to the banquet hall, and his banner ___ ___ ___ ___."

Answers

1. They had 7 children; 6 boys and 1 girl. **2.** She gave her maidservant Bilhah to Jacob so that Bilah could bear children for her **3.** Leah, Rachel, Bilhah, and Zilpah **4.** True (Genesis 16:1-6) **5.** She died giving birth to Benjamin **6.** The wife of his master, Potiphar **7.** He refused the advances of Potiphar's wife who then him of trying to rape her **8.** True. He married her after Nabal died (1 Samuel 25:39-40) **9.** The seventh commandment **10.** Solomon **11.** Michal **12.** His eldest daughter Merab **13.** Michal **14.** Michal put it in David's bed to deceive Saul's men **15.** over me is love

Quiz #5

1. Who wept when David requested that Michal be returned to him?

2. How many children did Michal and David have?

3. In 1 Kings, who did Solomon build a palace for?

4. Which town was given to Solomon's wife by her father as a wedding gift?

5. How many wives did King Solomon reportedly have?

6. In what way did Solomon do "evil in the eyes of the Lord"?

7. Which Egyptian rescued seven sisters and their flock of sheep from a group of shepherds?

8. Who arranged to have Naboth stoned to death so that she could give his vineyard to her husband?

9. True or false? Moses' wife was the prophetess, Deborah.

10. What were the names of Moses' two sons?

11. Who came to Moses in the desert and gave him good advice?

12. According to the book of Esther, who did Esther marry?

13. How did Esther save her husband's life?

14. By what other name was Esther known?

15. What is the name of the Jewish feast that celebrates the day when King Xerxes stopped the massacre of the Jews because of his love for Esther?

Answers

1. Paltiel, her second husband 2. None 3. His wife, Pharaoh's daughter 4. The town of Gezer, which Pharaoh had ransacked 5. 700 6. He did not obey the Lord completely but loved foreign wives who turned his heart to their gods 7. Moses 8. Jezebel 9. False. His wife was Zipporah, daughter of a priest of Midian (Exodus 2:16, 21) 10. Gershom and Eliezer 11. His father-in-law, Jethro (Reuel) 12. King Xerxes (King Ahasuerus) 13. She warned him of a plot by some of his officials to kill him 14. Hadassah 15. The Feast of Purim

Quiz #6

I. In the first chapter of Hosea, what does the Lord command Hosea to do?

2. What is the name of Hosea's wife?

3. Who is referred to in this passage from Hosea, "She decked herself with rings... and went after her lovers, but me she forgot"?

4. From which Old Testament book is the following passage taken: "How beautiful you are, my darling! Oh, how beautiful! Your eyes are doves"?

5. In the New Testament, how did the couple Ananias and Sapphira displease God?

6. What was Ananias and Sapphira's fate?

7. Who told Joseph not to divorce Mary?

8. True or false? Joseph chose the name Jesus for his son.

9. Which New Testament Gospel talks of Joseph and Mary's trip to Bethlehem?

10. Joseph was the descendant of which Old Testament king?

II. Why did Joseph and Mary go to Jerusalem each year?

12. Where did Joseph take his wife and child when he was told of Herod's plan to kill Jesus?

13. What were the names of John the Baptist's parents?

14. Which Old Testament couple were told that their descendants would be as many as the stars in the sky?

15. True or false? An angel told Zechariah that his son was to be called John.

Answers

I. To take an adulterous wife **2.** Gomer **3.** Israel **4.** Song of Songs **5.** They lied about the amount of money they had made from the sale of their property **6.** They both dropped down dead **7.** An angel appeared to Joseph in a dream **8.** False. The angel Gabriel told Joseph and Mary to name their son Jesus (Matthew 1:21) **9.** Luke's Gospel **10.** King David **II.** To celebrate the Feast of the Passover **12.** To Egypt **13.** Elizabeth and Zechariah **14.** Sarah and Abraham **15.** True (Luke 1:13)

Quiz #7

1. What was God's first command to Adam and Eve?

2. In which of Paul's letters does he write about marriage and being single?

3. From which part of Adam's body was Eve made?

4. Supply the four missing words from this statement made by Adam in the Garden of Eden: "She shall be called 'woman' for she was ___ ___ ___ ___."

5. After the Fall, in what way did God say that woman's relationship with man would change?

6. In which Gospel does Jesus meet the Samaritan woman who has had many husbands?

7. In the account of Jesus and the Samaritan woman at the well, how many husbands had she been married to?

8. Whose wife was Asenath, daughter of Potiphera, priest of On?

9. What were the names of Joseph's two sons?

10. From which Old Testament book does Paul quote when writing to the Ephesians, "For this reason a man will leave his father and mother and be united to his wife"?

11. In which book is the following passage found: "The sons of God saw that the daughters of men were beautiful, and they married any of them they chose"?

12. True or false? Immediately before setting out to go to Canaan, Abraham and Sarah were living in Ur.

13. Why did Lot's sons-in-law not leave Sodom with him and his daughters?

14. Name one of the two Old Testament kings who took Sarah from Abraham, thinking she was his sister.

15. In Egypt, why did Abraham pretend that Sarah was not his wife?

---

15. He thought that he would be killed because she was so beautiful **14.** Pharaoh, and Abimelech, king of Gerar **13.** Because they thought Lot was joking when he said that the city was about to be destroyed **12.** False. They were living in Haran (Genesis 12:5) **11.** Genesis **10.** Genesis **9.** Manasseh and Ephraim **8.** Joseph's **7.** 5 **6.** John's Gospel **5.** God said that woman's desire would be for her husband and that her husband would rule over her **4.** taken out of man. **3.** A rib **2.** 1 Corinthians **1.** To be fruitful and increase in number

Answers

190

Quiz #8

1. Where did Jacob first meet Rachel?

2. How did Jacob greet Rachel at their first meeting?

3. Which Old Testament couple saved their nephew, King Ahaziah's son Joash, from being murdered by Athalia, and then kept him hidden for six years?

4. What god did Jezebel persuade her husband to worship?

5. In the New Testament, who publicly condemned Herodias' marriage to Herod Antipas?

6. To whom was Joanna, one of Jesus' followers, married?

7. In the New Testament, Paul spoke to which governor and his wife about righteousness, self-control, and judgment?

8. Who was accused by Saul's son, Ish-Bosheth, of sleeping with Rizpah, one of Saul's concubines?

9. How did Jacob mark the site where Rachel was buried?

10. What was the occupation of Priscilla and Aquila?

11. What were Abraham and Sarah's names before God changed them?

12. How old was Abraham when Sarah gave birth to Isaac?

13. How old was Isaac when Rebekah agreed to marry him?

14. Which of David's sons visited Bathsheba and requested Abishag as his wife?

15. In which New Testament Gospel is there an account of the Parable of the Ten Virgins?

Answers

1. At a well, where she had come to water her sheep 2. With a kiss
3. Jehoiada and his wife Jehosheba (King Ahaziah's sister and King Jehoram's daughter) 4. Baal 5. John the Baptist
6. Chuza, manager of Herod's household 7. Felix, governor of Judea and his wife Drusilla, a Jewess 8. Abner
9. With a stone pillar 10. They were tent makers 11. Abram and Sarai 12. 100 years old 13. 40 years old
14. Adonijah 15. Matthew's Gospel

GREAT LOVE STORIES

Quiz #9

1. In the Parable of the Ten Virgins, how many virgins went into the wedding banquet with the bridegroom?

2. In 1 Timothy, whose wives must be "women worthy of respect, not malicious talkers but temperate and trustworthy in everything"?

3. In his letter to Timothy, what are the four things that the apostle Paul counsels young widows to do?

4. Which New Testament writer wrote, "But those who marry will face many troubles in this life"?

5. In the book of Ruth, who were witnesses to Boaz's statement that he intended to marry Ruth?

6. True or false? In the book of Ruth, Boaz was entitled to marry Ruth as he was her husband's nearest kin.

7. According to the book of 1 Samuel, how did Hannah's husband Elkanah express his love for her?

8. Why did Elkanah's other wife, Peninnah, continually provoke Hannah?

9. In the New Testament, who had no union with his wife until she gave birth to their child?

10. According to Matthew's Gospel, to whom was Jesus talking when he said, "What God has joined together, let man not separate"?

11. Supply the missing word from the teaching Jesus gave to the Sadducees: "At the ____ people will neither marry nor be given in marriage."

12. In the Parable of the Wedding Banquet, who accepted the invitation to come to the feast?

13. Jesus taught that anyone who looked at a woman lustfully had already committed what with her in his heart?

14. Who is the author of Revelation referring to when he writes of the bride, the wife of the Lamb?

15. In the Old Testament, who said to his wife, "Don't I mean more to you than ten sons?"?

Answers

1. 5 **2.** Deacons **3.** To marry, have children, manage their homes and give the enemy no opportunity for slander **4.** Paul **5.** The elders and all the people at the gate **6.** False. There was a closer relative, who was entitled to first refusal (Ruth 3:12) **7.** Whenever the day came for Elkanah to sacrifice to the Lord, he would give Hannah a double portion of the meat **8.** Because Hannah was barren **9.** Joseph **10.** Some Pharisees **11.** resurrection **12.** The people who were invited in off the streets **13.** Adultery **14.** The Church **15.** Hannah's husband, Elkanah

192

Quiz # 10

1. In which New Testament epistle is it written, "Husbands ought to love their wives as their own bodies"?

2. True or false? Paul said, "So guard yourself in your spirit and do not break faith with the wife of your youth."

3. Who does Paul encourage to, "Put to death, therefore, whatever belongs to your earthly nature: sexual immorality, impurity, lust, evil desires, and greed"?

4. Which Old Testament book contains the passage, "A wife of noble character who can find? She is worth far more than rubies. Her husband has full confidence in her"?

5. Who in the New Testament tells husbands to "be considerate as you live with your wives, and treat them with respect as the weaker partner"?

6. In Deuteronomy, what was the fate of a newly married wife who could not give evidence of her virginity?

7. Who was willing to travel hundreds of miles with a servant to marry a man she had never seen?

8. Which Old Testament wife cursed her husband for continuing to believe in God after his family and livestock had been killed and he had been inflicted with illness?

9. In the account of the wedding at Cana, who was surprised by the high quality of the wine served during the banquet?

10. Who in the Old Testament said, "I have made a covenant with my eyes not to look lustfully at a girl"?

11. In which New Testament letter are the faithful exhorted to keep the marriage bed pure, for God will judge adulterers and the sexually immoral?

12. True or false? In Old Testament times, men were encouraged to take foreign wives.

13. In the book of Isaiah, who is compared to a bridegroom rejoicing over his bride?

14. Who sought a suitable husband for her widowed daughter-in-law?

15. In Judges 1, who promised his daughter's hand in marriage to the man who attacked and captured the town of Debir, also called Kiriath Sepher?

Answers

13. God **14.** Naomi **15.** Caleb

12. False. They were told to marry from among their own people (1 Kings 11:2)

7. Rebekah **8.** Job's **9.** The master of the banquet **10.** Job **11.** Hebrews

3. The church of Colosse **4.** The book of Proverbs **5.** Peter **6.** She would be stoned to death

1. Paul's letter to the Ephesians **2.** False. It was the Old Testament prophet Malachi (Malachi 2:14-15)

193

Quiz #11

1. In the book of Judges, what did Caleb give his daughter Acsah as a dowry?

2. What was the name of King David's virgin companion who looked after him in his old age?

3. To which church is Paul writing when he suggests, "If they cannot control themselves, they should marry, for it is better to marry than to burn with passion"?

4. In 1 Timothy, who "should be the husband of but one wife"?

5. According to Deuteronomy, if a man refuses to marry his brother's widow, the widow is entitled to remove what from him in the presence of the elders?

6. In Paul's letter to Titus, who does he recommend to train young women to love their husbands and children?

7. In Paul's letter to Titus, what teaches people "to say "No" to ungodliness and worldly passions"?

8. What reason did Laban give to Jacob for tricking him into marrying Leah?

9. What did Laban give to his daughters when they got married?

10. Which unloved wife hoped that her husband would love her once she had given birth to a son?

11. Which couple is referred to in the following passage: "So she became his wife and he loved her"?

12. Apart from marriage, how were Leah and Rachel related to Jacob?

13. In the book of Esther, how did Queen Vashti anger the king?

14. In Deuteronomy, what person "must not take many wives, or his heart will be led astray"?

15. In Genesis, who pushed her son into deceiving her husband?

Answers

1. Land in the Negev and also the upper and lower springs of water 2. Abishag 3. To the church in Corinth 4. An overseer 5. One of his sandals 6. Older women 7. The grace of God that brings salvation 8. It was not the custom to give the younger daughter in marriage before the older daughter 9. He gave each of them a servant girl 10. Leah 11. Isaac and Rebekah 12. They were cousins 13. She refused to exhibit her beauty before his guests 14. The king of the Israelites 15. Rebekah

Facts 1

The Hanging Gardens of Babylon, one of the seven wonders of the world, is reported to have been built by King Nebuchadnezzar II for one of his wives, to remind her of her homeland.

People in Biblical times rarely married for love, although it was generally accepted that love would result from being married, hence Leah's prayer that Jacob would love her once she had borne him a son (Genesis 29:32).

Israelite marriage was a business affair. The bridegroom's family paid a bride-price, a *mohar*, to the bride's father. This was compensation for loss of the woman as a worker and also for the loss of her offspring.

As soon as the mohar, the bride-price, had been paid, the girl was legally married (betrothed). A betrothal could only be broken by divorce or death, hence Joseph's desire to divorce Mary quietly before they were married (Matthew 1:19). The marriage was not consummated until the wedding.

A betrothal was seen as a binding contract and the couple were commonly called husband and wife, even though they were not yet married. This is why Joseph is called Mary's husband in Matthew 1:19.

The bride-price could not be spent by the bride's father, but he could use interest that was earned on it. When the daughter's parents or husband died, the bride-price had to be given to her. In Genesis 31:15, Leah and Rachel are angry with their father Laban because he had spent theirs.

In Deuteronomy, 50 shekels of silver was the usual minimum bride-price. This could be paid in kind. Jacob paid it by working for his father-in-law. Pharaoh gave Solomon a city when he married his daughter (1 Kings 9:16).

In the Song of Songs, the bride is referred to as "sister." This affectionate term occurs frequently in Near Eastern love poetry, indicating how close a husband is to his wife.

Ruth's request to Boaz to "spread the corner of your garment over me" (Ruth 3:9) symbolized a request for protection through marriage. It alludes to a Hebrew wedding custom whereby a new wife is covered with the corner of a prayer shawl.

Facts 2

More than a hundred thousand inscribed clay tablets have been found dating from the Middle Bronze Age. These throw considerable light on the customs and laws of the ancient Near East in the time of Abraham.

It was customary for a childless couple to adopt a son to care for them during their lifetime and attend to their burial. The adopted son lost his rights if the couple subsequently had a son (Genesis 15:2).

An ancient law code, the Code of Hammurabi (c. 1750 B.C.), permitted a man to have a secondary wife (a concubine). The concubine, who was usually a slave, had well-defined rights.

One marriage contract, found at Nuzi, states, "If Gilimninu [the bride] does not bear children, she shall take a Lullu woman as a wife for Shennima [the bridegroom]...Gilimninu shall not send the handmaid's offspring away."

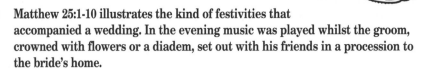

The Israelites were told not to marry foreigners, to avoid being tempted to worship foreign gods. As Numbers 36:6-9 explains, this prohibition also prevented the promised land being divided up by inheritance claims.

Matthew 25:1-10 illustrates the kind of festivities that accompanied a wedding. In the evening music was played whilst the groom, crowned with flowers or a diadem, set out with his friends in a procession to the bride's home.

The groom greeted his bride, who was given a blessing by her family. This was the only religious activity in the wedding. The bride was accompanied by bridesmaids who had helped her dress.

Descriptions of the bride's wedding dress in Jeremiah, Ezekiel and Revelation show that they were made from the finest linen and were richly embroidered. The bride was also adorned with many jewels and a thick veil, which explains why Jacob did not recognize Leah.

Facts 3

The bride and groom walked in a torchlight procession, amid dancing and singing, back to the groom's house or to their new home, where the bridegroom's family held a feast.

Celebrations lasted a week, or even a fortnight (Genesis 29:27). During this time there was considerable drinking and eating, and also games and contests. The bride and groom were seated on a dais, and were treated as king and queen.

Throughout the wedding, a friend of the bridegroom acted as master of ceremonies.

If a man seduced or raped an unmarried woman, he was obliged by law to pay the woman's father a bridal price and to take the woman as his wife. This is what Shechem tried to do with Dinah, Jacob's daughter.

To be married, but remain childless, was considered shameful and was thought to be a mark of God's displeasure. If a wife was barren, it meant that there would be no descendants to continue the family line.

According to the law of Moses, if a widow was childless, her husband's eldest brother had to marry her and produce a son. This was called a Levirate marriage and is the law referred to in Matthew 22.

When a brother married his brother's widow, the eldest son of that marriage belonged to the first husband and carried his name. Onan, Judah's second son, was killed by God because he did not want to produce offspring with his brother's widow.

If there was no brother-in-law for a widow to marry, then this duty could be passed to the next-of-kin, the "kinsman-redeemer," as recorded in Ruth chapters 3 to 4.

Since Naomi had no more sons for Ruth to marry, it was a sacrifice for Ruth to accompany her mother-in-law Naomi back to her homeland. Ruth was willing to put Naomi's interests above her own.

Facts 4

The Old Testament book Song of Songs, tells of deep human love. It looks at marriage sensitively from a woman's point of view and describes the purity and nobility of true love.

The Song of Songs is often interpreted as a devotional allegory in praise of the love of God and his people. Alternatively, it may be seen as a parable which, by celebrating human love, points beyond itself to the love of God.

The Parable of the Lost Coin in Luke 15 probably refers to a coin lost from a wedding headdress. Headdresses were made from coins strung together and were part of the bride's dowry.

A married man was absolved from military service for a period of one year after his marriage. This was to give him time to enjoy being with his wife, and probably also to give him time to produce an heir.

Israelites who strayed away from God and worshiped foreign gods were often described as committing adultery. This was often literally the case as worship of Canaanite deities sometimes involved sleeping with temple prostitutes.

Women were often given in marriage to seal treaties with foreign nations, hence the marriage of Solomon to Pharaoh's daughter.

In Old Testament times, if a man took a king's concubine, it indicated that he desired to become a ruler, hence Ish-Bosheth's concern for his inheritance when Abner slept with his father Saul's concubine (2 Samuel 3:7).

Hosea uses the courtship, marriage, and adultery of a husband and wife to describe God's relationship with his people.

When Abraham asked his servant to find a wife for Isaac, the servant had to place his hand under Abraham's thigh. This Babylonian custom emphasized the solemnity of the oath and the importance of continuing the family line. The thigh was often used to symbolize the "loins," the source of procreative power.

Facts 5

There is no word for a "bachelor" in Hebrew, suggesting that marriage was the norm in Biblical times.

In New Testament times, the legal age for marriage was set at thirteen for boys and twelve for girls. This was probably one reason why parents played a major part in choosing a bride for their son.

Deuteronomy 24:1 allowed divorce if a man found something "indecent" (some uncleanness) in his wife. In that case the man merely had to issue a certificate stating that he was divorcing his wife.

In Old Testament times a woman could not divorce her husband. This was because, in the eyes of the law, she was a chattel with no legal rights.

In the time of Jesus, the teachers of the law were divided about what was meant by "uncleanness" in Deuteronomy 24. Some had a strict approach, saying that the only grounds for divorce were adultery or unchastity.

One school of rabbinical teaching interpreted "uncleanness" as meaning anything that might offend the husband. A woman could therefore be divorced for spoiling the evening meal.

When Jesus spoke out strongly against a lax approach to marriage and divorce, he was addressing a lively, strongly-debated issue.

The common Hebrew word for husband is 'ba'al', which means owner, possessor or master. Hence Boaz's question to his foreman, "Whose young woman is that?" (Ruth 2:5).

Crime and Punishment

CRIME AND PUNISHMENT

Quiz #1

1. What is the first crime recorded in the Bible?

2. Under what pretext was Paul the apostle thrown into prison while in Philippi?

3. How did God protect Cain from being killed during his years as a wanderer?

4. In Genesis, what three punishments did God give the serpent for deceiving Eve?

5. In which Old Testament book is the following quotation found, "For dust you are and to dust you will return"?

6. How did God ensure that Adam and Eve could never return to Eden?

7. What two punishments did God give the woman for disobeying him in the Garden of Eden?

8. As recorded in Genesis, why did God want to flood the Earth?

9. Why did Noah curse Ham, his son, saying, "The lowest of slaves will he be to his brothers"?

10. What is the eighth commandment?

11. At the end of Abraham's pleading with God about Sodom and Gomorrah, God was prepared to save the cities if there were how many righteous men living there?

12. What deceit did Rebekah and Jacob commit against Isaac and Esau?

13. In which book of the Old Testament does the passage, "eye for eye, tooth for tooth" first appear?

14. In Genesis, what did Rachel steal from her father Laban?

15. When Joseph's brothers came to Egypt to buy food, which brother did Joseph imprison, while letting the others return to their homeland?

---

1. Cain's murder of his brother Abel **2.** It was claimed Paul was advocating customs that were unlawful for Romans to practice **3.** God put a mark on Cain **4.** The serpent had to crawl on its belly, eat dust and have humankind as its enemy **5.** Genesis **6.** God placed cherubim on the east side and a flaming sword that flashed in every direction **7.** Pains in childbirth and her husband would rule over her **8.** Because the Earth and the people in it were corrupt and full of violence **9.** Because Ham saw his father naked and told his brothers **10.** You shall not steal **11.** 10 **12.** Rebekah helped Jacob disguise himself as Esau in order to trick Isaac into blessing him **13.** Exodus **14.** Laban's household gods **15.** Simeon

Answers

202

Quiz #2

1. During the Israelites' flight from Egypt, how did the Lord punish them for worshiping a golden calf?

2. How old was Joseph when his brothers threw him into a pit?

3. Which Old Testament judge had Agag, king of the Amalekites, executed?

4. In the book of Revelation, where did the angel throw Satan?

5. What were the occupations of the two men that Pharaoh had thrown into prison with Joseph?

6. According to the book of Deuteronomy, how many witnesses to a crime were needed before a man could be put to death?

7. Which New Testament writer called himself "an ambassador in chains"?

8. In the Old Testament, to whom did God say, "Whoever sheds the blood of man, by man shall his blood be shed"?

9. When Moses was still a young man, why did he suddenly leave Egypt?

10. Which two towns in the Old Testament were considered so corrupt that God completely destroyed them?

11. What is the sixth commandment?

12. According to the laws that God gave to Moses, what was the penalty for premeditated murder?

13. According to the laws that God gave to Moses, what was the penalty for accidental murder?

14. Where did Rebekah send Jacob when she found out Esau was planning to kill him?

15. On which mountain did God give the Law to Moses?

Answers

1. He struck them down with a plague 2. 17 years old 3. Samuel 4. Into the abyss
5. Pharaoh's chief baker, and Pharaoh's chief cupbearer 6. 2 or 3 7. Paul 8. Noah and his family
9. Because someone had seen him kill an Egyptian 10. Sodom and Gomorrah 11. You shall not murder
12. Death 13. The murderer was to flee to a safe "city of refuge"
14. She sent him to her brother Laban in Haran 15. Mount Sinai

Quiz #3

1. When Joseph lived in Egypt, for what alleged crime was he thrown into prison?

2. In Matthew's Gospel, which commandment did Jesus quote when he said that anger and insults were also forbidden?

3. How did God punish Moses for not trusting in him "enough to honor me as holy in the sight of the Israelites"?

4. What wrongdoing was God referring to in Deuteronomy when he said it, "blinds the eyes of the wise and twists the words of the righteous"?

5. Out of the two men that Joseph met in prison, who was hanged and who was saved?

6. According to Deuteronomy, who did the Israelites have to consult if they could not solve a case in their courts?

7. True or false? It says in Deuteronomy that a person can be put to death for someone else's sin.

8. After Abner had made his peace with David, why did Joab, leader of David's army, lure him back to Hebron and kill him?

9. In the book of Daniel, who was King Nebuchadnezzar referring to when he said that they would be cut up into pieces and their houses turned into heaps of rubble?

10. How was Saul's son Ish-Bosheth murdered?

11. What was the punishment recorded in Leviticus when a man married both a daughter and her mother?

12. Why did Joab, David's army commander, find it easy to kill Absalom?

13. Which of David's sons did King Solomon execute?

14. What was the crime brought before King Solomon by two prostitutes?

15. When David sinned against God by carrying out a census of fighting men, what three punishments did God present to David to choose between?

Answers

1. Attempted rape of Potiphar's wife 2. You shall not murder 3. God did not let Moses lead the Israelites into the promised land 4. Bribery 5. The baker was hanged and the cupbearer was saved 6. The Levite priests and the judge 7. False. It says, "Each is to die for his own sin" (Deuteronomy 24:16) 8. Because Abner had killed Joab's brother, Asahel 9. Those who spoke against the God of Shadrach, Meshach and Abednego 10. He was stabbed and his head cut off 11. Both he and the women were to be burned to death 12. Because Absalom's head was caught up in the branches of a tree and he couldn't escape 13. Adonijah 14. One prostitute claimed that the other had stolen her newborn baby 15. 3 years of famine, 3 months of fleeing from his enemies, or 3 days of plague

Quiz #4

1. In which of his letters in the New Testament does Paul state that Christ is "the end of the law"?

2. In 1 Kings, what was the trumped-up charge that led Naboth the vineyard owner to be killed?

3. Name the crime of the woman who Jesus saved from being stoned.

4. What method of execution did King Xerxes use for Haman in the book of Esther?

5. In the book of Joshua, what crime did Achan commit after the fall of Jericho?

6. Who requested that Herod behead John the Baptist?

7. Which one of the disciples was the keeper of the money bag?

8. According to the book of Acts, who "dragged off men and women and put them in prison" in an attempt to destroy the church at Jerusalem?

9. In Romans, Paul quotes, "For it is written: 'It is mine to avenge; I will repay,' says the Lord." From which book in the Old Testament does this quotation originate?

10. In the book of Daniel, name the three Jews who King Nebuchadnezzar threw into the furnace.

11. On whose orders was Joab, commander of David's army, killed?

12. Which king had Daniel thrown to the lions for praying to God?

13. What crime was Hosea's wife guilty of?

14. True or false? According to the Law in Exodus, a man may legally kill a thief breaking into his home before sunrise, but after sunrise he cannot kill him.

15. Why did Herod arrest John the Baptist?

Answers

1. Romans 2. He was said to have cursed both God and the King 3. Adultery 4. The gallows 5. He coveted and stole gold and silver from Jericho instead of putting them into the Lord's treasury 6. Salome, Herodias' daughter 7. Judas Iscariot 8. Saul, later known as Paul 9. Deuteronomy 10. Shadrach, Meshach, and Abednego 11. King Solomon's 12. King Darius 13. Adultery 14. True (Exodus 22:2-3) 15. Because John told him that his marriage to Herodias, his brother's wife, was against the law

Quiz #5

1. What were the professions of Samuel's sons, Joel and Abijah?

2. Which prophet condemned shopkeepers for using dishonest scales?

3. True or false? Paul told his friend Onesimus to pay back any money he had stolen.

4. In 2 Chronicles, why did King Joash's officials conspire to bring about his death?

5. What were the names of the husband and wife who died suddenly after lying to the apostles about the money they had given to the church in Jerusalem?

6. Which famous New Testament figure was present at the stoning of Stephen?

7. In which of his letters does Paul preach, "He who rebels against the authority is rebelling against what God has instituted"?

8. True or false? The Jews wanted to stone Jesus several times.

9. Who was Jesus speaking about when he said, "He is a liar and the father of lies"?

10. What was the name of the island to which the apostle John was exiled as a punishment for preaching?

11. In 1 Kings, which group of people was sentenced to death and executed by order of Elijah?

12. In which book of the Old Testament is the verse, "My son, if sinners entice you, do not give in to them"?

13. Name the two crimes Barabbas had committed, as recorded in Mark and Luke.

14. At which feast was it the custom for Pilate to release a prisoner chosen by the people?

15. Who was killed on the orders of Joshua and buried under a heap of rocks in a place thereafter known as the Valley of Achor?

---

13. Murder and taking part in an insurrection in Jerusalem **14.** Feast of the Passover **15.** Achan
10. Patmos **11.** The prophets of Baal **12.** Book of Proverbs
6. Saul, later known as Paul **7.** Letter to the Romans **8.** True **9.** The devil
4. Because the king had murdered Zechariah (son of Jehoiada the priest) **5.** Ananias and Sapphira
1. They were judges **2.** Amos **3.** False. Paul offered to pay it back (Philemon 18)

Answers

Quiz #6

1. In 1 Kings, who was responsible for the death of Naboth the vineyard owner?

2. How did Samuel's sons, Joel and Abijah, upset the elders of Israel?

3. In 1 Kings, which king did Zimri, a chariot official, kill in order to become king himself?

4. In 2 Kings, which treacherous queen was killed during the coronation of her seven year-old nephew, Joash?

5. True or false? Manasseh, king of Judah, was famed for his love of God and his God-fearing rule.

6. What fate befell the youths who jeered at Elisha as he was on the road to Bethel?

7. On how many occasions did Paul the apostle receive 39 lashes from the Jews?

8. Who was imprisoned with Paul the apostle while they were in Philippi, Macedonia?

9. Who was converted while Paul the apostle was in prison in Macedonia?

10. While Paul and Silas were preaching in Thessalonica, why was their friend Jason dragged before the city officials?

11. According to Deuteronomy, what was the maximum number of lashes a guilty man could receive?

12. As he left Miletus to go to Jerusalem, who warned Paul the apostle that prison and hardships were facing him?

13. As recorded in the Gospels, if you look at a woman lustfully, what sin are you committing?

14. In the book of Revelation, to whom does John write, "I tell you, the devil will put some of you in prison to test you, and you will suffer persecution for ten days"?

15. Under which two Roman governors was Paul imprisoned in Caesarea?

Quiz #7

1. Who claimed he had been whipped, beaten, and stoned for being a servant of Christ?

2. Who was God punishing in the Old Testament when he said, "When you work the ground, it will no longer yield its crops for you"?

3. Why did the Pharisees condemn Jesus for healing a man with a shriveled hand?

4. True or false? According to the Law of Moses, it was a crime to consult a medium.

5. Two criminals were crucified with Jesus. What was their crime?

6. During the Israelites' time in the desert, a man was found breaking the Sabbath law and was stoned to death. What was he doing?

7. What was the name of the supreme law court of the Jews?

8. What was Jesus' answer to Peter's question, "How many times shall I forgive my brother when he sins against me? Up to seven times?"?

9. Who tried to persuade Pilate not to harm Jesus after he had been arrested?

10. Why did Judas Iscariot kiss Jesus when he found him in Gethsemane?

11. According to Jesus, what is the most important commandment?

12. In the account of Jesus being tried by the Sanhedrin, what crime had Jesus committed, according to two witnesses?

13. Why was Jeremiah arrested when he tried to leave the besieged city of Jerusalem to go to his property in the land of Benjamin?

14. Which Old Testament prophet described a plague of locusts, and said it was a foretaste of God's coming judgment on the Israelites?

15. When Paul and Silas were in prison in Philippi, what caused the prison doors to open and their chains to become loose?

Answers

1. The apostle Paul **2.** Cain **3.** Because it was the Sabbath day, and it was against the law to heal on the Sabbath **4.** True (Leviticus 19:31) **5.** Robbery **6.** Collecting wood **7.** The Sanhedrin **8.** "I tell you, not seven times, but seventy-seven times." **9.** Pilate's wife **10.** He had prearranged for the guards to arrest the man that he kissed **11.** "Love the Lord your God with all your heart and with all your soul and with all your mind and with all your strength." **12.** Jesus had said he was able to destroy the temple of God and rebuild it in 3 days **13.** It was thought that Jeremiah was deserting to the Babylonians **14.** Joel **15.** An earthquake

Quiz #8

1. During the siege of Jerusalem, officials complained to the king that Jeremiah was discouraging the people and soldiers. How did they try to stop him?

2. What did Jesus tell people to do if they had their tunic taken away from them?

3. What eventually happened with the thirty pieces of silver that Judas had received for betraying Jesus?

4. True or false? Paul said, "Money is a root of all kinds of evil."

5. Who persuaded the Sanhedrin to release the apostles, saying, "If their purpose or activity is of human origin, it will fail. But if it is from God, you will not be able to stop these men"?

6. Which of the twelve disciples did King Herod have put to death by the sword?

7. Why did King Herod arrest Peter?

8. How did Peter escape from prison and enter the city after King Herod had ordered four squads of soldiers to guard him?

9. True or false? Paul wrote his letter to the church of Colosse while he was in prison.

10. Which parable does Jesus tell the disciples to teach them that they must always forgive one another?

11. Who said, "We must obey God rather than men"?

12. Why did the magistrates who threw Paul and Silas into prison in Macedonia then come forward to appease them and escort them from the prison?

13. True or false? The chief priests approached Judas Iscariot to ask him to betray Jesus.

14. Why did Caiaphas and the chief priests and elders decide against arresting Jesus during the Passover?

15. The words of which prophet were fulfilled by the actions of Judas Iscariot?

Answers

1. They imprisoned him in a dry water cistern 2. To give their cloak too 3. The priests and elders used them to buy a field as a burial place for foreigners 4. False. Paul said that it was "the love of mone", not money itself (1 Timothy 6:10) 5. Gamaliel, a Pharisee 6. James, the brother of John 7. King Herod wanted to please the Jews 8. An angel caused his chains to fall off and led him out of the prison and into the city 9. True (Colossians 4:18) 10. The Parable of the Unmerciful Servant 11. Peter and the apostles 12. Because Paul told them he was a Roman citizen 13. False. Judas approached them 14. Because they wanted to avoid a riot 15. Jeremiah

Quiz #9

1. What is the royal law that James refers to in his letter in the New Testament?

2. Complete this quotation from the letter to the Hebrews: "God is a consuming ____."

3. What did God say would happen if Adam and Eve ate of the tree of the knowledge of good and evil?

4. In the Parable of the Sheep and the Goats, why were the goats sent into eternal punishment?

5. When harvesting grapes and olives, why was it a crime to double-check that all the fruit had been picked?

6. How many brothers did Abimelech murder as recorded in the book of Judges?

7. How did the Lord destroy Sodom and Gomorrah?

8. What punishment befell Aaron's sons Nadab and Abihu when they offered unauthorized fire in their censers before the Lord?

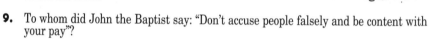

9. To whom did John the Baptist say: "Don't accuse people falsely and be content with your pay"?

10. Complete Jesus' teaching from Matthew 7: "____ is the gate and ____is the road that leads to destruction, and many enter through it."

11. Before he sent out his disciples to preach his message, what advice did Jesus give them about being arrested?

12. In Matthew 11, which three cities are denounced by Jesus because of their lack of repentance, despite miracles having been performed there?

13. In the Parable of the Talents, what happened to the man who hid his one talent in the ground?

14. When Paul despaired of getting justice in Palestine, he exercised his right as a Roman citizen and asked for his case to go to appeal. Who did he appeal to?

15. What happened to Lot's wife when she disobeyed God's command not to turn round and look back at Sodom?

Quiz #10

1. According to the book of Revelation, for how many years was Satan to be locked away?

2. According to Paul, who masquerades as an angel of light?

3. How did God punish the Israelites who were afraid to enter the Promised Land?

4. Which of Joseph's brothers tried to rescue Joseph after he had been thrown into a pit?

5. In 2 Samuel, to whom does Nathan compare David because of his adultery with Bathsheba and the killing of Uriah?

6. In which book of the Old Testament is it written, "An evil man is snared by his own sin, but a righteous one can sing and be glad"?

7. What punishment did Paul command to be given to the sexually immoral man in the church in Corinth?

8. In the Parable of the Good Samaritan, who were the two people who passed by the robbers' victim without helping him?

9. In his letter, what does James describe as, "a fire, a world of evil among the parts of the body"?

10. Why did Pilate give orders that Jesus' tomb should be sealed and guarded for three days?

11. In John's Gospel, to which group does Jesus say, "If you were blind, you would not be guilty of sin; but now that you claim you can see, your guilt remains"?

12. What reason did the Jews give for wanting to stone Jesus?

13. Why did the Israelites want to stone Joshua and Caleb after they had returned from exploring the Promised Land?

14. Who pelted King David and his officials with stones, but was not reprimanded by David?

15. According to Paul, what is the fate of someone who preaches a gospel other than the Gospel of Jesus Christ?

Answers

1. 1,000 years 2. Satan 3. They could not enter the promised land but died in the wilderness 4. Reuben 5. A rich man with lots of sheep and cattle, who takes away and kills the only lamb belonging to a poor man 6. Proverbs 7. The man was to be expelled from the church 8. The priest and the Levite 9. The tongue 10. It was thought the disciples would steal the body and claim Jesus had risen from the dead 11. Pharisees 12. Blasphemy 13. Because the two men accused the Israelites of rebelling against God 14. Shimei, son of Gera, a man from the same clan as Saul's family 15. Eternal condemnation

Quiz #11

1. Which Old Testament character refused to curse God and turn away from him, even though Satan brought all manner of evil and disaster upon him?

2. When a man said that he had killed King Saul, what did David do?

3. Which priest from the Old Testament had two sons, Hophni and Phinehas, who were killed by the Lord because of their wicked ways?

4. What crime did Joseph claim his brother Benjamin had committed?

5. What was Cain's motive for murdering Abel?

6. To whom was Paul writing when he said people should, "submit to the authorities, not only because of possible punishment but also because of conscience"?

7. Which New Testament writer tells his readers, "For whoever keeps the whole law and yet stumbles at just one point is guilty of breaking all of it"?

8. Why was Miriam, Moses' sister, struck with leprosy?

9. When God asked Cain where his brother Abel was, Cain lied and said, "I don't know." What did Cain then ask God?

10. In the parable about the landowner who leased a vineyard to tenants, what did the tenants do when the landowner's son went to collect his father's harvest?

11. Why did the Jews have Jesus tried by the Romans instead of judging him themselves?

12. According to John's Gospel, when did Satan enter Judas?

13. To whom did Paul say, "May your money perish with you because you thought you could buy the gift of God with money"?

14. True or false? The Law of Moses forbade the oppression of a foreigner.

15. Why did the Roman commander have the prisoner Paul transferred from Jerusalem to Caesarea?

Answers

1. Job 2. David had him killed 3. Eli 4. The theft of a silver cup 5. Jealousy 6. The Christians in Rome 7. James 8. Because Miriam instigated an open rebellion against Moses 9. Cain asked, "Am I my brother's keeper?" 10. They killed him 11. Because by Roman law they had no right to pass a death sentence 12. During the last supper, as soon as Judas had taken the bread from Jesus 13. Simon the sorcerer 14. True (Exodus 23:9) 15. Because a group of Jews were plotting to kill Paul

212

Facts 1

It was common practice among the nations of the ancient world to make two copies of a covenant or agreement. Each party then stored its copy in a holy place. This may be why the Ten Commandments were written on two tablets and kept in the ark of the covenant, the holy place of both God and Israel.

The idea of a "scapegoat" comes from the ceremony performed on the annual Day of Atonement. The high priest first laid both hands on the goat, symbolically putting on it all the sins of the people. Then he sent the goat into the desert as a sign that the people's sins had been taken away.

The Law of Moses stated that capital punishment was appropriate for eighteen different offences, including some, such as rape, that did not involve murder.

God's law was different from that of other nations, notably because it treated all people as equal - kings and rulers, as well as citizens, had to obey it.

The Law of Moses instituted cities of refuge to which murderers could flee until a trial could be held. They could remain in the city and be protected from anyone seeking vengeance.

The gallows mentioned in Esther was probably not scaffolding and rope, but a pole or stake upon which the criminal was impaled. This was a common method of execution in nations in the Near East at that time.

The Romans favored crucifixion when executing military and political criminals, but they never executed a Roman citizen in this way.

The Law of Moses decreed "an eye for an eye" in order to avoid excessive punishment. The point was that the punishment had to fit the crime.

Jeremiah was imprisoned in a private house, and later in a cistern, because there were no prisons in Israel before Roman times.

The Jews found Jesus guilty of blasphemy, but as they could not authorize a death penalty, they had to convince the Romans he had broken one of their laws. He was therefore charged with sedition because of his talk about the kingdom of God.

The authorities were pleased when Judas came forward to betray Jesus because they needed to arrest Jesus away from the crowds. Since Judas was a disciple, he knew the quiet places where Jesus went to be alone with his friends.

Facts 2

There was no police force in Palestine. In Roman times, order was kept by the Roman army. The Jews, however, had their own guards, chosen from among the Levites, to keep order in the Temple.

The name of the place where Jesus was crucified was called, "Golgotha," which means "the place of a skull." The name may have arisen because it was a place of execution, or the hill where it was located may have been shaped like a skull.

In Israel, the main form of execution was by stoning. This was seen as the responsibility of the whole community (Leviticus 24:14).

Traditionally, criminals who had been executed were buried outside the city and had stones flung on top of their graves. This is how Absalom was buried by Joab.

The cities of Sodom and Gomorrah were located in an area where the soil was full of bitumen, which burns easily. One school of thought suggests the cities were destroyed when this bitumen was set alight, perhaps by a meteoric thunderstorm.

The cities of Sodom and Gomorrah may be buried under the water at the southern end of the Dead Sea.

The first plague God sent the Egyptians turned the Nile into blood. This would have had a major religious significance as Egyptians held the Nile and certain species of fish and crocodile to be sacred.

Frogs were sacred to the Egyptians and it was forbidden to kill them. They would therefore have suffered intensely during the second plague.

The Egyptians deified cattle, so when God sent a disease which killed their cows, it would have been clear to the Egyptians that he was attacking their religion.

Facts 3

A unique feature of Hebrew law was that a master had to release a slave that he had harmed, thereby placing emphasis on the humane treatment of all people, regardless of rank or status.

If a woman was raped, the rapist had to pay compensation to her father because she was considered to be his property. Since the father had lost an eligible virgin, the payment had to be the amount he would have received as a bride-price.

In the Old Testament, the crime of negligence was considered as serious as murder or stealing. A goring ox that killed a person was itself killed. However, if the owner knew of its habit, and had neglected to tie it up, then the owner was also put to death.

In early Old Testament times, justice was administered by the chief of the tribe or clan, later by local or circuit judges. During the time of the monarchy, the elders of a town acted as judges at the town gate. The king was an appeal judge.

In New Testament times, the highest court in the land was the Sanhedrin. It had seventy-one members, which acted as a parliament and a court of law. The president of the Sanhedrin was the high priest.

No crucifixions are recorded in the Old Testament, although corpses were sometimes hung on a tree as a warning to others. This symbol of humiliation, with the body regarded as cursed, is described in Isaiah when he foretells Jesus' death.

The possession of animals in a semi-nomadic society was of prime importance, which may explain why the penalty for stealing animals involved a four or five-fold restitution rather than like for like, thereby acting as a deterrent to others.

It was common for Romans to chain guards to prisoners, especially those under house arrest.

Pontius Pilate was the Roman procurator (governor) of Judea during the time of Jesus' ministry. In 36 A.D. he was recalled to Rome because he had used Roman troops to massacre a religious gathering in Samaria.

As well as places of worship, synagogues served as schools, and local law courts. Offenders were sometimes excommunicated, which was a serious punishment, since a synagogue was the center of the community.

Jewish law laid down that the number of strokes in a whipping should not exceed thirty-nine.

War and
Peace

Quiz #1

1. How were the Israelites who took part in a war paid?

2. Who was the only judge who was also a prophetess?

3. Who said, "All who draw the sword will die by the sword"?

4. Which Philistine champion was over nine feet tall?

5. Gideon started with an army of 32,000 men. How many people did he allow to go home?

6. Which judge sang about the time when the Israelites did not have a shield or spear among 40,000 of them?

7. Who made this famous lament over the death in battle of Saul and Jonathan: "Your glory, O Israel, lies slain on your heights. How the mighty have fallen!"?

8. When the spies returned from exploring Canaan what was it about their cities that worried them?

9. Which New Testament letter talks about God's "armor of light"?

10. Speaking of the future glory of Zion who prophesied, "I will make your battlements of rubies, your gates of sparkling jewels, and all your walls of precious stones"?

11. Which Old Testament prophet described the penetrating characteristic of God's word as follows: "He made my mouth like a sharpened sword... he made me into a polished arrow"?

12. Which Old Testament prophet wrote, "I will make a covenant of peace with them; it shall be an everlasting covenant"? (KJV)

13. Who is referred to as "Lord of lords and King of kings" in the book of Revelation?

14. Which king of Judah "...made machines designed by skillful men for use on the towers and on the corner defenses to shoot arrows and hurl large stones"?

15. Manoah was the father of which famous Israelite champion?

Answers

1. By sharing the spoils 2. Deborah 3. Jesus 4. Goliath
5. 31,700, so he was left with just 300 men in his army 6. Deborah 7. David
8. They were fortified and very large 9. The letter to the Romans 10. Isaiah 11. Isaiah
12. Ezekiel 13. The Lord Jesus Christ 14. Uzziah 15. Samson

Quiz #2

1. What was the name of the Galilean who led an armed revolt against the Romans when Jesus was a boy?

2. True or false? A Roman centurion was an officer in charge of one hundred men.

3. Why did the Israelites give a "long blast" on their trumpets just before they advanced on Jericho?

4. When some soldiers asked John the Baptist, "And what should we do?" how did John reply?

5. After the Israelites crossed the Red Sea why did God say he would not lead them through the Philistine country?

6. Which Israelite leader said that if God was with you then you could rout a thousand people?

7. What happened to all of Pharaoh's chariots as they chased the Israelites?

8. Who told people living in Jerusalem, "Don't be afraid of them: Remember the Lord, who is great and awesome and fight for your brethren, your sons, and your daughters, your wives, and your homes"?

9. Which Psalm speaks about kings being bound with fetters?

10. Where in the Old Testament does the following verse come from: "Consider the blameless, observe the upright, there is a future for the man of peace"?

11. What, according to Psalm 119:165, do people have to do if they want "great peace"?

12. Who prevented a war by saying to Rehobam, "You should not fight against your brothers"?

13. In which Psalm is it written, "He makes wars cease to the ends of the earth; he breaks the bow, and shatters the spear in sunder; he burns the shields with fire"?

14. Who said, "Blessed are the peacemakers: for they shall be called sons of God"?

15. Who gave this piece of advice in one of his New Testament letters: "Do not let not the sun go down on your anger"?

Answers

1. Judas 2. True 3. A long blast on a trumpet signaled the beginning of an attack. It was intended to create confusion and panic. 4. "Don't exhort money and don't accuse people falsely–be content with your pay" 5. If they faced war, they might change their minds and return to Egypt. 6. Joshua 7. The wheels of their chariots came off and the entire army of Pharaoh that had followed the Israelites into the sea were drowned as the waters swept over them 8. Nehemiah 9. Psalm 149 10. Psalm 37:37 11. "Love the law" 12. Shemaiah 13. Psalm 46:9 14. Jesus 15. Paul

Quiz #3

1. The message of which Old Testament book can be summed up by the words, "everyone did as he saw fit"?

2. Who imposed a levy of 100 talents of silver and a talent of gold on Judah?

3. Where in the Old Testament is wisdom described as follows: "Her ways are ways of pleasantness, and all her paths are peace"?

4. What work were the men described in the following verse engaged in: "From that day on, half of my men did the work, while the other half were equipped with spears, shields, bows and armor"?

5. As Moses arrived with the Ten Commandments what did Joshua say to him about the noise in the Israelite camp?

6. Who was the first person to meet Abraham after he returned from defeating Kedorlaomer?

7. True or false? David killed Goliath with a bow and arrow.

8. Which Old Testament book contains this practical advice: "A soft answer turneth away wrath: but grievous words stir up anger"? (KJV)

9. Which king of Babylon did Ezekiel predict would "direct the blows of his battering rams against the walls of Jerusalem"?

10. Which king of Israel is the seventh most mentioned man in the Old Testament?

11. Who, on several occasions, promised the Israelites that they would be defeated in battle if they violated his covenant?

12. Who spoke to the Israelites after he had defeated Sihon king of the Amorites?

13. Which king of Israel was once King Saul's armor-bearer?

14. Joshua made a surprise attack on the Gibeonites after he had marched all through the night from where?

15. Who defeated Ben-Hadad three times and recovered the Israelite towns?

Quiz #4

1. Who wrote, "We do not wage war as the world does"?

2. True or false? In Old Testament days, spies were usually sent out before starting a battle.

3. Who said, "You come against me with sword and spear and javelin, but I come against you in the name of the Lord Almighty, the God of the armies of Israel, whom you have defiled"?

4. Which defeated enemy did David set to work making bricks?

5. Who said, "Bring out Samson to entertain us"?

6. On what animals did David's cavalry ride?

7. Which commander of the army of the king of Aram was a leper?

8. What is the name of the fortress in Jerusalem where the Roman army had its headquarters?

9. Which king of Israel told Amaziah, king of Judah, that he was arrogant?

10. A trumpet was blown to summon the Israelites to gather for war, as Gideon did when summoning the Abiezrites to follow him. What was the trumpet made from?

11. To which two groups of people did Moses say, "Shall your countrymen go to war while you sit here?"?

12. Which Old Testament book is made up of laments over the destruction of Jerusalem?

13. Which Old Testament book says, "His speech is smooth as butter, yet war is in his heart"?

14. True or false? Miriam was a judge who challenged the Israelites to fight against King Sisera and his 900 iron chariots.

15. When Joshua captured Jericho, who were the only ones spared from being killed?

Answers

1. Paul **2.** True (Joshua 2:1) **3.** David **4.** The Ammonites **5.** The rulers of the Philistines
6. Mules **7.** Naaman **8.** Antonia Fortress **9.** Jehoash **10.** A ram's horn
11. The Gadites and Reubenites **12.** The book of Lamentations **13.** The Psalms
14. False. It was Deborah (Judges 4) **15.** Rahab the prostitute and all who were in her house

Quiz #5

1. What is the name for the "Sea Peoples" against whom King Saul and David waged war?

2. When the Israelites were conquering Canaan did they ever fight as separate tribes?

3. Which town did Goliath come from?

4. What was Joshua told to hold out in his hand in the direction of Ai before attacking that town?

5. True or false? When laying a siege against an enemy city, the army was not allowed to cut down the enemy's fruit trees growing outside the walls.

6. When there was "war in heaven," what name was given to the ejected dragon?

7. Through whom, according to the apostle Paul, do we have peace with God?

8. Who named one of his daughters Eliezer because, "My father's God was my helper; he saved me from the sword of Pharaoh"?

9. The 32 kings who were once in their tents getting drunk were allies with whom?

10. Why were the Levites excused from military service?

11. Which king of Egypt was defeated by Nebuchadnezzar at Carchemish?

12. Who said, "Peace I leave with you; my peace I give you"?

13. What was the last thing King Zedekiah ever saw?

14. Which Old Testament prophetic book is all about Nineveh's sinfulness?

15. Which false prophet predicted that the Lord would "break the yoke of Nebuchadnezzar king of Babylon off the neck of all the nations within two years"?

Answers

1. The Philistines 2. Yes they did sometimes. One example is when the men of Judah attacked Jerusalem and took it. 3. Gath 4. A javelin 5. True (Deuteronomy 20:20) 6. The devil, or Satan 7. Our Lord Jesus Christ 8. Moses 9. Ben-Hadad 10. Because they were engaged in the ceremonies in the tabernacle. 11. Pharaoh Neco 12. Jesus 13. His sons killed by the Babylonians. 14. The book of Nahum 15. Hananiah

Quiz #6

1. "All the Israelites twenty years old or more who were able to serve in Israel's army were counted [by Moses and Aaron and the twelve leaders of Israel] according to their families." What was the total number?

2. Who asked the question, "What causes quarrels and fights among you?"?

3. What answer is given in the second part of the verse which is quoted in the previous question?

4. Why did David decline to wear King Saul's coat of armor and bronze helmet?

5. Who predicted that a time would come when people "would no longer train for war"?

6. Which famous warrior said, "He [God] trains my hands for battle; my arms can bend a bow of bronze"?

7. Which city was "kept under siege until the eleventh year of King Zedekiah"?

8. Which Old Testament prophet predicted that the king of the North would be defeated by the king of the South?

9. In which book of the Bible is this proverb found: "By long forbearing is a prince persuaded, and a soft tongue breaketh the bone"? (KJV)

10. True or false? Samson was a one-man army fighting the Philistine army. But he lost his strength when his hair was cut off.

11. Which two kings only ruled Judah for three months?

12. Who was the last king of Judah?

13. Who mistook the dawn sun shining on the water for blood and so lost a battle against the Israelites?

14. What remarkable event did Joshua record about "the day the Lord gave the Amorites over to Israel"?

15. Which Old Testament prophet identified himself completely with his people when he said, "Since my people are crushed, I am crushed"?

Answers

1. 603,550 2. James 3. "Don't they come from the desires that battle within you?"
4. Because David was not used to wearing them 5. Isaiah 6. David 7. Jerusalem 8. Daniel
9. Proverbs 10. True (Judges 16:17) 11. Jehoahaz and Jehoiachin 12. Zedekiah
13. The Moabites 14. The sun stood still. 15. Jeremiah

Quiz #7

1. What, according to Isaiah, would be made into plowshares and what would be made into pruning hooks, as a sign of a time of peace?

2. Who killed an Egyptian for mistreating an Israelite slave?

3. The angel of the Lord met which Israelite judge under the oak in Ophrah?

4. In which Old Testament book is this advice given: "If you wage war, obtain guidance"?

5. Which of the judges ruled Israel for the longest?

6. Which Old Testament book prophesied that war would be no more in the following words, "Bow and sword and battle I will abolish from the land, so that all may lie down in safety"?

7. In which Old Testament book is the following question found: "Has any god ever tried to take for himself one nation out of another nation, by testings, by miraculous signs and wonders, by war…?"?

8. In which of Paul's letters is the following instruction found: "If it is possible, as much as you can, live peaceably with all men"? (KJV)

9. Who was the first king of the northern kingdom of Israel?

10. Of which king did the Lord say, "He will not enter this city or shoot an arrow here"?

11. Who asked the Lord that he might die with the Philistines?

12. Which king took silver and gold from the temple and sent it as a gift to King Tiglath-Pileser?

13. Which king of Assyria imprisoned King Hoshea?

14. Who ruled the northern kingdom of Israel for only one month?

15. How, according to the letter of Hebrews, did the walls of Jericho fall?

Quiz #8

1. David had three exceptionally brilliant soldiers who are known as "The Three," or, "The Three Mighty Men." What were their names?

2. Who was said to be "as famous as the three mighty men"?

3. Which Old Testament prophet prophesied about a "Prince of Peace"?

4. Which warrior-king of Israel was described as being a man after God's own heart?

5. Which infamous queen is mentioned 23 times in the Old Testament?

6. Who said, "My kingdom is not of this world. If it were, my servants would fight"?

7. Which judge called herself "a mother in Israel"?

8. True or false? Moses fought the battle of Jericho.

9. Which famous Israelite warrior is the ninth most mentioned man in the Old Testament?

10. Which New Testament writer assured his readers that, "The peace of God, which transcemds all understanding, shall keep your hearts and minds in Christ Jesus"?

11. Which soldier did David deliberately get drunk?

12. Which king, who was on the point of death, was told by Isaiah that he would live another 15 years and that he would be delivered from the city of Jerusalem?

13. Who plotted to have all Hebrew people killed?

14. 2 Samuel 15 records one of David's sons leading a revolt against him? Which son?

15. In which New Testament letter is the following instruction given: "Follow peace with all men"? (KJV)

Answers

1. Josheb-Basshebeth, Eleazar, and Shammah 2. Benaiah 3. Isaiah 4. David 5. Jezebel
6. Jesus 7. Deborah 8. False. Joshua fought the battle of Jericho (Joshua 6:2) 9. Joshua
10. Paul 11. Uriah 12. Hezekiah 13. Haman 14. Absalom 15. Hebrews

Quiz #9

1. Which left-handed judge killed Eglon, King of Moab by plunging his sword into the king's belly?

2. What kind of musical instrument did each of Gideon's 300 men take with them when they fought against an enemy who were camped in the valley with more camels "than sand on the sea shore"?

3. Besides a musical instrument what else did each of Gideon's 300 men take with them when they fought against an enemy who were camped in the valley with more camels "than sand on the sea shore"?

4. Which defeated army did David make lie down on the ground so they could be measured with a length of cord? "Every two lengths of them were put to death, and the third length was allowed to live."

5. Who broke many vows he had made to David and tried to kill him several times?

6. What was King Herod's final command concerning John the Baptist?

7. Who was the first king of Judah?

8. Who ruled Judah for 41 years?

9. Who was Queen Jezebel's husband?

10. Which Old Testament king had an iron bed that measured more than 13 feet long and 6 feet wide?

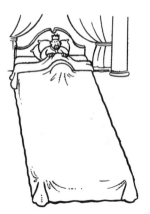

11. When Evil-Merodach became king of Babylon what did he do for Jehoiachin?

12. Over how many provinces did King Xerxes rule?

13. Where in the Bible is the statement "[There is] a time for war and a time for peace"?

14. Who said to Samson, "You have made a fool of me"?

15. How old was Darius the Mede when he became ruler of Israel?

Answers

1. Ehud 2. A trumpet 3. A torch hidden in a jug 4. The Moabites 5. Saul
6. That he should be beheaded 7. Rehoboam 8. Asa 9. King Ahab 10. King Og
11. He released him from prison 12. 127 13. Ecclesiastes 14. Delilah 15. 62 years old

Quiz # 10

1. When the Israelites attacked the town of Kir Hareseth they successfully deployed "men armed with slings". Who was their enemy?

2. David and some of his men were in the back of a cave when Saul came into the same cave. Why did Saul go into the cave?

3. Which king ruled the northern kingdom of Israel for the longest?

4. Against which army did the Lord give David this instruction: "As soon as you hear the sound of marching in the tops of the balsam trees, move quickly, because that will mean that the Lord has gone in front of you"?

5. Who boasted, "With a donkey's jaw-bone I have killed a thousand men"?

6. Once, when Elisha's servant woke up, he saw the enemy army surrounding his town. Elisha said, "Don't be afraid. Those people who are with us are more than those with them." When the servant looked again, what did he see?

7. Which judge "had thirty sons, who rode thirty donkeys"?

8. Who does Isaiah say will have no peace?

9. Who in the New Testament said, "Glory to God in the highest, and on earth peace, good will toward men"? (KJV)

10. When Jesus sent out 72 disciples ahead of him, what did he tell them to say when they went into someone's house?

11. Which three kings are said in the Bible to have ruled all of Israel?

12. How many priests did Saul have killed at Nob because they helped David?

13. Who carried out David's orders and placed Uriah in the middle of the fiercest fighting and then left him to be killed there?

14. Who took over from Moses as leader of the Israelites?

15. Which Old Testament prophet said, "The work of righteousness shall be peace"? (KJV)

Quiz #11

1. True or false? Before the Israelites embarked on a "holy war" they often made a sacrifice to God.

2. Some of the strongest and bravest of David's soldiers formed a group known as "The Thirty." But there were more than 30 of them. How many were there?

3. Who described the word of God as, "Living and active. Sharper than any double edged sword, it penetrates even to dividing soul and spirit, joints and marrow"?

4. Which army was completely captured by David except for "four hundred young men who rode off on camels and fled"?

5. When Gideon attacked the Midianite camp what did he tell his soldiers to shout out?

6. In which Old Testament book is the following complaint found, "I am a man of peace; but when I speak, they are for war"?

7. Who once "mobilized twenty-six thousand swordsmen"?

8. Which short Old Testament prophetic book says of the wicked people of Nineveh, "the sword will cut you down and, like grasshoppers, consume you"?

9. Micah 5:5 states, "When the Assyrian invades our land and marches through our fortresses, we will raise against him seven shepherds, even eight leaders of men." What do "seven" and "eight" denote?

10. What happened to Israel's last king, Zedekiah, before he was exiled in Babylon?

11. What does the psalmist call on God to do with nations who delight in war?

12. When Jesus predicted that we would hear of wars and rumors of wars, how did he say we should react to such news?

13. Which Old Testament prophet referred to God as his "war club"?

14. Which Old Testament book describes seven times how the Israelites rejected God and then were delivered when God raised up a military champion?

15. The reigns of how many judges are recorded in the book of Judges?

Facts 1

Israel did not engage in war like her surrounding neighbors. When Israel fought she fought a "holy war" because she only fought when God told her to fight. One of the names by which God was known to Israel was "the God of the armies of Israel" (1 Samuel 17:45).

Eliakim asked a field commander of the threatening Assyrian army to speak in Aramaic and not in Hebrew as he was in the hearing of the people on the wall of Jerusalem. The Assyrians wanted to demoralize the people of Jerusalem by negotiating in their earshot in their own language.

King Ahab discovered to his cost that the weak parts of armor were its joints. "But someone drew his bow at random and hit the king of Israel between the sections of his armor" (1 Kings 22:34).

Those whom God had appointed to destroy Moab were urged on with these words from Jeremiah, "A curse on him who keeps his sword from bloodshed" (Jeremiah 48:10). Such curses have been open to abuse, as when Pope Gregory VII used it as his motto.

The Israelites often celebrated their victories with a song of praise to God (Exodus 15:1-18) and with singing, and dancing and tambourines.

Gideon said, "I will not rule over you, nor will my son rule over you. The Lord will rule over you" (Judge 8:23). The idea of a theocracy, God ruling over the nation of Israel, is central in the book of Judges. Like Samuel, Gideon rejected the idea of a monarchy.

When David, like Moses and Joshua before him, led Israel into battle he thought of himself as fighting the Lord's battles (1 Samuel 25:28). David's victories over the Philistines were not for his personal advancement but to bring glory to the Lord.

"The Lord Almighty is mustering an army for war" (Isaiah 13:4). In this verse the Hebrew word for "army" is the word for "Almighty" in the singular form. God is the leader of the armies that are going to destroy Babylon.

Amos 2:11 states, "For three sins of Edom, even for four, I will not turn back my wrath. Because he pursued his brother with a sword". "Edom" stands for the descendants of Esau and his "brother" was Israel. Edom continually broke its relationship with Israel by its hostile actions.

Jesus said, "I did not come to bring peace, but a sword" (Matthew 10:34). His coming caused conflict within families, as well as among the religious hierarchy.

Zechariah 9:14 predicts, "I will bend Judah as I bend my bow and fill it with Ephraim." God is depicted as the Divine Warrior. He takes Judah as his bow and the northern kingdom of Ephraim as his arrow.

Facts 2

Numbers 21:14 is the only place in the Old Testament to mention "the Book of the Wars of the Lord." It no longer exists but was most probably an old collection of songs of war which praised God.

David had a royal bodyguard made up of mercenaries, the Kerethites and Pelethites, who were separate from the regular army. They were freed from doing forced labor and from paying taxes.

Nahum 3:3 describes the Assyrian army as causing "Many casualties, piles of dead, bodies without number, people stumbling over the corpses". The Assyrians tortured and mutilated the leaders of the cities they captured.

When Joshua was faced with an army as numerous as the sand on the seashore God told him not to be afraid and to "hamstring their horses" (Joshua 11:6). This was done by cutting the horses tendon above the hock so that it became lame.

When King of Aram's army surrounded Samaria, and famine threatened Samaria, God made the Aramaen army hear the sound of thousands of chariots and horses. They thought the Hittite and Egyptian armies were marching to save Samaria and so fled.

According to Exodus 15:3, "The Lord is a man of war" (KJV), "The Lord is a warrior". In the Old Testament God is often pictured as a warrior-king leading his people into battle.

Gideon was once asked by the officials of Succoth, "Do you already have the hands of Zebah and Zalmunna in your possession?" (Judges 8:6) The Egyptians and Assyrians amputated the hands of their enemies as proof of their victories.

Psalm 76 celebrates God's mighty power in defending Jerusalem. It recalls God's crushing defeat of Zion's enemies. "There he [God] broke the flashing arrows, the shields and the swords, the weapons of war" (Psalm 76).

When Elisha was dying, Jehoash king of Israel visited him and said, "My father! My father!... The chariots and horsemen of Israel!" (2 Kings 13:14) The king knew that Elisha was more important for Israel's success than any military weapons.

The Old Testament repeatedly teaches that Israel's security does not rest in military strength but in God himself. "When you go to war against your enemies and see horses and chariots and an army greater than yours, do not be afraid of them, because the Lord your God... will be with you" (Deuteronomy 20:1).

Abraham rescued Lot with "318 trained men born in his household" (Genesis 14:14). This demonstrates Abraham's great wealth. The Hebrew word for "trained men" only comes here in the Bible and probably refers to armed retainers.

Facts 3

Like the ancient Greeks, the Philistines sometimes decided the outcome of a war by choosing a champion from each army. The champions then fought each other on behalf of each army (See 1 Samuel 17:9).

Gideon overheard a Midianite telling his friend his dream in which "a round loaf of barley bread came tumbling into the Midianite camp" (Judges 7:13). God often revealed things in dreams in the Old Testament. The unusual feature here is that both the dreamer and the interpreter were not Israelites.

The minor prophets reminded God's people about the vital principle that God himself should be trusted and not any weapons of war. "I will save them–not by bow, sword or battle, or by horses and horsemen, but by the Lord their God" (Hosea 1:7).

Hezekiah "blocked the upper outlet of the Gihon spring and channeled the water down to the west side of the City of David" (2 Chronicles 32:30). The Siloam Inscription still exists in the middle of the 600 yard long tunnel, describing in Hebrew how the work to build this tunnel began at opposite ends and met in the middle.

After a battle the Israelites often observed a ban, called a herem. This meant that a whole city, including its people and possessions, were set apart for God. Israelites were not allowed to appropriate any spoils for themselves.

God did not want the Israelites to think that their own righteousness enabled them to conquer the Promised Land. "No, it is on account of the wickedness of these nations" (Deuteronomy 9:4).

David, on the run from King Saul, had the opportunity to kill Saul, and was urged to do so by his men, but said that he would not lift his hand against the Lord's anointed. David believed that Saul was king by the sanction of God and had been anointed for this purpose.

In Hebrew poetry the shield is often used as a symbol of the power and security that a believer finds in God. The poet-warrior David wrote, "The Lord is my strength and my shield; my heart trusts in him, and I am helped" (Psalm 28:7).

When the Assyrian army surrounded Jerusalem, God rescued the city in a remarkable way. "An angel of the Lord went out and put to death a 185,000 men in the Assyrian camp" (2 Kings 19:35).

Facts 4

The Philistines' weapons were far superior to anything the Israelites had because they knew how to work iron and other metals. Hence it says in 1 Samuel 13:19, "Not a blacksmith could be found in the whole land of Israel, because the Philistines had said, 'Otherwise the Hebrews will make swords or spears!' "

The Israelites used wooden shields covered with oiled leather once they settled in Canaan. These leather shields were rubbed with oil to preserve them. Hence Saul's shield was "defiled" because it was "no longer rubbed with oil" (2 Samuel 1:21).

The Israelites asked God if they should fight before waging war. They thought of entering the Promised Land, or defending it as a "holy" activity. "The Israelites went up and wept before the Lord until evening, and they enquired of the Lord. They said, 'shall we go up again to battle...?'" (Judges 20:23)

"The king of Assyria captured Samaria and deported the Israelites" (2 Kings 17:6). The Assyrians generally followed the policy of deporting the people they conquered.

"We have heard that the kings of the house of Israel are merciful" (1 Kings 20:31). In contrast with the Assyrians who inflicted torture on their captured enemies, the Israelite kings had a reputation for being compassionate.

On a number of occasions the Israelites killed everyone in a city they captured. "The city and all that is in it are to be devoted to the Lord" (Joshua 6:17). This refers to giving over things and people to God in an irrevocable way.

Leather-covered shields were sometimes soaked in water as a defense against the enemies burning arrows. Hence Paul writes, "take up the shield of faith, with which you can extinguish all the flaming arrows of the evil one" (Ephesians 6:16).

"The Philistines assembled to offer a great sacrifice to Dagon their god" (Judges 16:23). "Dagon," a popular Philistines god, means "grain" and so was probably a vegetation deity.

Jerusalem was a strongly fortified mountain-top citadel. David needed to use a clever plan to capture it. His men climbed up a secret tunnel—a water shaft leading from the city to a spring outside the city walls.

The Israelites were attacked by a war-like nomadic tribe from the region of Sinai, called the Amalekites. So long as Moses held his hands up the Israelites won the battle. Holding his hands up like this was a symbolic way of appealing to God for help.

1 Samuel 23:9 states, "When David learned that Saul was plotting against him, he said to Abiather the priest, 'Bring the ephod' ". He did this because this ephod contained the Urim and Thummin, a divinely appointed means of communicating with God.

Facts 5

Different types and sizes of shield were used in the Old Testament. In 2 Chronicles some soldiers were equipped with large shields and spears while other soldiers were armed with small shields and bows. The smaller meginah was usually carried by archers and the larger sinah by bowmen.

Psalm 127:5 says "Blessed is the man whose quiver is full of them [sons]". Leather quivers were carried by bowmen and fitted in chariots. Ordinary quivers held about 30 arrows and quivers in chariots about 50 arrows. A quiver full of children would have been a big family.

When Joshua approached Jericho he saw a man with a drawn sword in his hand. Joshua asked him "Are you for us or for our enemies?" "Neither," he replied, "but as commander of the army of the Lord I have come" (Joshua 5:13-14). This figure may have been God, or Jesus or an angel.

Lamentations 1:12 asks, "Is any suffering like my suffering... that the Lord brought on me in the day of his fierce anger?". The author of Lamentations sees that the Babylonians were but human agents and that God himself destroyed his temple and city.

The Lord used the elements of nature as one of his armaments to defeat Israel's enemies. In 1 Samuel 7:10 the "Lord thundered with loud thunder against the Philistines" so they were thrown into such a panic that the Israelites routed them.

After Samson lost his strength the Philistines gouged out his eyes. It was common for prisoners of war to receive such brutal and humiliating treatment.

Psalm 149:6-7 speaks of a double-edged sword inflicting vengeance on the nations. Vengeance was God's just retribution on anyone who attacked God's followers.

As Abimelech besieged a tower at Thebez a woman dropped an upper millstone on his head and cracked his skull. It was a great disgrace for a soldier to be killed by a woman. Hence Abimelech asked his armor-bearer to kill him.

When the Psalmist wrote about Jerusalem's famous fortifications, "Walk about Zion, go round her, count her towers, consider well her ramparts, view her citadels" (Psalm 48:12-13), he was saying that the strength of Jerusalem's towers and ramparts is God's presence.

In the Bible, the sword often symbolizes divine judgment. "Out of his mouth came a sharp double-edged sword" (Revelation 1:16). The double-edge sword was similar to a long, broad Thracian sword.

When God commanded Israel to destroy a nation it was because they were evil. The Amorites were spared until their sin became too great. "The sin of the Amorites has not yet reached its full measure" (Genesis 15:16).

Dollars and Sense

Quiz #1

1. In Mark's Gospel, what coin did Jesus ask to be brought to him when he was questioned about the paying of taxes?

2. What is Jesus referring to when he says, "I tell you the truth, you will not get out until you have paid the last penny"?

3. In the Gospel of Matthew, Jesus says, "Are not even the tax collectors doing that?" What is he referring to?

4. How much did Abraham pay for the field that he bought from Ephron the Hittite?

5. Why did Jeremiah buy a field from his cousin Hanamel?

6. According to the Law of Moses in Exodus, what must people not do when lending money to the needy?

7. What gifts was Rebekah given at the well?

8. Who stole gold and silver from the ruins of Jericho?

9. What was the name of the tax collector Jesus met as he was passing through Jericho?

10. Which Old Testament prophet did the Lord use to speak to the Israelites, saying, "You earn wages, only to put them in a purse with holes in it"?

11. In Matthew 17, what did Jesus tell Simon Peter he would find in the mouth of a fish?

12. In John's Gospel, who is said to have stolen money from the disciples' money bag?

13. In 1 Kings, which king attacked Jerusalem and carried off the treasures of the temple and the palace?

14. To whom is Paul writing when he says, "For the love of money is a root of all kinds of evil"?

15. Which one of Jesus' disciples was formerly a tax collector?

Answers

1. A denarius **2.** Settling matters with an adversary **3.** Loving those who love you **4.** 400 shekels of silver **5.** Because he was Hanamel's nearest relative and it was his duty to redeem and possess the field if asked to do so **6.** They must not charge interest **7.** A gold nose ring and two gold bracelets **8.** Achan **9.** Zacchaeus **10.** Haggai **11.** A four-drachma coin **12.** Judas Iscariot **13.** King Shishak of Egypt **14.** Timothy **15.** Matthew (called Levi in Mark and Luke)

Quiz #2

1. In the New Testament, how much was a day's wage to the hired men in the parable of the workers in the vineyard?

2. In a conversation between Simon Peter and Jesus, who was considered exempt when kings collected duty and taxes?

3. In 1 Kings, who took all the silver and gold left in the temple and persuaded Ben Hadad, to break his treaty with Baasha, King of Israel?

4. Fill in the missing word from Deuteronomy, "At the end of every ___ years you must cancel debts."

5. As recorded in Matthew's Gospel, how many sparrows cost a penny?

6. In Exodus, why did the Israelites have to pay a half-shekel offering to God?

7. Which famous person from the Old Testament owned, "7,000 sheep, 3,000 camels, 500 yoke of oxen, and 500 donkeys and had a large number of servants"?

8. In which Old Testament book is it written, "But remember the Lord your God, for it is he who gives you the ability to produce wealth"?

9. Which Gospel does not mention the money-changers being chased out of the temple by Jesus?

10. Fill in the missing word from Proverbs: "A ___ woman gains respect, but ruthless men gain only wealth."

11. Which disciple said at the feeding of the 5,000 that eight month's wages would not buy enough bread for all the people?

12. In Genesis, why does the Pharaoh of Egypt give Abraham a large quantity of livestock and servants?

13. In the Parable of the Lost Coin, how many does the woman have to begin with?

14. In Mark's Gospel, when Jesus is being questioned about the payment of taxes, whose head is on the coin that Jesus looks at?

15. In the Parable of the Rich Fool, what happens to the man who plans to build bigger barns to store all his crops, so he can take life easy?

DOLLARS AND SENSE

Quiz #3

1. Who does Paul tell to: "command those who are rich in this present world not to be arrogant nor to put their hope in wealth which is so uncertain"?

2. In which book of the Old Testament is it written, "Therefore I command you to be open handed towards your brothers and towards the poor and needy in your land"?

3. In Luke, when Jesus is telling the crowds what to do to become a disciple, he uses an example of a man wanting to build a tower. What does he do before he starts to build?

4. In 2 Kings, who did Mesha, King of Moab, have to supply with 100,000 lambs and the wool of 100,000 rams?

5. What did King Solomon exchange for the cypress trees to build his temple?

6. Which queen gave King Solomon, "120 talents of gold, large quantities of spices, and precious stones"?

7. Fill in the missing word from 1 Kings 16:24: "Omri became king of Israel. He bought the hill of ___ from Shemer for two talents of silver and built a city on the hill."

8. What is the rich young man's response when Jesus tells him to sell all of his possessions?

9. Which Old Testament king gave Hiram, the King of Tyre, 20 towns in Galilee in repayment for the cedar, pine, and gold that he had provided?

10. Which Old Testament person became so rich that the Philistines envied him and blocked up his wells?

11. In the New Testament, who gave two silver coins to an innkeeper on behalf of another?

12. True or false? Matthew the Gospel writer was originally a tax collector.

13. Which Old Testament prophet passes judgment on Israel saying that, "they sell the righteous for silver, and the needy for a pair of sandals"?

14. In the Old Testament, who bought a threshing floor and oxen from Araunah the Jebusite for fifty shekels of silver in order to build an altar on it?

15. After which parable does Jesus say, "There is rejoicing in the presence of the angels of God over one sinner who repents"?

Answers

1. Timothy 2. Deuteronomy 3. He estimates the cost to see if he has enough money to finish the tower
4. The King of Israel, King Joram 5. Grain (wheat) and olive oil 6. The queen of Sheba 7. Samaria
8. He goes away full of sadness 9. King Solomon 10. Isaac 11. The Good Samaritan
12. True (Matthew 9:9) 13. Amos 14. King David 15. The Parable of the Lost Coin

Quiz #4

1. Who does Jesus tell to visit the lost sheep of Israel, but, "do not take along any gold or silver or copper in your belts"?

2. In Genesis, when Joseph's brothers return to Egypt for a second time to ask for food, how much silver do they take with them?

3. In 2 Kings, where did Hezekiah, king of Judah, get the silver and gold that he needed to pay Sennacherib, King of Assyria?

4. In the Old Testament, who gave Saul a quarter of a silver shekel for a gift to Samuel?

5. In the Parable of the Shrewd Manager, what did the manager do after being told he would lose his job?

6. After Jacob's marriage to Rachel and Leah, he continued to work for his father-in law, Laban. What agreement did he reach with Laban for wages?

7. Which Old Testament king said, "I now give my personal treasures of gold and silver for the temple of my God, over and above everything I have provided for this temple"?

8. Through Moses, what three metals did the Lord ask the Israelites to bring him as an offering for the Tabernacle?

9. Why did Abimelech give Abraham 1,000 shekels of silver?

10. In the Parable of the Pearl, what did the merchant do when he found one of great value?

11. In which Old Testament book does the following command appear: "Do not hold back the wages of a hired man overnight"?

12. The words from Deuteronomy, "There will always be poor people in the land" are repeated by Jesus in which Gospel?

13. In which Gospel is the story of the rich man and Lazarus?

14. Which four groups of people benefited from tithes, according to the book of Deuteronomy?

15. When Jesus says, "Do not let your left hand know what your right hand is doing" what is he referring to?

Answers

1. The 12 disciples 2. Double the amount they took first of all 3. From the temple of the Lord and the palace treasuries 4. Saul's servant 5. He reduced the debts of his master's debtors 6. Jacob was to have every dark, speckled, or spotted lamb and goat from Laban's flock 7. King David 8. Gold, silver and bronze 9. As compensation for taking Sarah away from Abraham 10. He sold everything he had to buy it 11. Leviticus 12. Matthew 13. Luke 14. The Levite, the alien, the fatherless, and the widow 15. Giving to the needy

Quiz #5

1. Which New Testament writer says "has not God chosen those who are poor in the eyes of the world to be rich in faith and to inherit the kingdom…?"?

2. In the Old Testament, who said that he had taken great pains to provide a hundred thousand talents of gold and a million talents of silver for the Lord's temple?

3. What is "a pledge," as described in the Old Testament in relation to a loan?

4. In 1 Kings, how much weight in gold is Solomon reported to have received yearly?

5. In the book of Job, what cannot be bought, "with the finest gold, nor can its price be weighed in silver" and "neither gold nor crystal can compare with it"?

6. In the book of Nahum, which city is referred to when it says, "Plunder the silver! Plunder the gold! The supply is endless, the wealth from all its treasures"?

7. In the Old Testament, who got wealth and riches and wisdom from God when all he asked for was wisdom?

8. According to Leviticus, in what year does any property sold previously have to be returned to its owner?

9. Did Joseph's brothers sell Joseph to Babylonian or Ishmaelite merchants?

10. During the long siege of Samaria, people began to grow desperate for food. What animal's head sold for eighty shekels of silver?

11. In Acts, to whom did Peter say, "Silver or gold I do not have, but what I have I give you. In the name of Jesus Christ of Nazareth, walk!"?

12. The chief priests bribed the guards guarding Jesus' tomb to tell what lie?

13. In the Parable of the Talents in Matthew's Gospel, how many talents did the master give each of his three servants?

14. At the Last Supper, when Jesus told Judas to do what he had to do quickly, what did the disciples think Judas was going to do?

15. Who said in the New Testament, "provide purses for yourselves that will not wear out"?

Answers

1. James **2.** King David **3.** Security for a loan **4.** 666 talents (about 25 tons; 23 tonnes) **5.** Wisdom **6.** Nineveh **7.** King Solomon **8.** The year of Jubilee **9.** Ishmaelites (Midianites) (Genesis 37:28) **10.** A donkey's **11.** A crippled beggar **12.** That the disciples stole Jesus' body during the night while they slept **13.** He gave five to the first, two to the second and one to the third **14.** They thought Jesus was asking Judas to buy things what was needed for the feast or to give something to the poor **15.** Jesus

Quiz #6

1. In 2 Kings, to whom did Naaman give two silver talents after he had been cured of leprosy?

2. Where did the disciples normally keep their money, according to Mark's Gospel?

3. In the Parable of the Talents in Matthew's Gospel, what did the servant who had received one talent do with it?

4. In Genesis, during the famine in Egypt, who was in charge of collecting money and distributing corn?

5. In the New Testament, which couple sold a piece of property, and kept some of the money for themselves, before taking the rest to the apostles?

6. In Acts, who sold their lands and houses and had the money distributed to people as they had need?

7. Who tried to buy the "gift of God" with money in the New Testament?

8. Which governor hoped that Paul might offer him a bribe to get out of prison?

9. In 2 Kings, who were the first to plunder the camp of the Arameans after the siege of Samaria was lifted?

10. True or false? Joseph was sold for 20 shekels of gold.

11. Fill in the missing word from Psalm 112, "Good will come to him who is ___ and lends freely."

12. In Matthew's Gospel, what three things are said to destroy treasures on earth?

13. Which believers did Paul instruct to set aside money, each week, according to their income, for those in Jerusalem?

14. Why didn't the chief priests and elders put Judas' money back into the treasury?

15. In Acts, who made money by fortune-telling in Philippi?

Quiz #7

1. During the famine in Egypt, what two things did the Egyptians and Canaanites sell after they had used up all their money and had sold their livestock?

2. In the New Testament, who dropped down dead after lying to the apostle Peter about the money she and her husband had received from selling some land?

3. In Psalm 112, in which man's house is wealth and riches?

4. For how many silver pieces was Jesus betrayed?

5. In the Old Testament, who is Micah rebuking when he says, "Her leaders judge for a bribe, her priests teach for a price, and her prophets tell fortunes for money"?

6. In the book of Esther, which man tells the king that he will put 10,000 silver talents in the royal treasury for the men who take part in the massacre of the Jews?

7. In 2 Kings, Menahem, king of Israel, exacted 50 shekels of silver from every wealthy man to secure the support of the king of which country?

8. In Numbers, to whom did Moses give the sanctuary shekel?

9. In James' letter, what did he say had happened to the rich people's clothes and money?

10. In the book of Nehemiah, which group of people are accused by the prophet of exacting usury from the Jews?

11. Which three Gospels document the discussion between Jesus and the Pharisees about paying taxes?

12. In Exodus, the law states that a man must pay compensation if an animal he has borrowed is injured or dies. What are the two exceptions?

13. Who did Jesus meet and eat with at Matthew's house?

14. According to the book of Exodus, what payment weighed 20 gerahs?

15. In 2 Kings, to whom did Jehoiakim pay the silver and gold demanded of him?

Answers

1. They sold themselves and their land 2. Ananias and Sapphira 3. The man who fears the Lord 4. 30 5. Israel 6. Haman 7. Assyria 8. Aaron and his sons 9. Their clothes have been eaten by moths and their gold and silver has corroded 10. The nobles and officials of Jerusalem 11. Matthew, Mark, and Luke 12. If the owner is present, or if the animal is hired 13. Tax collectors and sinners 14. The sanctuary shekel 15. The Pharaoh (Neco)

DOLLARS AND SENSE

Quiz #8

1. Which king wrote a letter to Ezra telling him to take lots of silver and gold and buy livestock and produce for sacrificing in the temple in Jerusalem?

2. In the New Testament, whom does James compare to a mist that appears for a little while and then vanishes?

3. In the book of Exodus, how much was the sanctuary shekel?

4. To the king of which nation did Elisha prophesy, "about this time tomorrow, a seah of flour will sell for a shekel and two seahs of barley for a shekel"?

5. In the time of Elisha, how was the widow of one of Elisha's prophets saved from creditors?

6. In the New Testament, which field was bought with Judas' thirty pieces of silver?

7. After which parable does Jesus say, "so if you have not been trustworthy in handling worldly wealth, who will trust you with true riches"?

8. What was the name of the beggar, in one of Jesus' parables, who was laid at the gate of a rich man?

9. Which church does Paul exhort to, "just as you excel in everything... see that you also excel in this grace of giving"?

10. According to Paul's letter to Timothy what kind of people, "fall into temptation and a trap and into many foolish and harmful desires that plunge men into ruin and destruction"?

11. Who was Jesus talking to when he told the story of the two men who did not have any money to pay off the debts they owed to a moneylender?

12. True or false? Just before they left Egypt, the Israelites asked the Egyptians for articles of silver and gold and clothing and were given them.

13. According to Exodus, if you buy a Hebrew servant, how long should he serve you for before he goes free?

14. According to Proverbs 22, what is more desirable than great riches?

15. When Solomon asked Hiram, King of Tyre, to supply him with cedars for building the temple, what did Hiram ask for in return?

Quiz #9

1. When Joseph's brothers went to Egypt to buy corn, which brother stayed at home?

2. In the New Testament, what was the field bought with Judas' thirty pieces of silver used for?

3. In which letter is it written, "No immoral, impure or greedy person—such a man is an idolater—has any inheritance in the kingdom of Christ and of God"?

4. In the Parable of the Sower, what did the seeds that fell among the thorns stand for?

5. True or false? In the Parable of the Prodigal Son, it was the older son who squandered his wealth in a distant country.

6. Who is worth far more than rubies in Proverbs 31?

7. As recorded in Paul's letter to Timothy, for what job must a man be, "not violent but gentle, not quarrelsome, not be a lover of money"?

8. In which New Testament letter is it said that in the last days people will be lovers of themselves and of money?

9. In the New Testament, who told Titus that slaves should be taught not to steal from their masters?

10. Who is responsible for receiving tithes in the Temple?

11. Which letter writer in the New Testament exhorts believers not to discriminate against the poor and favor the rich?

12. Fill in the missing words, "Has God not chosen those who are ____ in the eyes of the world to be ____ in faith."

13. Who was angry with Job for saying, amongst other things, that if he had put his trust in gold, or rejoiced over his wealth then he would have sinned against God?

14. In the Old Testament, who did Balak, King of Moab, want to reward handsomely, if only he would put a curse on the Israelites?

15. Which Old Testament prophet, when talking of the daughter of Zion, says, "you were sold for nothing and without money you will be redeemed"?

DOLLARS AND SENSE

Quiz # 10

1. Who did Paul ask Philemon to welcome, saying that if he owed anything, then he, Paul, would pay?

2. Which Old Testament book says that riches and pleasures are meaningless?

3. In James' warning to rich oppressors, who cried out against the rich because their wages were not paid?

4. Which Old Testament prophet writes, "Why spend money on what is not bread, and your labor on what does not satisfy?"?

5. Which New Testament letter states: "Keep your lives free from the love of money and be content with what you have"?

6. Which king did Ezekiel say was the model of perfection but corrupted his wisdom because of his splendor?

7. Who did Peter appeal to in the New Testament, saying that they should not be greedy for money, but eager to serve, not lording it over others, but making examples of themselves?

8. Which Old Testament prophet told a Moabite king that even if he was given a palace filled with silver and gold, he could not do anything the Lord had not commanded?

9. In James chapter 2, who does James say is exploiting the believers by dragging them into court?

10. In the Old Testament, which two nomads had such a large number of flocks and herds and tents that the land could not support both of them, causing them to separate?

11. In the book of Revelation, who is said to be, "wretched, pitiful, poor, blind, and naked" although they think they are rich and wealthy and lack nothing?

12. Who rescued Lot and all of his possessions from captivity?

13. What happens to a thief who cannot compensate his victim, according to the law of Moses?

14. In 2 Thessalonians who are told to settle down and earn the bread they eat?

15. In which Gospel is the parable of the man who plans to build bigger barns to store his crops and goods so that he can take life easy?

Quiz # 11

1. According to the book of Exodus, is a person allowed to kill a thief caught breaking into their property?

2. Fill in the missing word from the book of Ecclesiastes: "Whoever loves money never has money enough; whoever loves wealth is never satisfied with his____."

3. Fill in the missing word from Proverb 23: "Cast but a glance at riches, and they are gone, for they will surely sprout wings and fly off to the sky like an____."

4. Which Old Testament prophet describes the day of Judgment as a day when God will come and sit as a refiner and purifier of silver, purifying the Levites?

5. When Paul received the blessing of the apostles to preach to the Gentiles, they asked him to remember which group of people?

6. Which church does Paul thank for sending him, "aid again and again when I was in need"?

7. What did Laban's sons say about the growth in Jacob's prosperity?

8. Who does Jesus tell to, "stay in that house, eating and drinking whatever they give you, for the worker deserves his wages"?

9. In the New Testament, who was told, "You have been faithful with a few things; I will put you in charge of many things. Come and share your master's happiness"?

10. Fill in the missing word from Romans 16: "If the____ have shared in the Jew's spiritual blessings, they owe it to the Jews to share with them their material blessings"?

11. Who did Abraham refuse to accept anything from so that he could never say that he had made Abraham rich?

12. Who is Jeremiah criticising when he says that, "your eyes and your heart are set only on dishonest gain, on shedding innocent blood and on oppression and extortion"?

13. In the reign of King Artaxerxes, who championed the poor, telling Jewish nobles and officials that they had to stop the exacting of usury from their own countrymen?

14. Which famous Old Testament judge prophesised that if the Israelites had a king he would extort a tenth of their grain, wine, and flocks and give it to his officials?

15. What was the name of the silversmith who caused a riot in Ephesus by telling fellow traders that Paul was damaging their business?

Answers

1. Only if they catch him before sunrise 2. Income 3. Eagle 4. Malachi
5. To remember the poor 6. The church in Philippi
7. They said he had taken everything away from their father and become wealthy at Laban's expense
8. The seventy two appointed to go to towns ahead of him 9. The servants who had invested wisely in the Parable of the Talents 10. Gentiles 11. The King of Sodom 12. Shallum, King of Judea (son of Josiah) 13. Nehemiah
14. Samuel 15. Demetrius

DOLLARS AND SENSE

Quiz #12

1. In the Old Testament, whose palaces were filled with gold, as, "nothing was made of silver, because silver was considered of little value"?

2. In one of Jesus' parables, what is likened to treasure found in a field?

3. In Luke's Gospel, what did Jesus see the widow put in the collection box?

4. Who should not be in pursuit of dishonest gain according to Paul's letter to Timothy?

5. What do the rich and the poor have in common according to Proverbs 22?

6. To whom did Abraham give a tenth of everything in Genesis 14?

7. In the Old Testament, who cheated who by changing his wages ten times?

8. What happened to Jesus to cause him to say to his followers, "You will always have the poor among you, but you will not always have me"?

9. Which wealthy old man provided for King David during his stay in Mahanaim?

10. Which churches does Paul praise, saying, "out of the most severe trial, their overflowing joy and their extreme poverty welled up in rich generosity"?

11. In 1 Samuel, who overcharged the Israelites for sharpening their axes and plowshares, because there were no blacksmiths in Israel?

12. "Let no ___ remain outstanding, except the continuing ___ to love one another." Which one word is repeated twice in this passage from Romans 13?

13. In Judges, whose mother paid 200 shekels of silver to make him a silver image and idol, which was later stolen by the Danites?

14. In the Old Testament, who did the Lord tell to return to his country and relatives and he would make them prosper?

15. Which Psalm says, "Do not be overawed when a man grows rich... for he will take nothing with him when he dies, his splendor will not descend with him"?

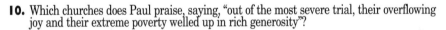

11. The Philistines 12. Debt 13. Micah 14. Jacob 15. Psalm 49

7. Laban cheated Jacob 8. He was anointed with a jar of perfume 9. Barzillai 10. The Macedonian churches

4. Deacons 5. The Lord is the Maker of them all 6. Melchizedek, king of Salem

1. King Solomon's 2. The Kingdom of heaven 3. 2 small copper coins

Answers

247

Quiz # 13

1. In the Old Testament, who became poverty-stricken because of Satan?

2. How was the prodigal son reduced to poverty?

3. Which person from the Old Testament prepared a large peace offering of livestock for his brother and sent it ahead of him as he traveled to Seir?

4. Why should you not invite your rich neighbors to lunch or dinner according to Luke's Gospel?

5. What did the prodigal son do when he found himself penniless?

6. To whom did Paul give the rule, "If a man will not work, he shall not eat"?

7. Which Old Testament woman praised God in a psalm, saying, "The Lord sends poverty and wealth; he humbles and he exalts. He raises the poor from the dust"?

8. Which New Testament writer says, "If anyone has material possessions and sees his brother in need but has no pity on him, how can the love of God be in him?"?

9. Which two Gospels record the beatitudes?

10. According to the law of Moses, what were the Israelites told to do if their tithe was too large to carry to "the place the Lord will choose to put his name"?

11. Which New Testament writer forbids favoring a rich man over a poor man?

12. Fill in the missing word, "Watch out! Be on your guard against all kinds of___; a man's life does not consist in the abundance of his possessions."

13. What advice does Jesus give to the rich fool who wants to inherit eternal life?

14. Which prophet quotes Ephraim who boasts, "I am very rich; I have become wealthy. With all my wealth they will not find in me any iniquity or sin"?

15. What event is Jesus referring to in Luke's Gospel when he says, "all these people gave their gifts out of their wealth; but she out of her poverty put in all she had to live on"?

Answers

1. Job **2.** He squandered his wealth on wild living **3.** Jacob
4. Because they may invite you back and so you will be repaid **5.** He took a job feeding pigs
6. The Thessalonians **7.** Hannah **8.** John **9.** Matthew and Luke
10. Convert it into silver, travel to the chosen place, then buy their tithe there instead **11.** James **12.** Greed
13. Keep the commandments and sell all your possessions, giving the money to the poor **14.** Hosea
15. The widow who put two small coins into the collection box

DOLLARS AND SENSE

Quiz # 14

1. Complete the verse from Ecclesiastes, "Wisdom is a shelter as ____ is a shelter, but the advantage of knowledge is this: that wisdom preserves the life of its possessor."

2. The writer of Proverbs 30 asked the Lord to give him neither poverty or riches. If he was poor he might shame God. What did he fear he would do if he was rich?

3. In which Old Testament book are the rules for the redemption of property laid out?

4. In the time of King Joash, which priest bored a hole in a chest, giving instructions that all the money brought to the temple was to be placed inside, to pay the temple workmen?

5. Where in the Old Testament is it written, "Better a poor man whose walk is blameless, than a rich man whose ways are perverse"?

6. If a man redeems any of his tithe, how much must he add to the value of it, according to the book of Leviticus?

7. In the Parable of the Great Banquet in Luke's Gospel, what excuses did three of the guests give for not being able to come to the wedding?

8. Who bribed Delilah with silver so that she would betray her husband?

9. Whose sons, Joel and Abijah, were appointed judges but, "turned aside after dishonest gain and accepted bribes and perverted justice"?

10. In 2 Kings, what did the King of Assyria do after King Ahaz had sent him silver and gold from the Lord's temple and the palace treasuries?

11. During the temptation in the desert, what was Jesus's reply when Satan offered him all the kingdoms of the world and their splendor, if only Jesus would worship him?

12. What is the first instance recorded in the Bible of someone buying something?

13. Who is Paul writing to when he says that slaves should be taught to be trustworthy rather than steal?

14. When Jericho was attacked by Joshua and his people, what did they do with all the gold and silver they found there?

15. Why did David make plans for building the temple but then leave the building of it to Solomon?

Answers

1. Money 2. He feared he might disown God 3. Leviticus 4. Jehoiada 5. The book of Proverbs 6. Fifth 7. One had just bought a field, one had just bought some oxen, and one had just got married 8. The Philistines 9. Samuel's 10. He captured Damascus, deported its inhabitants and killed Rezin, king of Aram 11. "Away from me Satan! For it is written: 'Worship the Lord your God, and serve him only.'" 12. Abraham buying a tomb for Sarah 13. Titus 14. They put it in the temple treasury 15. God had told him not to build the temple himself because he was a warrior and had shed blood

Quiz #15

1. What name did Jacob give to the land that he bought from the sons of Hamor for a hundred pieces of silver?

2. In Ecclesiastes, what turns a wise man into a fool?

3. According to Proverbs 22, what will the man who oppresses the poor to increase his wealth have in common with the man who gives gifts to the rich?

4. What was the value of a male between the ages of twenty and sixty in terms of being dedicated to the Lord?

5. Which New Testament letter states, "the world and its desires pass away, but the man who does the will of God lives for ever"?

6. In Nehemiah, the Israelites promised God they would not buy things on which days?

7. Fill in the missing word, "_____ is the man who accepts a bribe to kill an innocent person."

8. In John's account of Jesus overturning the moneychangers' tables in the temple, what animals were also ejected?

9. True or false? Jesus met and talked with tax collectors, but never ate and drank with them.

10. Who, according to Jesus, announced their gifts to the needy with trumpets in the synagogues and on the streets?

11. According to Matthew's Gospel, what should a person do if they are offering a gift at the alter and then remember that their brother has something against them?

12. According to Proverbs 11, what happens to the one who withholds his riches unduly?

13. Moses and the Israelites were commanded by God to bring offerings for the Tabernacle. What precious metal was offered in the form of jewellery?

14. In Deuteronomy, who is said to give the ability to produce wealth?

15. True or false? Talents could be made of gold, silver, bronze or iron.

Quiz #16

1. Who levied a tax of 100 talents of silver and one talent of gold on Judea and dethroned King Jehoahaz?

2. Which area in the Old Testament was famous for the gold it produced?

3. Which Old Testament king from Babylon stole articles from the temple and put them in his own temple?

4. Which wealthy Old Testament king ruled over 127 provinces stretching from India to Cush?

5. Which king of Judah defeated the Ammonites and forced them to pay him silver, wheat, and barley for three years?

6. Fill in the missing word, "Of what use is money in the hand of a fool, since he has no desire to get___."

7. In the book of Judges, who hired "reckless adventurers" to kill Jerub-Baal's sons for 70 silver shekels?

8. In the Old Testament, if someone wanted to make a special vow to dedicate a person to the Lord, but was too poor to pay the specified amount, what could he do?

9. As recorded in Numbers, how old did a baby have to be before it was redeemed at the temple for the price of five shekels of silver?

10. Who received a tithe from the Levites' tithe?

11. Who settled in the hill country of Seir because his possessions were too great to live in the same place as Jacob?

12. Why should you not take millstones as security for a debt?

13. In the Old Testament, who received a piece of silver and a gold ring from each of his friends and family after suffering great hardships?

14. Under what circumstances could an Israelite charge another Israelite interest?

15. True or false? According to Deuteronomy 24, you should pay the wages of a hired Israelite each day before sunset, but not the wages of an alien.

Answers

1. The Pharaoh of Egypt (Neco) 2. Ophir 3. Nebuchadnezzar 4. King Xerxes
5. King Jotham 6. "Wisdom" 7. Abimelech 8. Present the person to the priest who decided what the man could afford
9. One month 10. Aaron 11. Esau 12. Because it would take away a man's livelihood
13. Job 14. They were not allowed to charge fellow Israelites interest under any circumstances
15. False. Both Israelite and alien should be paid each day (Deuteronomy 24:14-15)

DOLLARS AND SENSE

Quiz # 17

1. Which Old Testament king said to his official Haman, "Keep the money, and do with the people as you please"?

2. In the book of Judges, who asked each of the Israelites to give him an earring from their plunder after the defeat of the Midianites?

3. Moses and Eleazar the priest led the Israelites into battle, after which the commanders offered to the Lord all the gold they had plundered. Against whom did they battle?

4. In the Old Testament which prophet bought his wife for fifteen shekels of silver and some barley?

5. True or false? After all the trials that Job went through, God made him more prosperous that he had been before.

6. In the book of Joel the nations are condemned for selling the people of Judea and Israel to whom?

7. Who, according to Jesus, had to depend on the generosity of the people in the towns and villages that they passsed through?

8. True or false? Jesus overturned the moneychanger's tables in the temple because he disagreed with paying the temple tax.

9. Who told Jacob to leave Laban's household when arguments about his wealth and wages began to surface?

10. What is the "work" referred to in the following passage, "The expenses of these men are to be fully paid out of the royal treasury, from the revenues of Trans-Euphrates, so that the work will not stop"?

11. In the New Testament, why is it said that God and Money cannot be served at the same time?

12. In the Old Testament, who paid who to nurse her own child?

13. In Malachi, on the Day of Judgment who will testify against those who defraud laborers of their wages?

14. Where did Jeremiah store his deeds of purchase for the field he had acquired from his cousin?

15. How did the gold that Gideon requested from the Israelites become a snare to him and his family?

Quiz # 18

1. Which Old Testament prophet prophesised that where there were a thousand vines worth a thousand silver shekels, there would be only briers and arrows?

2. What reason did Abraham give the Hittites for wanting to buy a field from them?

3. Who in the Old Testament, "collected all the money that was to be found in Egypt and Canaan in payment for the corn they were buying"?

4. If a man gave a neighbor his silver or goods for safekeeping and they were stolen and then the thief was caught, what must the thief do?

5. Levites were entitled to sell their houses, but what were they not allowed to sell, according to the book of Leviticus?

6. Who betrayed Samson for a fortune in silver shekels?

7. From whom did King Ahab try to buy a vineyard, so he could use it as a vegetable garden?

8. In the Old Testament, why did Naomi's kinsman redeemer decline to buy the land she was selling?

9. In the reign of Joash, what was done with the money offerings that were left over after the temple had been rebuilt?

10. In the book of Ezra, what did the Lord ask the Israelites to do with the money that they received from Babylon once they had returned to Jerusalem?

11. In Luke, Jesus tells a parable about two men who owed money to a moneylender. One owed 500 denarii and the other 50. How did the parable end?

12. Who claimed in the New Testament that he had not coveted anyone's silver, gold, or clothing and had used his own hands to supply all that he and his companions needed?

13. What was the other name for half a shekel, as described in the book of Exodus?

14. Who supplied Solomon with gold?

15. According to the book of Leviticus, if a man dedicated part of his land to the Lord, how was the value of it determined?

Answers

1. Isaiah 2. He wanted to use it as a burial site 3. Joseph 4. He must pay the owner double what he stole 5. Their land 6. Delilah 7. Naboth 8. Because it he had to marry Ruth as well 9. They were made into articles for the temple 10. He told them to buy animals, grain and drink offerings to sacrifice at the temple in Jerusalem 11. The moneylender canceled the debts of both 12. Paul 13. Beka 14. Hiram, King of Tyre 15. By how much seed it required

Quiz #19

1. True or false? Slaves could be part of an inheritance as they were the property of their owner.

2. For what job did Jethro tell Moses to select capable men, "men who fear God, trustworthy men who hate dishonest gain"?

3. Complete the following verse from Deuteronomy, "Do not have two differing ___ in your bag—one heavy, one light."

4. How were the disciples expected to survive without money as they preached the Gospel throughout the land?

5. Where did the buying and selling of goods take place in Jerusalem?

6. Who wrote to the church in Smyrna telling them that although they were afflicted and poor, they were, in fact, rich?

7. According to Mark's Gospel, who was begging for money by the roadside as Jesus and his disciples approached Jericho?

8. In the book of Ruth, who wanted to sell land that had belonged to Elimelech?

9. What parable does Jesus tell to illustrate how hard it is for the rich to enter the kingdom of God?

10. Which group of people in the New Testament are described as lovers of money?

11. In which Old Testament book is it written, "The sleep of a laborer is sweet, whether he eats little or much, but the abundance of a rich man permits him no sleep"?

12. In Matthew's Gospel, to whom did Jesus tell Simon Peter to give a four-drachma coin?

13. Which prophet at the end of the Old Testament admonishes the Israelites for robbing God of his tithes and offerings?

14. According to the Law of Moses what were masters required to give their servants when they were released from service?

15. Who pleaded in the Old Testament, "Give me, O God, the pledge you demand. Who else will put up security for me?" ?

Answers

1. True (Leviticus 25:46) **2.** Judges **3.** Weights **4.** They were to rely on the hospitality of the places they visited **5.** Outside the temple and at the city gates **6.** John **7.** Bartimaeus **8.** Naomi (his widow) **9.** The Parable of the Rich Ruler (Rich man in other gospels) **10.** The Pharisees **11.** Ecclesiastes **12.** The collectors of the temple tax **13.** Malachi **14.** They were required to give liberally from their flocks, threshing floor, and winepress **15.** Job

Quiz #20

1. In the New Testament, which nation is said to have made merchants grow rich from its excessive luxuries?

2. Zephaniah prophesied to which nation, saying, "Wail, you who live in the market district; all your merchants will be wiped out, all who trade with silver will be ruined"?

3. Fill in the missing word. Paul in his letter to Timothy recommends that the wealthy be, "___ in good deeds."

4. In Genesis 37, who bought Joseph from his brothers?

5. What is the city pictured in Revelation chapter 21 made of?

6. After Ezra and the exiled Israelites had left Babylon and returned to Jerusalem, they rested for three days. What did they do on the fourth day?

7. Who redeemed Ruth and her father-in-law's land in the book of Ruth?

8. In the Old Testament, who went to the King of Israel laden with silver talents, gold shekels, and clothing in the hope that he might be cured of leprosy.

9. In Old Testament times, could an Israelite sell himself to another as a slave?

10. In the book of Revelation who does John counsel to, "buy from me gold refined in the fire, so that you can become rich"?

11. In which Old Testament book is there a chapter that begins, "The Lord abhors dishonest scales, but accurate weights are his delight"?

12. True or false? Abraham brought a field from the Hittites because it contained a cave that he wished to bury Sarah in.

13. Who in the Old Testament gave his three daughters the same inheritance as his seven sons?

14. Fill in the missing word from Exodus 30:16, "Receive the _____ money from the Israelites, and use it for the service of the Tent of Meeting."

15. In the book of Esther, who boasted to his wife and friends about his vast wealth, his many sons, and his close relationship with the king?

Quiz #21

1. What was Jesus' reply to those who asked him, "Is it right to pay taxes to Caesar or not? Should we pay or shouldn't we?"?

2. What New Testament parable ends with the protagonist saying, "Don't I have the right to do what I want with my own money?"?

3. Who said, after he met Jesus, "Here and now I give half of my possessions to the poor, and if I have cheated anybody out of anything, I will pay back four times the amount"?

4. Which Old Testament figure grew prosperous as a rearer of livestock and came to own large flocks of sheep and goats?

5. In Matthew's Parable of the Talents, when the master spoke to the servant who had received only one talent, what did he tell him he should have done with it?

6. In Exodus, what is a man told to do if, through no fault of his own, his bull injures another bull, which then dies?

7. According to Exodus, if you take your neighbor's cloak as a pledge, when should you return it to him?

8. In which Gospel are we told to love our enemies and lend to them without expecting repayment?

9. What was Jesus doing when he said, "It is not the healthy who need a doctor, but the sick"?

10. Which Old Testament king "made silver as common in Jerusalem as stones"?

11. Which Old Testament book laments that gold had lost its luster?

12. In 2 Kings, how did Jehoiakim find the money to pay the tribute tax demanded of him?

13. In 2 Kings, why did the widow of one of Elisha's prophets come to Elisha for help?

14. In the book of Revelation, what was the rider of the third horse holding?

15. What was the name of the field that the priests and elders bought with Judas' money?

Answers

1. "Give to Caesar what is Caesar's and to God what is God's" (Mark 12:17).
2. The Parable of the Workers in the Vineyard **3.** Zacchaeus **4.** Jacob **5.** He should have put it on deposit with the bankers so that it earned interest **6.** Sell the live bull, then divide up the dead bull and money equally between owners **7.** By sunset **8.** Luke's Gospel **9.** When he sat and ate with Matthew and other tax collectors and sinners. **10.** King Solomon **11.** The book of Lamentations **12.** He taxed people for the land they owned **13.** Her husband's creditors were threatening to take her boys as his slaves **14.** A pair of scales **15.** The field of blood

Facts 1

In the Old Testmant, Abraham was considered a very wealthy man (Genesis 13:2). A person's wealth was measured by the number of livestock they owned and the amount of precious metal they had.

Silver was the most common precious metal in the Near East during biblical times.

Money changers were a common but necessary sight in the outer areas of the temple in Jerusalem, as the temple tax had to be paid with a Tyrian silver half-shekel although there were coins of several different origins in circulation in the city.

The Jewish temple tax had to be paid in coins from Tyre (Matthew 21:12), as the coins from Antioch did not have enough silver in them.

King Solomon's wealth was apparent in the many gold articles he owned, such as 200 gold shields, each containing 600 bekas of gold, which amounts to approximately seven and a half pounds (3.5 kilograms) of gold per shield.

Before coins were in circulation, precious metal, such as gold, silver, and bronze were used as currency. Merchants carried scales to weigh the amount being traded.

Jewish coins had scenes from Israel's history and pictures of plants on them instead of people's heads as the second commandment forbade the making of idols or use of images.

In the account of the widow's mite in Mark's Gospel, the word "mite" refers not to a unit of currency but to a very small amount of money. The widow put in two small copper coins called "leptons", which amounted to a Roman "quadrans", or penny.

A shekel was originally just a unit of weight rather than a unit of currency ("shekel" comes from the Hebrew word for "weight"). King Solomon imported a chariot from Egypt for 600 shekels of silver, which weighed approximately 7 kilograms.

In Biblical times the Israelites had to pay a temple tax of two drachmas. In Matthew, Jesus asked Simon Peter to pay both of their temple taxes with a four-drachma coin, a "stater". This coin was more common than a two-drachma coin, so people may often have paid their tax in pairs.

Facts 2

The Roman word for money was *"pecunia"*, from the word "pecus" meaning cow or cattle, reflecting the importance of livestock as a sign of wealth and as a item of barter before money was in common usage.

In the account of Jesus' anointing with perfume in Bethany (Mark 14), the jar of perfume is said to be worth more than a year's wages. The Greek translation puts this as more than 300 denarii, the basic Roman coin, made of silver.

A tribute-tax, such as that paid by several kings of Israel and Judea to Assyrian kings, was levied by a conqueror in order to subdue and weaken hostile nations.

There are few references in the Old Testament of an Israelite king receiving tribute-tax, possibly because it was rare for the Israelites to be powerful enough to exact it. One exception is King David who in 2 Samuel 8:9-11 dedicated the tax to the Lord.

Jews did not just hate tax collectors because of their habit of extorting money, but because their regular contact with Gentiles made them unclean.

Tithes, the giving of one-tenth of your income or produce for religious purposes, was practised by many nations before it was included in the Law of Moses (Genesis 14:18; Gen 28:22).

Tithes were given by the Israelites to the Levites as payment for their duties to the Tabernacle, as the Levites had no income of their own. The Levites then had to pay a tenth of this payment to the priests (Numbers 18:26).

"Numbered, weighed, and divided" is a literal translation of the writing on the wall in Daniel. It could have a double meaning; "Mene" also means mina, or about 50 shekels, "Tekel" can mean a shekel, and "Parsin", the plural of "Peres", can mean a half shekel.

In the famous Pauline saying, " the love of money is the root of all kinds of evil" the word translated as "money" in the NIV is the Greek word for "silver". Silver was used so often to buy things that the Hebrew word for "silver", "kesep", came to mean "money".

Because silver was so commonly used, the word was often omitted from the text and just the weight of it, in shekels, was recorded, as in 2 Kings 7:1.

The word "talent" comes from the Latin word "talenta" meaning sum of money, and the Greek word "talanton" which means weight or unit of money.

Facts 3

In Leviticus and Deuteronomy, the Lord tells the Israelites not to use dishonest weights when measuring metals. To ensure there was no cheating, the purchaser usually weighed out the metal and the vendor checked it in front of witnesses, as mentioned in Genesis 23:16.

Throughout the Bible there are repeated references to dishonesty in weighing, such as in Micah 6. It could be comparatively easy to use false weights. Hebrew weights inscribed with the same standard have been found to vary in weight, with an error margin of up to 6%.

Egyptian monuments from biblical times show gold in the form of rings being weighed.

"*Nechosheth*" is translated as "brass" in the KJV and "bronze" in the NIV, but usually refers to copper. Copper was used as currency in the Old Testament. It is listed beside gold and silver as a suitable offering to the Lord for the Tabernacle.

Ancient weights used for measuring metal were made of carved stone and carried in pouches (Deuteronomy 25:13). Purchasers could check the weights of the merchants to see if they were getting a fair deal.

Gold was commonly kept in the form of jewellery or ingots, whereas silver was used in pieces or lumps.

Perfumes and ointments were of great value, hence the inclusion of myrrh and frankincense with the gold brought to Jesus by the Magi.

Each city or nation set its own standards of weights and measures. For example, there were heavy and light Phoenican shekels made of silver and heavy and light Babylonian shekels made of gold.

Although gold was rarely used as currency in transactions, it was highly prized and was symbolic of great wealth and riches in the Old Testament. It is mentioned more than any other metal in the Bible with more than 500 references in all.

The belt that the disciples were told not to fill with money was probably a sash, a piece of folded cloth that would have been wound several times around the waist. It not only served for carrying money, but for carrying other valuables, even food.

Canaan, the land of "milk and honey", was an ideal location for the Israelites to settle in as it was situated on the main trade routes between Egypt in the south, Syria and Phoenicia in the north, and the Babylonian empire in the east.

Facts 4

The word "dross" refers to the residue left after a metal ore has been smelted to separate the impurities from the pure metal. It is used in the Bible to signify Israel's sinfulness (Isaiah 1:25).

Wages were more commonly paid in livestock, property, or services rather than in money in Old Testament times. Jacob, for example, was paid in livestock by Laban. This kind of payment was more suited to a semi-nomadic lifestyle.

The Hittites, Semites, and early Egyptians shaped the precious metals they were trading into nodules, rings, or bars, which were easier to transport.

Even after coins had been introduced, they were still weighed to ensure that they had not been filed or tampered with in any way.

Among the earliest known coins are ones made in Lydia by King Croesus, famous for his Anatolian gold and silver mines. Cyrus the Great probably brought the idea of coins back to Persia after conquering Croesus.

Israel did not have many natural resources, but the major trading routes that crossed its territory gave access to precious metals that the people could use as currency.

The first mention of the Jews minting their own coins comes in the Apocrypha, in 1 Maccabees 15:6 when Simon Maccabaeus is granted permission to issue coins by the reigning Roman emperor, Antiochus VII.

Cloth and clothing are often mentioned in Biblical passages about treasure on earth, alongside silver and gold. Israel had a thriving textile industry and was famous for its rich purple cloth manufactured in Tyre that was popular throughout the Mediterranean region.

Israel's wealth was further enhanced by the trade routes that passed through Isrealite territory, especially during the reigns of David and Solomon Israelite territory. This meant the Israelites could impose large import and export duties, and excise tax, on merchants.

In God's Garden

Quiz #1

1. In John 15, who did Jesus say was the gardener?

2. What name is given to the festival that celebrated the gathering in of the wheat harvest?.

3. By which trees was Abraham sitting when he was visited by angels?

4. Why did Jesus curse a fig-tree?

5. In the parable, what kind of seed, when it is full grown, offers shelter to birds?

6. Who died in the Field of Blood?

7. In the Parable of the Vineyard Workers, how much was each worker paid?

8. When Adam and Eve were banished from the garden, the land was cursed to produce what?

9. According to the parable, why did the farmer allow the wheat and the weeds to grow together until harvest?

10. Who allowed Ruth to glean in his fields?

11. Who wore a crown of thorns?

12. From which tree were Adam and Eve not allowed to eat?

13. In what way was an oak tree instrumental in the death of Absalom?

14. Whose barley crop was set on fire because he refused to meet with Absalom?

15. Which king wanted possession of Naboth's vineyard?

Answers

1. His Father 2. Pentecost 3. The great trees of Mare 4. It had no fruit 5. Mustard
6. Judas 7. A denarius (the usual daily wage) 8. Thorns and thistles 9. By picking out the weeds, he may have picked the wheat too 10. Boaz 11. Jesus 12. The tree of the knowledge of good and evil
13. Absalom's head got caught in the branches as he was escaping from his enemies on his mule
14. Joab 15. Ahab

Quiz #2

1. According to John's Gospel, who mistook Jesus for a gardener?

2. Which of the ten plagues of Egypt consisted of hail and lightning that destroyed vegetation?

3. Who had a vision of an angel standing among the myrtle trees?

4. Which fruit, the size of an orange, is embroidered round the edge of the high priest's robe?

5. According to the parable in Matthew 21, who did the landowner eventually send to his vineyard?

6. Palm Sunday commemorates which event in the life of Jesus?

7. What caused the plant that was shading Jonah to die?

8. Which Old Testament character said, "At least there is hope for a tree. If it is cut down, it will sprout again"?

9. In the Song of Songs, which animals are said to ruin the vineyards?

10. Who had a dream of a tree that grew large and strong and touched the sky?

11. According to Matthew's Gospel, who bought the Potter's Field?

12. In ancient Israel, with which oil were kings and priests anointed?

13. Who had an almond rod that flowered and produced fruit overnight?

14. In the book of Genesis, who had a dream that there would be seven years of plenty followed by seven years of famine?

15. In which book of the Bible do we find the words, "I am a rose of Sharon, a lily of the valleys"?

12. Olive oil 13. Aaron 14. Pharaoh 15. Song of Songs

7. A worm 8. Job 9. Foxes 10. Nebuchadnezzar 11. The chief priests

6. Jesus entering Jerusalem on a donkey

1. Mary 2. Seventh 3. The prophet Zechariah 4. Pomegranate 5. His son

Answers

Quiz #3

1. In the Parable of the Sower, what happened to the seed that fell on the path?

2. The river in the Garden of Eden separated into four rivers, the Euphrates and the Tigris are two them, name one of the other two.

3. True or false? Abel kept flocks and Cain worked the soil.

4. Who planted crops in the land and reaped a hundredfold because of the Lord's blessing?

5. According to Paul's teaching to Timothy, who should be the first to receive a share of the crops?

6. What name is given to the last tree mentioned in the Bible?

7. True or false? There are no oak trees in the Bible.

8. In Isaiah 32, what is poured out to make the desert a fertile field and the fertile field seem like a forest?

9. In Psalm 23, what type of pastures does the Lord make the writer lie down in?

10. In which of Paul's letters is there a list of nine characteristics described as the fruit of the Spirit?

11. From James 5, name the two kinds of rain the patient farmer waits for.

12. In Peter's first letter, he wrote, "The grass withers and the flowers fall," but what did he say would last for ever?

13. What did the serpent tell Eve would happen if she ate the forbidden fruit?

14. In which garden was Jesus arrested?

15. Finish off this sentence from Paul's letter to the Galatians, "Do not be deceived. God is not mocked. A man reaps…"

Answers

1. Birds took it **2.** Pishon or Gihon **3.** True (Genesis 4:2) **4.** Isaac
5. The farmer **6.** The tree of life **7.** False (Genesis 35:4) **8.** The Spirit **9.** Green pastures
10. Galatians **11.** Autumn and spring rains **12.** The word of the Lord
13. "You will be like God, knowing good and evil." **14.** Gethsemane **15.** "what he sows"

Quiz #4

1. According to Isaiah, what building stands in the vineyard?

2. True or false? Jesus' tomb was in a garden.

3. In how many Gospels does the Parable of the Sower appear?

4. Talking of the church, Paul says, "I planted the seed." Who does he say watered it?

5. If you have faith, what type of tree can you tell to be uprooted and planted in the sea?

6. Which Old Testament prophet was appointed to uproot and tear down, destroy and overthrow, to build and to plant?

7. Who sold a field and gave all the money to the apostles?

8. In which Old Testament book do we find the words, "a time to plant and a time to uproot"?

9. Who in the Garden of Eden called out, "Where are you?"?

10. In Genesis, a cherubim and a flaming flashing sword guard the way to which tree?

11. What type of tree is Gethsemane most famous for?

12. In the vision of Ezekiel 47, the leaves of the trees served what purpose?

13. According to John the Baptist, what will happen to trees that fail to bear good fruit?

14. Who asked, "Do people pick grapes from thorn bushes, or figs from thistles?"?

15. Fill in the missing word in this verse taken from the book of Job: "They skim past like boats of ___."

Quiz #5

1. True or false? The Bible tells us that the fruit Eve ate in the Garden of Eden was an apple.

2. When Abram and Lot separated, which way did Lot go?

3. Who in the book of Genesis, took fresh cut branches and made white stripes on them by peeling back the bark and exposing the inner wood?

4. Which king of the Philistines did Isaac go to during a time of famine?

5. To what use did the king of Samaria want to put Naboth's vineyard?

6. In John 12, what must a grain of wheat do to produce many seeds?

7. The roots of which tree produce charcoal to make incendiary arrows?

8. Which prophet wrote these words: "The harvest is past, the summer has ended, and we are not saved"?

9. In Hosea, what will you reap if you sow the wind?

10. In the Parable of the Sower, where did the third lot of seed land?

11. At the Passover, what plant did Moses use to sprinkle blood on the doorposts of houses?

12. What type of fungus, regarded as God's punishment on the disobedient, did Solomon pray for deliverance from in his prayer at the dedication of the temple?

13. True or false? Jesus asked the people whether they had gone out into the desert to see sand blown by the wind.

14. In Isaiah 42, what kind of reed will the servant of the Lord not break?

15. Who said, "I knew that you are a hard man, harvesting where you have not sown and gathering where you have not scattered seed"?

Answers

1. False. The fruit is not named (Genesis 2:17) **2.** Lot went to the plain of Jordan, which was "well watered, like the garden of the Lord" **3.** Jacob **4.** Abimelech **5.** Vegetable garden **6.** Fall in the ground and die **7.** Broom tree **8.** Jeremiah **9.** The whirlwind **10.** Among thorns **11.** Hyssop **12.** Mildew **13.** False. Jesus said, "a reed swayed by the wind" (Matthew 11:7) **14.** A bruised (bent) reed **15.** The servant who hid his one talent in the ground

Quiz #6

1. In Psalm 92, who spring up like grass?

2. Which king was driven away from his people and ate grass like cattle?

3. In the parable, what is the mustard seed likened to?

4. Complete the sentence: "A king's rage is like the roar of a lion, but his _____ is like dew on the grass."

5. In the feeding of the 5,000, what special detail does Mark tell us about the grass?

6. In the Parable of the Weeds, the weeds are burned. What happens to the wheat?

7. During the wheat harvest, who went out and found some mandrake plants for his mother Leah?

8. True or false? In Exodus 34, keeping the Sabbath instructions did not apply during harvest time.

9. In the Parable of the Weeds, who came when everyone was sleeping and sowed weeds among the wheat?

10. Complete the sentence: "Do not plant your field with _____ kinds of seed."

11. In the New Testament, who said, "The ax is already at the root of the trees"?

12. According to the Sermon on the Mount, what kind of fruit does a good tree bear?

13. In Deuteronomy 24, the Israelites were told not to over-harvest their vines, but to leave grapes for three types of people, the alien (foreigner) and two others. Who were they?

14. Where was the cave where thirty chief men visited David during the harvest?

15. Complete the sentence: "He who sleeps during harvest is a disgraceful ___."

Answers

1. The wicked 2. Nebuchadnezzar 3. The kingdom of God 4. Favor 5. It was green 6. The wheat is gathered and put into the barn 7. Reuben 8. False (Exodus 34:21) 9. An enemy 10. Two 11. John the Baptist 12. Good fruit 13. The fatherless and the widow 14. Adullam 15. Son

Quiz #7

1. In Matthew 13, who are the harvesters at the end of the age?

2. To whom in Luke's Gospel does Jesus say, "The harvest is plentiful"?

3. Which Old Testament prophet spoke of the purchase of a field for thirty silver coins?

4. Who in the New Testament said of Jesus, "His winnowing fork is in his hand"?

5. In Matthew 24, Jesus speaks of two men in a field, what happens to them?

6. According to Leviticus 19, when entering a new land, in which year is the fruit of a new tree allowed to be eaten?

7. In the Old Testament, what name is given to the fiftieth year, when no sowing or reaping was allowed?

8. Which Old Testament prophet bought a field from his cousin Hanamel?

9. In Genesis 4, who was killed in a field?

10. At the threshing floor of Atad, who observed a seven-day period of mourning for his father Jacob?

11. True or false? Seed that fell on good soil produced a crop of a 100, 60 or 30 times what was sown.

12. Which Old Testament prophet spoke of untold destruction by swarms of locusts?

13. In Mark's Gospel, who found himself naked in a garden?

14. Who placed a wool fleece on a threshing-floor to get guidance from God?

15. At the instruction of her mother-in-law, who went to a threshing-floor to meet her future husband?

Answers

1. Angels **2.** The 72 (or 70) disciples **3.** Jeremiah **4.** John the Baptist **5.** One is taken and one is left **6.** Fifth **7.** Jubilee **8.** Jeremiah **9.** Abel **10.** Joseph **11.** True (Mark 4:8) **12.** Joel **13.** A follower of Jesus (possibly Mark) **14.** Gideon **15.** Ruth

Quiz #8

1. In the book of Judges, who told the story of trees anointing a king for themselves?

2. In 2 Kings 6, when a man was cutting down a tree, what fell in the water?

3. In Matthew 9, who are the disciples to ask to send workers into the harvest field?

4. Complete the sentence, "The harvest is plentiful but the workers are _____."

5. True or false? The fruit of the righteous is a tree of life.

6. Who saw a vision of an almond tree?

7. In which parable do we find the excuse of just having bought a field?

8. Which king could describe all types of plant life?

9. Name one of two animals that should not be yoked together for plowing?

10. Complete the sentence, "No one who puts his hand to the plow and looks back is fit for service in the _____."

11. Who had a dream about sheaves of grain bowing down?

12. True or false? Boaz grew barley and wheat.

13. Why did Zacchaeus climb a tree to see Jesus?

14. In support of whom does Paul write to the Corinthians quoting from the Old Testament, "Do not muzzle the ox while it is treading out the grain"?

15. Who in Genesis is called a man of the soil?

Answers

1. Jotham 2. An ax head 3. The Lord of the harvest (God) 4. Few 5. True (Proverbs 11:30)
6. Jeremiah 7. The Parable of the Great Banquet 8. Solomon 9. Ox or donkey 10. Kingdom of God
11. Joseph 12. True (Ruth 2:23) 13. He was a little man
14. The elders who were leaders, preachers and teachers in a church 15. Noah

Quiz #9

1. Which of Job's companions said that the man who forgets God is like a well-watered plant in the sunshine, which entwines its roots around rocks?

2. The word "orchard" or "orchards" only appear in three books of the Bible, name one of them.

3. Complete the sentence: "A shoot will come up from the stump of _____ ; from his roots a Branch will bear fruit."

4. True or false? During the Passover Festival, the Jews were not allowed to eat bread.

5. Who did the Lord call "a thriving olive tree with fruit beautiful in form"?

6. In the parable, how long was the fig-tree given to bear fruit before it would be cut down?

7. Who said, "The man who plants and the man who waters have one purpose"?

8. Complete the sentence from 1 Corinthians: "Who plants a vineyard and does not eat of its _____?"

9. According to Job 40, what lies under the lotus plant and is hidden among the reeds in the marsh?

10. According to Proverbs 31, what sort of wife plants a vineyard?

11. In the Parable of the Sower, why were some plants scorched when the sun came up?

12. How would God provide for the Israelites during every seventh year when they neither sowed nor harvested?

13. In Exodus 10, what covered the ground until it was black and devoured everything left in the fields and on the trees?

14. The spies who Moses sent to explore the promised land returned with grapes and two other types of fruit. Name one of the other two.

15. According to 1 Kings 4, where would you find hyssop growing?

Answers

1. Bildad 2. Isaiah or Jeremiah or Song of Songs 3. Jesse 4. False. They could eat bread, but it had to be made without yeast (Deuteronomy 16:3) 5. The people of Judah 6. 12 months 7. The apostle Paul 8. Grapes 9. The behemoth (or hippopotamus or elephant) 10. A wife of noble character 11. The ground was rocky, and the soil was shallow, so they had no roots 12. There would be a threefold harvest in the sixth year 13. Locusts 14. Pomegranates and figs 15. Out of walls

Quiz #10

1. In the Parable of the Sower, who went out to sow the seed?

2. Who was responsible for a servant losing his ear in a garden?

3. Who said, "Take my yoke upon you and learn from me"?

4. What did Solomon want to do with the cedar and pine logs that he bought from King Hiram?

5. In Genesis 2, how was the ground watered?

6. Who beat out wheat in a winepress to hide it from the Midianites?

7. In the ancient world, which biblical city was famed for its hanging gardens?

8. Why did God bring all the animals to Adam in the garden?

9. True or false? The first people were vegetarians.

10. In the Old Testament, what plant is Israel compared to?

11. In Matthew 15, which plants will be pulled up by their roots?

12. When Jesus was on the cross, on the stalk of which plant was a sponge of wine vinegar placed to give Jesus a drink?

13. In 1 Chronicles 27, who was in charge of the vineyards?

14. Complete this verse from the psalms: "He who goes out weeping, carrying seeds to sow, will return with songs of joy, carrying ___ with him."

15. In the book of which prophet do we find the question, "Is there yet any seed left in the barn?"?

Answers

1. The farmer 2. Peter 3. Jesus 4. Build the temple 5. By underground streams 6. Gideon 7. Babylon 8. So that Adam could name them 9. True (Genesis 1:29) 10. A vine 11. Those not planted by the heavenly Father 12. Hyssop 13. Shimei 14. Sheaves 15. Haggai

Quiz #11

1. In Nebuchadnezzar's dream, what did the command to leave the stump of the tree with its roots in the ground signify?

2. In Mark 11, what happened to the fig-tree cursed by Jesus?

3. Who in the New Testament is said to come from the root of Jesse?

4. In which of his letters does Paul write, "If the root is holy, so are the branches"?

5. What is the root of all kinds of evil?

6. In Genesis 41, what came out of the river and grazed among the reeds?

7. In Revelation 11, what was John told to measure with a reed?

8. Jesus said the Pharisees gave a tenth of their spices. One spice was dill. What were the other two?

9. Who, according to the book of Acts, declared, "He has shown kindness by giving you rain from heaven and crops in their seasons"?

10. Fill in the gap: the spies reported that the promised land flowed "with milk and ___."

11. True or false? God told the Israelites to add salt to all their grain offerings.

12. In which book of the Bible do we find the words, "There is a time for everything, and a season for every activity under heaven"?

13. Which Old Testament prophet records the words, "Sow for yourselves righteousness, reap the fruit of unfailing love"?

14. When Jesus cursed the fig tree, which Gospel records the fact that it was not the season for figs?

15. True or false? When the disciples saw the fig tree Jesus had cursed, Jesus said "Have faith in yourselves."

Answers

1. When Nebuchadnezzar acknowledged God, his kingdom would be restored 2. It was withered from the roots 3. Jesus 4. Romans 5. The love of money 6. Seven cows 7. The Temple (or altar) 8. Mint and cummin 9. Paul 10. Honey 11. True (Leviticus 2:13) 12. Ecclesiastes 13. Hosea 14. Mark 15. False, He said, "Have faith in God" (Mark 11:22)

Quiz #12

1. In the purification rites of Leviticus 14, what plant was used?

2. Fill in the missing word in David's prayer in Psalm 51, "Cleanse me with ___, and I will be clean."

3. Which New Testament writer heard a sound like a voice saying, "A quart of wheat for a day's wages, and three quarts of barley for a day's wages, and do not damage the oil and wine!"?

4. In order to stop him becoming conceited, what does Paul say he was given?

5. In Numbers 33, who would become barbs in the eyes of the Israelites and thorns in their sides?

6. In Luke 13, what type of seed did a man plant in his garden?

7. In 1 Samuel 6, when harvesting the wheat, what did the people of Beth Shemesh see to make them rejoice?

8. True or false? The first people in the Bible were builders.

9. In the book of Judges, who burned down a field of corn?

10. What plant did Jesus say he was?

11. In 1 Chronicles 21, what did Araunah see when threshing wheat?

12. What wood did Noah use to build his ark?

13. In which Old Testament book is there a reference to trees clapping?

14. Who was told in Jeremiah 41, "Don't kill us! We have wheat and barley, oil and honey, hidden in a field"?

15. To whom did Jesus say, "Satan has asked to sift you as wheat"?

Answers

1. Hyssop **2.** Hyssop **3.** John in the book of Revelation **4.** A thorn in the flesh **5.** People who had been living in the Promised Land before the Israelites arrived and had been allowed to stay on in the land **6.** A mustard seed **7.** The ark of the covenant **8.** False. They were gardeners (Genesis 2:15) **9.** Samson **10.** Vine **11.** An angel **12.** Cypress wood (or gopher wood) **13.** Isaiah **14.** Ishmael **15.** Peter

273

Quiz #13

1. In the Parable of the Sower, what metaphor is used to describe Satan taking away the word that was sown?

2. Complete the sentence from the Song of Songs, "Like a _____ among thorns."

3. In Genesis, who was told, "When you work the ground, it will no longer yield its crops for you"?

4. In which book of the Bible do we find the words, "Flowers appear on the earth, the season of singing has come"?

5. Fill in the missing word: on every ___ year the people were not to sow their fields or prune their vineyards because the land had to have a year of rest.

6. In the interpretation of the Parable of the Sower, what does the seed represent?

7. In the book of Esther, who gave a party in his garden lasting for seven days?

8. In Genesis, what did Jacob buy from the sons of Hamor?

9. When the Israelites were in the wilderness, what appeared on the ground like flakes of thin frost?

10. True or false? It was Elisha, not Elijah, who features in the account of Naboth's vineyard.

11. True or false? After the flood, Noah first of all sowed seed in the ground.

12. Fill in the name of the flower: "The wilderness will rejoice and blossom. Like the ___ it will burst into bloom."

13. In which Old Testament book do we find the words, "I will pour water on the thirsty land, and streams on the dry ground; I will pour out my Spirit on your offspring"?

14. In John's Gospel, who did Jesus see under a fig tree?

15. True or false? Zacchaeus climbed a sycamore tree.

IN GOD'S GARDEN

Quiz # 14

1. In Haggai, what had the people neglected to do, causing God to withhold dew from heaven and crops from the earth?

2. In the Parable of the Rich Fool, why did the farmer decide to pull down his barns?

3. True or false? Jesus told the Parable of the Rich Fool to warn the people to be on their guard against worry.

4. In Exodus, what was on fire and not burning up?

5. On the Egyptian building site, what was mixed with clay and water to make bricks?

6. Who wandered around in the fields of Shechem looking for his brothers, before finding them near Dothan?

7. In Genesis 47, why did the Egyptians have to sell their land?

8. True or false? Before the famine began in Egypt, Joseph stored up huge quantities of rice.

9. In Genesis 47, what percentage of their crop did the Egyptians have to give to Pharaoh?

10. What percentage of their crops did God ask of the Israelites?

11. Why did Abraham and Sarah travel down to Egypt?

12. Who learnt that the portions of grain, wine and oil assigned to the Levites had not been given and that the Levites and singers had therefore returned to their fields?

13. Which book of the Bible gives the advice, "Finish your outdoor work and get your fields ready; after that, build your house"?

14. Which Old Testament prophet would rejoice, even though "the fig tree does not bud and there are no grapes on the vines"?

15. In the parable, what did the man find hidden in a field?

Quiz #15

1. Complete the phrase from John 4, "____ months more and then the harvest."

2. In the account of creation, on what day did God make all the plants and trees?

3. Houses were lit by lamplight: what oil was used?

4. In Isaiah's image of peace, what will spears be turned into?

5. True or false? When harvesting, the Israelites were told to reap to the very edge of their fields.

6. In Jeremiah's vision of two baskets of fruit, what was the fruit?

7. True or false? As a result of the Fall, farming became hard work.

8. According to the book of Joshua, who gave his daughter the "upper and lower springs"?

9. Who shot an arrow in a field, as a sign that David's life was in danger?

10. Who told his servants to burn Joab's field of barley?

11. Near a field full of lentils, from whom did the Israelites flee?

12. True or false? Joseph had a dream in which he and his brothers were harvesting grain.

13. In 2 Kings 19, of which nation is it said, "They are like plants in the field, like tender green shoots, like grass sprouting on the roof, scorched before it grows up"?

14. Which Old Testament prophet records, "All the trees of the field will know that I the Lord bring down the tall tree and make the low tree grow tall"?

15. A leaf from which plant was brought by the dove to Noah as a sign that the flood water had receded?

Quiz # 16

1. Which two Old Testament prophets both spoke of a tree with the birds of the air nesting in its boughs?

2. Which Old Testament prophet declared that Zion would be plowed like a field and thickets would grow over the temple mound?

3. The wild flowers are dressed more beautifully than which king?

4. In the Parable of the Weeds, what does the field represent?

5. From which Old Testament book is the following quotation: "I will make Samaria a heap of rubble, a place for planting vineyards"?

6. True or false? Luke writes that Ananias and Sapphira sold a field.

7. In Judges 6, what remained dry when all the ground around it was covered in dew?

8. Fill in the missing word: "During Solomon's time Judah and Israel lived in safety, each man under his own vine and ___."

9. According to Acts 1, did Judas or the priests buy a field?

10. True or false? The law of Moses allowed an Israelite to eat as many grapes as he wanted from his neighbor's vineyard, but not to take any away in a container.

11. True or false? The vineyard in Isaiah 5 yielded only bad grapes.

12. In Luke 13, what type of tree was growing in the man's vineyard?

13. Which Old Testament prophet records, "There I will give her back her vineyards, and will make the Valley of Achor a door of hope"?

14. In the Parable of the Two Sons, which son, when asked by his father, went and worked in the vineyard?

15. According to Proverbs, what sweeps away the abundant food from a poor man's field?

Answers

1. Ezekiel and Daniel **2.** Micah **3.** King Solomon
4. The world **5.** Micah **6.** False. It was a piece of property (Acts 5:1) **7.** A fleece **8.** Fig-tree
9. Judas **10.** True (Deuteronomy 23:24) **11.** True (Isaiah 5:2) **12.** Fig-tree **13.** Hosea
14. The first son, who said, "I will not." **15.** Injustice

Quiz # 17

1. A Nazirite must not eat the seeds or skin of which fruit?

2. In Isaiah 32, when justice dwells in the desert, what will live in the fertile field?

3. True or false? Cinnamon was mixed with olive oil for anointing priests.

4. What natural disaster made Amos cry out, "How can Jacob survive? He is so small!"

5. In Numbers 22, what appeared standing in a narrow path between two vineyards?

6. Having created all vegetation, how, in one word, did God describe it?

7. In Deuteronomy 28, what will eat the grapes from the vineyards?

8. True or false? Lebanon was famous for its fine pine trees.

9. Fill in the missing word from Ezekiel's prophecy, "He took some of the seed of your land and put it in fertile soil. He planted it like a ___ by abundant waters."

10. According to Matthew 24, what does it mean when the fig tree becomes green and puts out its leaves?

11. In 1 Samuel 4, why did the ground shake when the ark of the covenant entered the camp?

12. Who found Elisha plowing with twelve yoke of oxen?

13. Who was told, in the first chapter of his book, "The oxen were plowing and the donkeys were grazing nearby, when the Sabeans attacked"?

14. In Judges 21, what did the Benjamites watch for when hiding in the vineyards?

15. Who said, "If you had not plowed with my heifer, you would not have solved my riddle"?

Answers

1. Grape 2. Righteousness 3. True (Exodus 30:24) 4. A swarm of locusts 5. The angel of the Lord 6. Good 7. Worms 8. False. It was cedar trees (1 Kings 5:6) 9. Willow 10. Summer is near 11. The Israelites shouted 12. Elijah 13. Job 14. Girls (or future wives) 15. Samson

Quiz #18

1. In Isaiah 1, who is left like a hut in a field of melons?

2. According to Proverbs, why does the sluggard find nothing at harvest time?

3. True or false? Jesus called his Father a gardener.

4. In the words of Jesus, who do not sow or reap or store away in barns?

5. Which Bible book has the most references to gleaning?

6. Naboth's vineyard was in Jezreel close to which building?

7. In Gethsemane, who did Jesus ask to keep watch with him?

8. According to Isaiah 2, where do oaks come from?

9. Name one of the things that Jacob buried under the oak at Shechem?

10. In John's vision in the book of Revelation, what stood on each side of the river that flowed down from the throne?

11. What sort of tree did Abraham plant at Beersheba?

12. True or false? According to Moses, the gardens of Egypt were watered by hand.

13. Who was buried in his palace garden?

14. In 1 Chronicles 27, what was Zabdi in charge of?

15. Where did the old prophet live who met a man of God under an oak tree?

Answers

1. The Daughter of Zion (Israel) 2. Because he has not plowed (sown any seed) 3. True (John 15:1) 4. Birds of the air 5. Ruth 6. The palace 7. Peter, James and John 8. Bashan 9. Foreign gods and earrings 10. The tree of life 11. Tamarisk 12. False. They were watered by foot (Deuteronomy 11:10) 13. Manasseh 14. The produce of the vineyards 15. Bethel

Quiz #19

1. According to Psalm 104, in which kind of tree does the stork nest?

2. Which Old Testament prophet urged the pine and oak to wail?

3. According to Psalm 92, who will flourish like a palm tree?

4. Who said, "I made gardens and parks and planted all kinds of fruit trees in them"?

5. In the account of the trees in Judges 9, what can come out of the thornbush to consume the cedars of Lebanon?

6. True or false? Jesus said that if you have faith as small as a mustard seed you can tell a mulberry tree to go into the sea and it will?

7. In Revelation 8, how much of the tree was burned up at the sound of the first trumpet?

8. To cover their nakedness, what type of leaves did Adam and Eve sew together?

9. In the book of Numbers, who said that the Israelites were spread out like gardens beside a river?

10. Who said, "To each kind of seed he [God] gives its own body"?

11. Complete this phrase quoted in Galatians, "_____ is everyone who is hung on a tree."

12. From Revelation, name the tree that bore its fruit every month.

13. According to Hosea, what tree is God like?

14. In Psalm 1, who is like a tree planted by streams of water?

15. Which two cereal crops are usually intended by the use of the term "grain"?

Answers

1. The pine (or fir) 2. Zechariah 3. The righteous 4. The teacher (Solomon, the writer of Ecclesiastes) 5. Fire 6. True (Luke 17:6) 7. One third 8. Fig 9. Balaam 10. Paul 11. Cursed 12. The tree of life 13. A green pine tree 14. Someone who studies God's word 15. Barley and wheat

Quiz #20

1. In which garden did Adam and Eve live?

2. Why did Jesus stop under a sycamore-fig tree?

3. Under the shelter of what tree did the angel sit when visiting Gideon?

4. In the thunderstorm described in Psalm 29, what tree is twisted by the voice of the Lord?

5. In the Garden of Gethsemane, how many times did Jesus return to find his disciples asleep?

6. In which of the four Gospels is the Parable of the Growing Seed?

7. Who wrote, "All over the world this gospel is bearing fruit and growing"?

8. Is the Mount of Olives nearer Bethlehem or Jerusalem?

9. Who left Jerusalem at night, by way of the king's garden?

10. In the parable of Luke 20, how many servants did the owner send to his vineyard?

11. True or false? The Garden of Gethsemane was on the Mount of Olives.

12. To whom did Jesus say, "For if men do these things when the tree is green, what will happen when it is dry"?

13. Complete this promise from Isaiah, "You will be like a ___ garden."

14. In the seven "I am" sayings of Jesus in John's Gospel, how many refer to a plant or tree?

15. What common form of vegetation is used in the Bible to describe both the flourishing and the mortality of people?

Quiz #21

1. True or false? There were only two trees in the Garden of Eden.

2. Who wrote to the Jews in Babylon, "Plant gardens and eat what they produce"?

3. In the New Testament, who wrote that the rich man would pass away "like a wild flower"?

4. In Jesus' illustration of the vine, who are the branches?

5. According to the book of Job, what can revive a dead tree stump?

6. True or false? Naboth sold his vineyard for a great price.

7. In Jesus' illustration of the vine, what does the gardener do to fruitful branches?

8. Fill in the missing word, "Like the coolness of ___ at harvest time is a trustworthy messenger."

9. In Ecclesiastes 11, when are you told to sow your seed?

10. In which Bible book is a locked garden used as an analogy?

11. How is the garden in the Song of Songs shared?

12. In Isaiah 2, which two gardening tasks will replace warfare?

13. Pentecost celebrates the wheat harvest. What is the festival that celebrates the end of the fruit harvest?

14. For what virtue does James praise the farmer?

15. In Hosea, what is likened to poisonous weeds?

Answers

1. False (Genesis 2:9) **2.** Jeremiah **3.** James **4.** All Jesus' disciples
5. Water **6.** False. Naboth was stoned to death and his vineyard was taken (1 Kings 21:15)
7. He prunes them so they will produce more fruit **8.** Snow **9.** In the morning **10.** Song of Songs **11.** By its fragrance
being blown abroad **12.** Pruning and plowing **13.** Tabernacles (Booths, Ingathering) **14.** Patience
15. Lawsuits caused by broken promises and false oaths

Facts 1

Many burial chambers belonging to wealthy families have been found on the sides of the hills to the north, south and east of Jerusalem. The tombs were cut out of the soft limestone rock, and often a garden was made in front of the tombs.

When the grapes were being harvested, vineyard workers camped in a stone watchtower in the orchard or slept in the open. By doing this, they were able to guard the grapes against thieves.

Vineyard watchtowers were expensive to build. Jesus told a parable about a farmer who started to build a watchtower, but could not afford to finish it.

In the towns, houses were crowded together, and there were not many gardens. Sometimes a rich person would have a walled courtyard garden, with a fountain and flowering trees.

The well-to-do had shady gardens on the hills outside the city walls. These were orchards rather than flower gardens.

Large solitary oak trees often became landmarks. They were a favorite place to sit beneath (Judges 6:19), and were also used as burial sites (Genesis 35:8).

Summer houses were a regular feature of most royal gardens.

In the early stages of growth, it is hard to distinguish wheat from a poisonous weed, the darnel grass. This explains Jesus' parable about allowing the wheat and the weeds to grow together until harvest, when they are clearly distinguishable.

When Jesus spoke of the "lilies of the field," he was speaking of wild flowers such as the blue hyacinth, the poppy, anemone and crown daisy.

Straw is the stubble that remains after harvesting wheat. It was mainly used as bedding for animals and people and for animal fodder. Isaiah likens Moab's fate to straw being trampled down among dung (Isaiah 25:10).

Facts 2

When there was no space for a vegetable garden, vegetables were planted between the rows of vines in the vineyard.

In Egypt, ditches, filled with water by hand, would criss-cross vegetable gardens. Irrigation of small plots was achieved simply by breaking the ditch wall with one's foot (Deuteronomy 11:10).

The exact location of Eden is unknown: some say it was in the land between the Tigris and Euphrates rivers, others that it was in the Arabian peninsula.

The palm trees referred to in the Bible were date palms. They were tall, slender trees, and were seen as gracious and elegant. The Hebrew word for palm, *tamar*, was often used as a girl's name.

Palm trees were a national symbol of victory and rejoicing. The people who waved palm branches as Jesus entered Jerusalem were therefore making a political statement.

Cedar wood was prized for its durability and was used in major building projects. Ships' masts were also made of cedar wood. The finest cedar wood came from the cedars of Lebanon (Song of Songs 5:15).

Pharisees referred to those with no religious education as "people of the land," suggesting that those who tended gardens and farmed were not held in high regard.

The village threshing floor was located in a windy spot to help with the winnowing. After the grain had been threshed, it was thrown into the air with a winnowing fork. The wind blew away the lighter straw and chaff while the grain fell to the ground.

In Bible times, flax was the only plant grown for cloth. Flax plants were pulled up by the root, and laid out to dry, often on the flat roofs of houses (Joshua 2:6). Linen cloth was made from the stems of the plants.

Identifying plants in the Bible is difficult because the plants found in the Middle East today were not necessarily native to the region in biblical times.

Facts 3

Acacia trees flourished in the desert, providing the Israelites with timber for the construction of the tabernacle and its furnishings.

Several times a fruit is mentioned which has characteristics similar to an apple. It has been suggested that Proverbs' "apples of gold" could be apricots, and this should be the translation elsewhere. There is no evidence that the apricot was known in biblical times.

Grapes, melons and cucumbers were a source of much needed liquid during the dry summer months.

God's agricultural principles laid down in Leviticus are proven practice to this day. These include leaving a field fallow every seven years to aid conservation. of the soil Another principle was not to plant two different crops in one field.

When poorer people had gardens in the villages, they used them to grow vegetables and herbs.

Green pastures are not a permanent sight in Israel, but last only for a short while after rain. Grass is thus a fitting symbol for the temporary nature of human life (Psalm 90:5-6).

The biblical description and use of hyssop indicates that it is not the plant we now know as hyssop, which does not grow in Palestine.

The hyssop used in Jewish cleansing ceremonies was probably the white Syrian marjoram. It belongs to the mint family and is scented like mint. Its hairy stems hold water, making it a good sprinkler (Exodus 12:22).

The "hyssop that grows out of walls," referred to in 1 Kings 4:33, may be the prickly caper, which grows in the crannies of walls in Palestine.

According to John, when Jesus was on the cross, a man fixed a sponge soaked in wine- vinegar on the stalk of a hyssop and gave it to Jesus. But a hyssop stalk was too feeble to hold a sponge. It has been suggested that the Greek word *hussopo*, has at some point been copied in error, and the word should be *hysso*, which means "lance."

Facts 4

A number of different Hebrew words are used for briars, brambles, nettles, thistles, and thorns, and no one is sure of the exact plant indicated by each Hebrew word. They all represent fruitlessness and evil.

Thorn hedges were sometimes grown to make defensive barriers (Hosea 2:6).

Exemption from military service was granted for men working in a vineyard.

In Mark's account of the feeding of the five thousand, the unique detail that the grass was "green," is a reference to the time of the year in which the miracle occurred—shortly after the rains.

Mildew is a common form of fungus that attacks plants and was seen in biblical times as a punishment from God for disobedience.

Plows were made of light wood so that farmers could lift them easily over the numerous stones and rocks in their fields.

Wormwood is a small shrub with a bitter, poisonous taste which grows in dry places. The Hebrew name means "accursed plant," and wormwood symbolized calamity and punishment (Lamentations 3:19).

Mulberry trees grow near water, very often on river banks, which makes sense of Jesus' statement that faith the size of a mustard seed is enough to send a mulberry tree into the sea.

Passers-by could, by law, eat ears of grain as they passed by fields of grain—but not on the Sabbath, since the plucking and breaking was thought to be threshing and winnowing, which was forbidden work.

The pink blossom of the almond tree appears at the end of January, before the leaves. Its Hebrew name, *shaqed*, sounds like the Hebrew word for "be wakeful," "watch over." It is as if the tree is keeping watch to announce the coming of spring (Jeremiah 1:11-12).

The small tree that is a variety of the pistachio tree grew wild in Canaan, but not in Egypt. The small round pistachio nuts that Jacob sent as a gift to the governor of Egypt would have been a rare delicacy (Genesis 43:11).

Facts 5

The most important crop was grain, which comes first in the lists of the main crops: grain, grapes and olives. Wheat and barley were the major grain crops. Millet was also grown, but not corn or maize.

Wheat was grown in the better soil and made into very fine and expensive white flour: the best of foods (Psalm 81:16). When thank-offerings of grain were given to God, it was wheat that had to be offered.

Barley could be grown on poorer soil, and had a shorter growing period. Loaves made from barley were a poor man's food and animal fodder. The flour was coarser than wheat flour and two or three times cheaper.

When confessing to jealousy, whether legitimate or groundless, a man was to take his wife to the priests for cleansing, together with an offering of barley. He could not add oil or incense to this offering.

Millet provided food for animals and for the very poor. Bread made from millet was rather like rye bread.

The main obstacles to working the land were: drought, strong winds which could lift and take away vast quantities of dry soil, locusts and invading armies.

The costly ointment lavished upon Jesus (Mark 14:1-11) was nard from India. It was imported in sealed alabaster jars to preserve its perfume.

The "first rains" came in October to November, and without these there could be no crop. Winter was the rainy season, and the winter rains kept the ground fertile. The rains stopped in March.

The "latter rains" came in April when the ear of grain was beginning to grow. For a good crop it was important that these rains came in early April. According to the Talmud, the latter rains brought more blessing than the ox and the yoke.

When Jesus told the parable about a man's enemy sowing weeds into his field of wheat, he probably knew that Roman law specified this was a criminal activity.

Facts 6

The rose was not known in Israel in Old Testament times. In some translations of Solomon's Song of Songs, the loved one's lips are compared to a "rose of Sharon." The red tulip or scarlet anemone may be the reference to that flower.

The rose seems to have been introduced into Palestine just before the Christian era. In Acts, Luke talks of a servant girl called Rose (Rhoda).

Olives were cooked, or pickled in salt water; the juice was extracted for cooking, for burning in lamps, for putting on wounds, for rubbing into the skin and hair (as a refreshing beauty treatment), for pouring on offerings given to God and for anointing kings and priests.

Olive wood was hard and could be rubbed into a high polish. The cherubim in the temple were made of wild olive wood.

The fig-tree was often grown with the vine (1 Kings 4:25), and its broad leaves gave a welcome shade. A fig-tree stood for peace, and it was customary to sit and meditate under its branches (John 1:48).

Papyrus is a marsh plant that grows in the Huleh swamp in northern Palestine, and used to grow in the Nile delta. Not only was paper made from papyrus, but also boats (Isaiah 18:2).

The land of Canaan was God's gift to the Israelites. The land was allocated to the tribes by lot. God determined the fall of the lot, so each tribe's area of land was God-given.

Within the tribes, each family was given its own plot of land which was to be treasured by the family for all generations (Isaiah 34:17).

When Naboth refused to sell his land to King Ahab, he was not being churlish. To sell would have been to rebel against God, who had given the land. Queen Jezebel, who was a foreigner, did not understand this.

If a family fell into debt and had to sell its land, the nearest relative bought it, to keep it within the family. Every fifty years all land had to be returned to the family. This preserved equality.

In the time of the kings, rich families bought the lands of poor people, and built up large estates, while the poor, unable to grow their own crops, became very poor. The prophets spoke out against this (Micah 2:2).

Facts 7

When a man was plowing a field, he had to keep his eyes straight ahead and not look back (Luke 9:62). This was not only to keep a straight furrow, but because the ground was often hard, in spite of the rains, and full of stones.

The roots of the broom tree were an excellent source of charcoal (Psalm 120:4).

The gardens of Assyrian and Babylonian kings were famous for their many varieties of trees and shrubs.

The plant that grew up to shelter Jonah from the sun was probably a castor oil plant, which is noted for the rapidity of its growth.

Boundary stones marked the edges of land belonging to one family. The Israelites were to resist the temptation to move an ancient boundary stone in an attempt to grab more land for themselves (Deuteronomy 19:14).

Frankincense is a resin obtained from the gum of trees in the Boswellia family, which grow in Arabia, Ethiopia, and India. When the bark is cut, the resin oozes out and hardens into whitish drops which are then collected and processed.

Frankincense was often carried by camels along the ancient spice routes. The traders added their overheads, and frankincense was very expensive by the time it reached Jerusalem.

Frankincense was the most important ingredient in the incense which priests burnt on the altar to make a sweet-smelling smoke. It was also added to the olive oil with which priests were anointed, and was made into a perfume.

Myrrh is an aromatic resin collected from a prickly shrub which grows in the deserts of north-east Africa and southern Arabia. When the branches are cut the brownish resin oozes out and hardens.

Like frankincense, myrrh was very expensive. It was made into a perfume (Song of Songs 3:6) and was added to oil for anointing priests. Myrrh was also one of the aromatic substances that was rubbed on a corpse in preparation for burial.

Miraculous
Events

Quiz #1

1. Who was struck blind on the road to Damascus as he sought to persecute Christians?

2. Who did Paul strike blind as a punishment?

3. How many of Jesus' recorded miracles took place on the Sabbath?

4. In the Old Testament who was told that the Lord would take away all sickness from them?

5. When the Israelites were fleeing from the Egyptians, what happened when Moses raised his staff and stretched his hand over the sea?

6. True or false? The word "miracle" never occurs in the New Testament outside the four Gospels.

7. Who saw a bush on fire that did not burn?

8. How long had Lazarus been dead when Jesus raised him to life?

9. When did the sun and moon stand still?

10. True or false? Elijah went up to heaven in a chariot of fire.

11. Who wrote that the apostles did many wonders and miraculous signs?

12. When Philip the deacon cast out evil spirits what noise was heard?

13. Which of Jesus' half-brothers experienced a resurrection appearance of the risen Lord Jesus Christ?

14. Who did an angel of the Lord tell to go to the desert road that links Gaza and Jerusalem?

15. As they had no boats, how were the Israelites able to cross the river Jordan?

Answers

1. Saul who was later called Paul 2. Elymas 3. 7 4. The Israelites 5. The waters divided 6. False (Galatians 3:5) 7. Moses 8. 4 days 9. When Joshua defeated the Amorites 10. False. Elijah went up in a whirlwind (2 Kings 2:11) 11. Luke 12. Shrieking 13. James 14. Philip 15. The waters stopped flowing

Quiz #2

1. True or false? Jesus never healed a woman.

2. What happened when Elijah struck the waters of the river Jordan with his cloak?

3. Which famous general was healed of his leprosy by dipping himself in a river?

4. How many times did this general dip himself in the river?

5. What was the first thing the general said after he was healed?

6. Which Old Testament prophet had a vision in which he was lifted up by the hair of his head?

7. True or false? Jairus' daughter was twelve years old when Jesus brought her back to life.

8. Which of Jesus' apostles walked on water?

9. Which Old Testament book mentions twice, "miracles that cannot be counted"?

10. Who became silent when Barnabas and Paul recounted the miracles they had performed among the Gentiles?

11. Which Gospel writer records the healing of the official's son as the second miraculous sign Jesus did?

12. After Elijah prayed, how long did the drought last?

13. The first miracle the Bible records is the creation of the world by God. Which Bible book is this in?

14. What happened to Moses' hand when he put it inside his cloak to perform a miraculous sign?

15. What was the first of the plagues with which God punished Pharaoh?

Answers

1. False (Matthew 8:14-15) **2.** The waters divided **3.** Naaman **4.** 7 times
5. "Now I know that there is no God in all the world except in Israel!" **6.** Ezekiel
7. True (Luke 8:42) **8.** Peter **9.** Job **10.** The council at Jerusalem **11.** John **12.** Three and a half years
13. Genesis **14.** It became leprous **15.** The water of the river Nile was turned into blood

Quiz #3

1. Luke 9:1-2 records Jesus sending out his twelve disciples to preach about the kingdom of God. What else did Jesus tell them to do?

2. True or false? When a blind beggar kept calling out to Jesus, those around Jesus told him to be quiet.

3. If the Greeks looked for wisdom, what did Jews demand?

4. When James' letter refers to the miraculous drought in Elijah's time, what in particular about Elijah does James remind his readers about?

5. Who was promised, "The jar of flour will not be used up and the jug of oil will not run dry until the day of the Lord gives rain on the land"?

6. Which Old Testament prophet likened the glory of God to a rainbow on a rainy day?

7. On which day did the religious leaders object to Jesus healing people?

8. Who raised the son of the widow of Zarephath from the dead?

9. Who was healed after she touched the edge of Jesus' cloak?

10. What was the second of the plagues God punished Pharaoh with?

11. Against the people of which town did God send an outbreak of tumors?

12. True or false? Jesus never told his disciples to heal the sick and to raise the dead.

13. Which New Testament book, outside the Gospels, mentions at least four resurrection appearances of Jesus?

14. Why did Jesus do so few miracles among the people of his own home town?

15. Matthew explains in his Gospel that Jesus' conception was miraculous. Which Old Testament prophet does he quote in support of this?

Answers

1. To heal the sick 2. True (Luke 18:39) 3. Miraculous signs 4. Elijah's earnest prayer
5. The widow at Zarephath 6. Ezekiel 7. The Sabbath (our Saturday) 8. Elijah
9. A woman who had been bleeding for 12 years 10. A plague of frogs 11. Gath 12. False (Matthew 10:8)
13. 1 Corinthians 14. Because of their lack of faith 15. Isaiah

Quiz #4

1. True or false? According to John very few believed in Jesus when they saw his miracles.

2. After being cursed by Elisha how many youths were killed by two bears?

3. True or false? Peter went into the empty tomb, where Jesus had been, before John did.

4. How many of Jesus' miracles are linked to him having authority over the forces of nature?

5. Who visited Jesus at night and said that nobody could do the miracles Jesus did if he was not from God?

6. After Elijah was taken to heaven in a whirlwind what was the first thing Elisha did?

7. What was the third of the plagues with which God punished Pharaoh?

8. Where was the angel of the Lord standing when the plague that killed 70,000 Israelites stopped?

9. Who said that it was impossible for anyone to do a miracle in his name and then say something bad about him?

10. Whose son did Elisha raise from the dead?

11. What happened to King Jeroboam's arm when he ordered that a man of God should be seized?

12. About whom was this question asked, "Why do you look for the living among the dead"?

13. What musical instrument was being played when Elisha had a vision about water being supplied for armies and cattle?

14. When Jesus visited the place where Lazarus had been buried, what did he do?

15. Which married couple dropped down dead after lying about the price they sold a piece of property for?

Answers

1. False. "Many" people believed (John 2:23) **2.** 42 **3.** True (John 20:6) **4.** 9
5. Nicodemus **6.** Elisha picked up Elijah's cloak and struck the waters of the river Jordan so they parted
7. A plague of gnats **8.** The threshing-floor of Araunah the Jebusite **9.** Jesus **10.** The son of a Shunammite woman
11. It shriveled up **12.** The risen Jesus **13.** The harp **14.** Jesus wept **15.** Ananias and Sapphira

Quiz #5

1. True or false? Jesus healed Peter's father-in-law.

2. When Moses, Aaron, Aaron's two eldest sons and seventy of Israel's elders saw the God of Israel, what did they see under God's feet?

3. Who said that he had to boast about visions and revelations he had from God?

4. What happened to some of the immoral men of Sodom just before Lot was rescued?

5. If a Christian is ill in bed who should be called in, according to James?

6. Who saw amazing visions when he was in the Spirit on the Lord's day?

7. True or false? There are more miracles in the New Testament linked to Paul than to Peter.

8. Which Old Testament king was told that he would be healed and that the shadow of the sun would go backwards?

9. How many of Jesus' miracles in John's Gospel took place on the Sabbath?

10. Whose staff did Gehazi lay on a dead boy in a vain attempt to bring him back to life?

11. What were the names of the two people the risen Jesus spoke to on the road to Emmaus?

12. God promised that a married couple would miraculously have a child. The husband was a hundred years old and the wife ninety years old. What were their names?

13. Who was turned into a pillar of salt for looking back at the cities of Sodom and Gomorrah?

14. Isaac prayed to the Lord that his barren wife might become pregnant. God miraculously answered this prayer and Rebekah had twins. What were the names of the twins?

15. About whom is it said in the book of Genesis that God remembered her, listened to her and opened her womb?

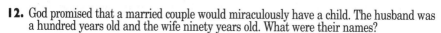

Answers

13. Lot's wife 14. Esau and Jacob 15. Rachel

11. We are only told the name of one of them: Cleopas 12. Abraham and Sarah

5. The elders 6. John, the writer of the book of Revelation 7. True 8. Hezekiah 9. 2 10. Elisha's

1. False. It was Peter's mother-in-law (Mark 1:30) 2. Something like a pavement 3. Paul 4. They were blinded

Quiz #6

1. In John's Gospel, just before the feeding of the 5,000, a great crowd followed Jesus because of the miracles he had performed on whom?

2. Which Old Testament prophet promised that "the ears of the deaf would be unstopped"?

3. Who, in Genesis 38, did the Lord kill because of his wickedness?

4. True or false? Anybody who saw Jesus' miracles automatically became a believer in Jesus.

5. Who did Paul predict would display all kinds of counterfeit miracles?

6. Who was killed in the tenth and final plague that struck Egypt?

7. True or false? Four times in his letters Paul mentions that ill Christians should be anointed with oil.

8. Which Old Testament prophet made bad spring water wholesome?

9. Just before he became the first Christian martyr, who saw a vision of God's glory with Jesus standing at God's right hand?

10. What did God do as a result of people trying to make a name for themselves by building the tower of Babel?

11. What was the fourth of the plagues with which God punished Pharaoh?

12. Which Old Testament prophet increased a widow's supply of oil?

13. Which two people from the Old Testament appeared with Jesus at his transfiguration?

14. After Jesus healed a man who was blind and mute, who did the Pharisees say Jesus used to drive out demons?

15. Which Old Testament prophet had a dream about four beasts?

Answers

1. The sick **2.** Isaiah **3.** Er

4. False. Many people did not believe in Jesus, even though they witnessed his miracles

5. The lawless one **6.** All the firstborn of Egypt **7.** False. This is only mentioned in James' letter (James 5:14)

8. Elisha **9.** Stephen **10.** The Lord confused the language of the whole world **11.** A plague of flies

12. Elisha **13.** Moses and Elijah **14.** Beelzebub **15.** Daniel

Quiz #7

1. To whom did Jesus say, "Daughter your faith has healed you. Go in peace and be freed from your suffering"?

2. The three women who went to Jesus' tomb wondered who would roll the stone away for them. Who, according to Matthew, did this?

3. True or false? Miraculous powers are included by Paul in his list of spiritual gifts.

4. Which Old Testament prophet was credited with the ability of knowing the words the king of Aram spoke in his bedroom?

5. Where was Paul when the islanders thought he was a god because he did not die after being bitten by a snake?

6. Which is the only miracle of Jesus recorded in all four Gospels?

7. What was the fifth of the plagues with which God punished Pharaoh?

8. Which army did Elisha strike blind?

9. True or false? After appearing to the two people on the road to Emmaus, the risen Jesus appeared to the eleven disciples who thought he was a ghost.

10. Who was seen in the fiery furnace with Shadrach, Meshach, and Abednego?

11. What explanation did Daniel give for not being mauled to death when he was in the lions' pit?

12. When Jonah was thrown overboard into a raging sea, what happened to the sea?

13. What did God send to rescue Jonah from the sea?

14. What did God provide Jonah with as he sat in the sun, east of the city of Nineveh?

15. Where did Jesus' ascension take place according to Luke's Gospel?

Answers

1. The woman who had been suffering from bleeding for twelve years 2. An angel of the Lord 3. True (1 Corinthians 12:10) 4. Elisha 5. Malta 6. The feeding of the 5,000 7. A plague of livestock 8. The Syrian army 9. True (Luke 24:37) 10. One who looked like the son of the gods 11. Because God sent his angel to shut the mouths of the lions 12. The sea became calm 13. A great fish 14. A vine (NIV), gourd (KJV) 15. The vicinity of Bethany

Quiz #8

1. True or false? The woman Jesus cured of bleeding had been ill in this way for twelve years.

2. Who, according to Paul in 2 Thessalonians 2:10, would be deceived by counterfeit miracles?

3. Some Jews said that since Jesus had opened the eyes of the blind could he not have prevented a friend of his from dying Jesus went on to raise his friend to life. Who was the friend?

4. What was the sixth of the plagues with which God punished Pharaoh?

5. True or false? More than thirty miracles are associated with Moses.

6. True or false? When Mary Magdalene first saw the risen Jesus she mistook him for a shepherd.

7. While listening to Paul speaking Eutychus fell out of a window and died. What did Paul do?

8. How did Joseph know that he had to take Jesus and Mary and flee to Egypt?

9. Who did Jesus heal because of Peter's action?

10. Who stopped a man from driving out demons in Jesus' name?

11. What was the result of Peter healing Aeneas?

12. What did Paul do to a slave girl who was able to predict the future?

13. What did the psalmist tell the descendants of Abraham and the sons of Jacob to remember?

14. When the risen Jesus told some of his disciples to throw their nets into the water to catch fish, did he say to throw the nets over the right or the left hand side of the boat?

15. How many baskets full of broken pieces were left over after Jesus fed 4,000 people?

Answers

1. True (Luke 8:43) **2.** Those who are perishing **3.** Lazarus **4.** A plague of boils **5.** True **6.** False. She mistook him for the gardener (John 20:15) **7.** Paul brought him back to life to the Lord **12.** Commanded the spirit in her to come out of her **13.** God's wonders and miracles **8.** The Lord appeared to him in a dream **9.** Malchus **10.** John **11.** The people who lived in Lydda and Sharon turned **14.** The right hand side of the boat **15.** 7

Quiz #9

1. What was the ninth plague with which God punished Pharaoh?

2. Who met Moses in the desert, kissed him and then was told by Moses about all the miraculous signs God had commanded him to perform?

3. Who did Paul write to telling him not to ignore his gift?

4. As he was holding two stone tablets whose face was seen to be radiant because he had been in the Lord's presence?

5. During Jesus' transfiguration, what did Peter suggest they should assemble?

6. During Jesus' transfiguration, what did he speak about?

7. After one person was healed on a certain island, all the people came to be healed by whom, according to Dr. Luke?

8. Who gave an interpretation which came true about a dream concerning seven fat cows and seven lean cows?

9. Who said, "If you forgive anyone his sins, they are forgiven"?

10. During Jesus' transfiguration, what words did the three disciples hear?

11. Which Old Testament prophet told a king that there "is a God in heaven who reveals mysteries" ?

12. What miracle took place after Jesus' transfiguration?

13. Who demanded that his dream should be interpreted but would not say what his dream was?

14. Through what kind of message did Timothy receive his spiritual gift?

15. To whom did Jesus say, "Everything is possible for him who believes." ?

Quiz #10

1. What kind of prayer, according to James' letter, will make a sick person better?

2. Who saw Peter and John laying hands on people and asked if he could buy this ability to give the Spirit?

3. How many days, according to Daniel's vision, would there be between the daily sacrifice being abolished and the setting up of the abomination that caused desolation?

4. Which Old Testament king wrote, "It is my pleasure to tell you about the miraculous signs and wonders that the Most High God has performed for me"?

5. After the disciples had caught no fish all night long Jesus told them to go out into the deep and let down their nets. What happened?

6. What did Peter say to Simon the sorcerer as he tried to buy the Holy Spirit?

7. True or false? When Jesus healed ten lepers, only two came back to thank Jesus.

8. How many of Jesus' miraculous signs are recorded in John's Gospel?

9. What was distinctive about the healed leper who returned to thank Jesus?

10. What did the Psalmist say took place in the land of Egypt, in the region of Zoan?

11. At what time of day did the first miracle recorded in the book of Acts take place?

12. How old was the man who was the first person to be healed in the book of Acts?

13. According to Deuteronomy, if a prophet predicts a miraculous sign that does take place, how can you tell if he is false prophet?

14. When Jesus turned water into wine at Cana, John says that the master of the banquet was unaware of this. But who was aware?

15. When false messiahs come what did Jesus say they would do?

Answers

1. The prayer offered in faith 2. Simon 3. 1,290 days 4. Nebuchadnezzar
5. They caught so many fish that their nets began to break 6. May your money perish with you, because you thought that you could buy the gift of God with money 7. False. Only one came back to thank Jesus (Luke 17:16)
8. Eight 9. He was a Samaritan 10. Miracles 11. At three in the afternoon 12. Over 40 years old
13. He is a false prophet if he says, "Let us follow other gods"
14. The servants who had filled the six stone water jars 15. Perform signs and miracles

301

Quiz #11

1. Which Old Testament prophet said, "I will pour out my Spirit on all people"?

2. When God's Spirit is poured out on all people what will sons and daughters do?

3. When God's Spirit is poured out on all people what will old men do?

4. When God's Spirit is poured out on all people who will see visions?

5. After Jesus called out, "Lazarus, come out!" what is the very next thing that happened according to John's Gospel?

6. After Jesus had raised Lazarus from the dead what did the chief priests plan to do to Lazarus?

7. After Philip had baptized the Ethiopian eunuch why did he not see Philip again?

8. When Paul asked the disciples at Ephesus if they had received the Holy Spirit how did they reply?

9. What outward sign did Paul use as the Holy Spirit came on the disciples at Ephesus?

10. When the crowds saw the miraculous signs Philip did in the city of Samaria how did they respond?

11. True or false? When the disciples at Ephesus received the Holy Spirit they spoke in tongues.

12. True or false? When the disciples at Ephesus received the Holy Spirit they prophesied.

13. Approximately how many disciples at Ephesus received the Holy Spirit through Paul's ministry?

14. What did the people of Lydda and Sharon do when they saw the man who had been healed by Peter?

15. Jesus predicted that with false 'Christs' another group of people would also appear? Who would they be?

Facts 1

After being involved in the miraculous incident with Eutychus Paul did not comment on the miracle. He carried on teaching until dawn as his overriding concern was to build up the believers at Troas.

The temple tax which Jesus told Peter to find in a fish's mouth (Matthew 17:24-27) was the tax that every male from the age of 20 had to pay each year and was used to pay for looking after the temple.

Jesus told his 72 disciples that he saw Satan fall as a result of them exorcizing demons. This was a clear indication that Satan was being defeated.

In Jacob's dream at Bethel he saw a "ladder" (KJV) extending from earth to heaven. Angels were able to go up and down it because it was not a ladder with rungs, but rather a stairway as would have been found at the side of ziggurats.

Jesus said that his followers would do greater miracles than he had done (John 14:12). Once Jesus returned to the Father, he would send the Holy Spirit in whose power these miracles would be performed.

Miracles often appear in clusters in the Bible. For example, as Ahab and Jezebel tried to make Baal the official deity of Israel the miraculous ministries of Elijah and Elisha were empowered by the Lord.

One of the Greek words used for miracles in the New Testament is *dunamis* (Acts 2:22) from which we derive the word "dynamite".

When the Pharisees accused Jesus of driving out demons using Beelzebub's power Jesus said that the Pharisees were guilty of blasphemy against the Spirit. Beelzebub, the prince of the demons, was the name used of Satan.

When Jonathan and his armor-bearer won a victory over the Philistines, the Israelites gave God the credit for a miraculous deliverance. Even the panic that overtook the Philistines was attributed to the Lord.

General Naaman was told to dip himself in the river Jordan. He was upset at the thought of a 25 mile journey to a muddy, meandering river. He considered the rivers of Damascus, Abana and Pharpar, superior to any waters of Israel.

Facts 2

One of the greatest groupings of miracles in the Bible are the twenty-one miracles associated with Elijah and Elisha. They witnessed to God's power as the Israelites were called back to the Lord, the true God.

Paul wrote that he was once caught up into the "third heaven" (2 Corinthians 12:2-3). If the first heaven is the earth's atmosphere, and the second heaven is the heaven of space, the "third" heaven is God's presence.

Jesus performed his miracles in a different way from anybody else. Prophets healed in the name of God. Jesus healed with the same authority that he forgave sins.

When the Israelites fled from Egypt, all night long a strong east wind drove the water back so Moses and the Israelites could cross over the sea on dry land. This natural phenomena is said to be the work of the Lord as it happened at the precise moment that it was so desperately needed.

Two of the wise men, sorcerers and Egyptian magicians who opposed Moses (Exodus 7:11) are, according to tradition, named by Paul in 2 Timothy 3:8 as Jannes and Jambres.

Mark 16:18 speaks about people being able to pick up snakes in the hands, drink poison and be unharmed and heal the sick. There is serious doubt about the authenticity of Mark 16:9-20 as it is missing in the earliest manuscripts of Mark's Gospel.

When a dead man's body touched the bones of the prophet Elisha the dead man came alive. The was the final time that Elisha demonstrated God's life-giving power.

The first thing Matthew's Gospel records after Jesus died is that the curtain in the temple was torn from top to bottom. This was a vivid symbol of Jesus' death providing access to God, as this curtain cut everyone off from God's presence.

Jesus' miracles did not always create faith. They gave people the opportunity to choose between faith and unbelief. After Lazarus was brought back to life some Jews believed while other Jews reported the matter to the Pharisees.

A mother from outside Palestine asked Jesus to help her demon-possessed daughter. Jesus said, "It is not right to take the children's bread and toss it to the dogs." This suggests that the the gospel was for the Jews first of all.

Facts 3

In the Old Testament one of the purposes of the miracles was to demonstrate that the God of Israel was completely different from the local gods. He was the one and only true and living God.

The letter to the Hebrews states that miracles, such as the supernatural healing of the sick, as well as signs and wonders, confirm the gospel message of salvation (Hebrews 2:3-4).

Mark states that Jesus touched and healed a leper. According to the Mosaic law you became defiled if you touched a leper. However, Jesus' great compassion for the leper overrode any ceremonial traditions.

When Jesus forgave the sins of the paralytic who had been let down by his four friends from the roof, the teachers of the law objected. Jesus had dealt with his greatest need. To show his authority to do this Jesus healed the paralytic.

After the miraculous catch of fish Jesus called his first disciples to follow him. Only great rabbis had the prerogative to gather round them a group of disciples. This was seen as a claim to authority and angered the Pharisees.

Jesus' resurrection was quite different from the raising to life of other people in the New Testament. They all died again. Jesus was raised to life and now lives for ever.

In the Old Testament a miracle is never an isolated fact. It is linked to other events. God's extraordinary interventions always said or announced something. To an Israelite the question to ask was, "What is the meaning of the miracle?"

When Jesus healed Peter's mother-in-law's fever he held her hand. Her healing was instantaneous and complete so she was able to serve them food immediately.

Jesus told his 12 disciples not to rejoice so much that the spirits were subject to them but to rejoice that their names were written in heaven. Jesus taught that salvation is more important than having miraculous power.

After Abraham's servant had found Rebekah he worshiped God. He took this meeting as a sign of God's intervention believing he had been divinely led on his journey to the house of his master's relatives.

Facts 4

The appearance of Moses and Elijah at Jesus' transformation are taken to represent the law and the prophets, and that Jesus was now fulfilling everything spoken in them.

Matthew's Gospel is the only one to record that just after Jesus died tombs broke open and holy people were brought to life. If an earthquake opened the tombs, Jesus' resurrection made the rising of these people possible.

Matthew 9:27-31 records Jesus healing two blind men. He told them not to tell anyone about it. Jesus would choose when the time was right for his miracles to be made public.

When Jesus told his 72 disciples that he had given them power over snakes and scorpions he may have been referring to evil spirits as he went on to say that they would overcome the enemy, who was Satan.

In the New Testament a divine action which might have an ordinary outward appearance, is seen, through the eye of faith, as a miracle. But an extraordinary phenomenon, unrelated to faith, is not a miracle.

The earliest form of ministry in the New Testament was charismatic. It was a supernatural gift or endowment and bore witness to the power and presence of the Holy Spirit.

Many of the miracles recorded in the Bible were meant for the encouragement of God's people and were not primarily for unbelievers.

When Jesus healed Jairus' daughter he said in Alamaic, "Talitha koum!" ("Little girl, I say to you, get up!" Mark 5:41) Alamaic was probably the language Jesus spoke.

The healing of the blind man at Bethsaida is the only miracle of Jesus that happened in two stages. With Jesus' first touch the blind man saw but he needed Jesus' second touch to see things as they really were.

Isaiah ordered that a poultice made from figs should be applied to King Hezekiah's boil. This healed him. God uses ordinary remedies but remains the divine healer.

Facts 5

The Bible offers no explanation about how King Hezekiah was able to see the shadow of the sun go back ten steps on a stairway. It was a dramatic symbol of extra time being given.

The Pharisees accused Jesus of breaking the Sabbath because when he healed a blind man he applied mud to his eyes. This involved mixing saliva and mud from the ground and the Pharisees said this was work.

In the book of Acts the first person to have performed great wonders and miraculous signs who was not an apostle was Stephen. The working of miracles was not exclusive to the apostles.

Jesus went up to a fig tree to see if it had any fruit in mid-April. The leaves of the fig trees in Palestine appear in March accompanied by a crop of edible knobs called *taksh*. If there are no *taksh*, there will be no edible fruit that year.

When Jesus cursed the fig tree for having no fruit he enacted out a piece of dramatic symbolism. Just as the fig tree had leaves but no fruit, so the Jews made a great show of outward religious observance but produced no spiritual fruit.

Among the spiritual gifts Paul lists is healing. Paul actually uses a double plural "gifts of healings" (1 Corinthians 12:9). This suggests a variety of healings to deal with a variety of diseases.

When Mary Magdalene, Mary the mother of James, and Salome went to Jesus' tomb they found that the stone across the entrance of the cave had already been rolled back. This was not to let Jesus out, but to let the women in.

People who do not have faith in God nearly always missed God's miraculous interventions. So Pharaoh, despite the extraordinary plagues in his land, saw nothing divine in them. They only hardened his heart against God.

When Jesus started his ministry it was a time when the Jews were running after people who performed miracles. Jesus, however, rejected the temptation to be a wonder-worker (Matthew 4:5-6).

Most of the miracles recorded in the Bible took place at critical times in the history of God's people. They took place leading up to and during the Exodus, in the days of Elijah and Elisha, and in the ministry of Jesus.

Facts 6

2 Kings 4:42-44 records how 20 loaves of bread, similar to our rolls, miraculously feed 100 men. The loaves were multiplied as a result of God's word without Elisha doing anything.

An ax-head fell into a river so Elisha threw a stick after it and it floated. As the ax-head was expensive and was borrowed the prophet who used it might have had to become a bond-slave until he had paid back the value of the ax-head.

In Isaiah's vision of the Lord the prophet also saw seraphs. Only in this place in the Bible are they are mentioned. The root meaning of seraphs in Hebrew is "burn" indicating their purity as they ministered in God's presence.

The miracles of the Bible had a specific purpose. For example, the plagues in Egypt were performed by the Lord as "wonders" so that the Israelites would be freed.

On the Day of Pentecost Peter said in his sermon that "Jesus of Nazareth was a man accredited by God to you by miracles, wonders and signs" (Acts 2:22). Peter meant that such miracles demonstrated that Jesus was the Messiah.

When Jesus healed a deaf and mute man he put his fingers in the man's ears and spat and touched the man's tongue. In this way Jesus communicated to the deaf and mute man what he was about to do. Saliva was thought to have healing properties.

Some modern writers accuse Jesus and the Gospel writers of confusing mental illness with demon possession. Mark clearly distinguishes (1:32-34) between the sick and the demon-possessed, who were both healed by Jesus.

When Elisha was told in a vision that the Lord would provide water for the kings of Israel, Judah and Edom, the Lord also told him what to do. He was told to make the valley full of ditches. God provided water through flash floods because of Elisha's obedience.

Joshua 10:13 records that the sun stopped and delayed going down. Many possible interpretations have been suggested but the Bible offers no explanation, beyond it being a dramatic sign of divine intervention.

When Jesus gave sight it was a sign that he was fulfilling what God had promised his Messiah would do. "Then the eyes of the blind will be opened" (Isaiah 35:5).

Angels Among Us

Quiz #1

1. How many angels persuaded Lot to leave the city of Sodom before it was destroyed?

2. Which animals had their mouths shut by an angel in the book of Daniel?

3. The Old Testament prophet Zechariah met an angel among which type of tree?

4. Which prophetic book records the destruction of Sennacherib's army by an angel of God?

5. How many angels appeared to the shepherds at the time of Jesus' birth?

6. In the Old Testament, how many men were killed by an angel following David's census of his fighting men?

7. Who, according to Paul in his letter to Timothy, was "vindicated by the Spirit and seen by angels"?

8. When an angel appeared to Peter in prison how did he wake the apostle?

9. An angel appeared to Hagar, concerning her son. What was the name of her son?

10. According to Acts which believer had the face of an angel?

11. True or false? Jesus never spoke about angels.

12. In Galatians, what does Paul say was put into effect through the mediation of angels?

13. During his escape from prison in Acts how many guards did the angel lead Peter past?

14. In Revelation 8 an angel fills a censer with fire and flings it where?

15. According to Luke what proof did the angel give to Mary that his words were true?

Answers

1. 2 **2.** Lions **3.** Myrtle **4.** Isaiah **5.** A multitude of the heavenly host **6.** 70,000 **7.** Jesus **8.** He struck him in the side **9.** Ishmael **10.** Stephen **11.** False (Matthew 18:10) **12.** The law **13.** 2 guards **14.** On earth **15.** The fact that her cousin Elizabeth was pregnant

Quiz #2

1. What was the name of the angel who told Mary she was going to have a baby?

2. After his confrontation with the prophets of Baal, Elijah fell asleep only to be woken by an angel who told him to do what?

3. An angel appeared to Mary in the sixth month of what?

4. How did angels help Jesus during and after his temptation in the desert?

5. In the book of Kings an angel found Elijah sleeping under which type of tree?

6. In the Old Testament, who claimed an angel had rescued Shadrach, Meshach and Abednego from the fiery furnace?

7. According to the Gospels, where did the angel tell the women Jesus had gone after his resurrection?

8. True or false? Paul says that nothing can separate Christians from God's love, not even angels.

9. To whom did an angel say, "Greetings, you who are highly favored!"?

10. What sort of angel is Michael?

11. According to Psalm 34, whom does the angel of the Lord encamp around?

12. In Acts an angel appears to Paul during a storm telling him he would stand trial before whom?

13. In Judges, what did an angel ask Gideon to place on a rock?

14. In Revelation 20, an angel is seen holding what?

15. In Acts, where was Stephen when his face was said to be like that of an angel?

Answers

1. Gabriel **2.** To get up and eat some food **3.** Of Elizabeth's pregnancy
4. They attended him **5.** A broom tree **6.** Nebuchadnezzar **7.** To Galilee **8.** True (Romans 8:38-40)
9. Mary, the mother of Jesus **10.** An archangel **11.** Those who fear him **12.** Caesar
13. Meat and unleavened bread **14.** The key to the abyss **15.** In the Sanhedrin

Quiz #3

1. When Zechariah refused to believe his wife was going to have a son how did the angel punish him?

2. True or false? When he was arrested, Jesus told his followers that if necessary he could call upon more than ten legions of angels to help him.

3. After his meeting with the angel in 1 Kings, where did Elijah travel to?

4. Where was Gideon when he was visited by an Angel?

5. According to Matthew, how many times did an angel appear to Joseph?

6. In Revelation 8, how many angels were given trumpets?

7. In Luke, what did the angel say that Zechariah's son must not do?

8. In Matthew 28, to whom did the angels tell the women to go?

9. Which angel's name means "Who is like God"?

10. In the New. True of false? The angels who came to rescue Lot and his family from Sodom spent the night in the town square.

11. The angel Gabriel told Mary that her child would be called the son of whom?

12. In Matthew 25, what does Jesus say is prepared for the devil and all his angels?

13. According to Matthew what noise will accompany the sending of angels when the Son of Man appears?

14. In Genesis 16, what did the angel tell Hagar to do?

15. In the Old Testament where was Lot sitting when the angels appeared to him?

Answers

1. He made him unable to speak until the child was born 2. False, Jesus said more than 12 legions (Matthew 26:53)
3. Horeb 4. At the threshing floor of Araunah the Jebusite 5. 3 times 6. 7 angels
7. Drink wine or fermented drink 8. To the disciples 9. Michael 10. False, they stayed in his house
11. Son of the Most High 12. The eternal fire 13. A loud trumpet call
14. Return to Sarah 15. In the gateway of the city of Sodom

Quiz #4

1. In Genesis as Jacob set out to meet Esau where did he encounter the angels of God?

2. In the New Testament, what name did the angel tell Zechariah to give to his son?

3. True or false? In Psalm 78 the manna eaten by the Israelites is called the bread of angels.

4. In Matthew's Gospel, where was the angel when he addressed the women after the resurrection?

5. According to Luke, why did Zechariah doubt the angel's words?

6. According to Revelation 16, angels held bowls containing what?

7. In Acts what did the angel rescuing Peter from prison tell him to put on?

8. At what point after his rescue from prison did the angel leave the apostle Peter?

9. What did Paul charge Timothy to do in the sight of the elect angels?

10. In Genesis, why did angels come to Sodom?

11. True or false? Mary did not question the pronouncement made by the angel Gabriel.

12. According to the apostle Paul, what should be the fate of an angel who attempts to preach a different gospel?

13. In Revelation 8, which musical instruments were given to the angels?

14. In Judges, when Manoah the father of Samson asked an angel for his name, what was the angel's reply?

15. What fact, according to Jesus in Matthew 24, are angels ignorant of?

Answers

1. Mahanaim **2.** John **3.** True (Psalm 78:25) **4.** Sitting on the rolled back entrance stone **5.** He and Elizabeth were old **6.** God's wrath **7.** His clothes and sandals **8.** After they had walked the length of one street **9.** To keep the instructions he had given him, without partiality **10.** To destroy it **11.** False. Mary asked how, as a virgin, she could have a child (Luke 1:34) **12.** Eternal condemnation **13.** Trumpets **14.** It is beyond understanding **15.** The day of Christ's return

Quiz #5

1. How does Paul describe Satan in his second letter to the Corinthians?

2. As recorded by Deborah's song in Judges, who did the angel command to be cursed?

3. Who were told of the birth of Jesus by a huge number of angels?

4. At Jesus' birth, where did the shepherds go when the angels had left them?

5. In 2 Kings 1 an angel appears to Elijah with a message for which king?

6. In Genesis, an angel likened Hagar's son to which animal?

7. What did the angel that Balaam saw have in his hand?

8. True or false? Paul says that a destroying angel killed some people for grumbling.

9. True or false? In Numbers the angel told Balaam to return home.

10. What happened to Jesus when Satan left him after tempting him in the wilderness?

11. The angel told Zechariah that his son would come in the power of which Old Testament prophet?

12. In John's Gospel, when a voice from heaven was heard, who thought it was an angel?

13. True or false? Cherubim are angels.

14. Who, did Paul say, were a spectacle to the whole universe, including angels?

15. Who, according to Psalm 8, was made a little lower than the angels?

Quiz #6

1. In Genesis, which crying mother was found by an angel of the Lord in the desert of Beersheba?

2. Which apostle was rescued by an angel the night before he was due to stand trial?

3. According to the book of Jude, which angel argued with the devil concerning the body of Moses?

4. True or false? Two angels appeared to Jesus as he prayed on the Mount of Olives.

5. True or false? The Galatians welcomed Paul as if he were an angel.

6. In Numbers, when Balaam met with an angel, who was he on his way to see?

7. "For he will command his angels concerning you" comes from which Psalm?

8. In 1 Kings, what did an angel tell the exhausted Elijah to eat?

9. In Genesis, what did the angel of the Lord do when Pharaoh's army approached the fleeing Israelites?

10. In Genesis, Lot asked angels if he could flee to which city?

11. According to Revelation 16, how many angels held bowls containing God's wrath?

12. Who stopped Abraham from slaying his son Isaac?

13. True or false? An angel said that Ishmael would live in peace with his brothers.

14. According to Hebrews 1, what is the task of angels?

15. After his meeting with the angel in 1 Kings, how long did Elijah travel for?

Answers

1. Hagar 2. Peter 3. The archangel Michael 4. False, only one angel appeared (Luke 22:43)
5. True (Galatians 4:14) 6. Balak 7. Psalm 91 8. A cake of bread 9. He moved behind the Israelites
10. Zoar 11. Seven 12. An angel calling from heaven 13. False, he said he would live in hostility (Genesis 16:12)
14. To worship God's Son 15. 40 days and 40 nights

Quiz #7

1. According to the prophet Hosea, who struggled with an angel and overcame him?

2. What was the name of the Roman centurion who saw an angel at Caesarea?

3. In Chronicles God sent an angel to destroy which city?

4. According to the book of Job, what did the angels do at the act of creation?

5. What attitude towards angels is condemned by Paul in Colossians chapter 1?

6. In Genesis chapter 24, Abraham told his servant that an angel would go before him. For what purpose?

7. In which of his temptations of Jesus does Satan mentions angels?

8. Who is the first person in the New Testament who sees an angel?

9. In Numbers, what did the angel say he would have done to Balaam if his donkey had not seen him?

10. In Matthew 1, what did an angel prevent Joseph from doing?

11. In Genesis, when Hagar fled from Sarah, an angel found her beside which geographical feature?

12. According to the apostle Paul who will judge the angels?

13. Why did an angel call out to Abraham in the region of Moriah?

14. Where was the angel standing when Balaam's donkey saw it the second time?

15. According to Matthew, when did an angel appear to Joseph for the last time?

Answers

1. Jacob 2. Cornelius 3. Jerusalem 4. Shout for joy 5. Angel worship 6. To find a wife for Isaac
7. The second temptation 8. Zechariah 9. He would have killed him
10. Divorcing Mary 11. A spring
12. Christians 13. To stop him killing his son Isaac
14. Between two vineyards 15. After Herod's death

Quiz #8

1. How did an angel of the Lord first appear to Moses?

2. How did an angel appear to Joseph telling him not to divorce Mary?

3. An angel appeared to Gideon under which type of tree in Ophrah?

4. In Acts, Cornelius was told by an angel to send messengers to which city?

5. In which chapter of Isaiah does the prophet see seraphim and receive his call?

6. In Revelation 15 the plagues are held by how many angels?

7. In the Parable of the Weeds in Matthew 13, who does Jesus say represents angels?

8. According to Revelation 15 what did the angels hold?

9. According to Matthew what phenomenon was caused by the angel at the tomb of Jesus?

10. Who thought she saw Peter's angel when the apostle arrived at Mary's house after his escape from prison?

11. In Judges, how does the angel address Gideon when he first appears?

12. What did Manoah the father of Samson sacrifice to the angel?

13. True or false? In Luke's Gospel, the angel which appeared to Zechariah was standing on the left-hand side of the altar of incense.

14. In Genesis 16 what did Hagar name the place where she met an angel?

15. According to the angel why should Joseph and his family flee to Egypt?

Answers

1. In a burning bush 2. In a dream 3. An oak tree 4. Joppa 5. Isaiah 6
6. Seven 7. The harvesters 8. Plagues 9. An earthquake 10. Rhoda 11. Mighty Warrior
12. A goat 13. False. The angel was standing at the right hand side (Luke 1:11)
14. Beer Lahai Roi, Well of the Living One Who Sees Me 15. Herod was trying to kill Jesus

Quiz #9

1. In the book of Acts, Philip is told to go where by an angel?

2. The writer to the Hebrews describes someone who is far greater than angels. Who is this person?

3. In Genesis, what do angels inflict upon the men of Sodom?

4. What did David do that caused God to send an angel to destroy Israel?

5. How many times did an angel appear to Elijah after his ordeal with the prophets of Baal?

6. What happened to the meat and unleavened bread which the angel told Gideon to place on the altar?

7. True or false? According to Jesus in Matthew 22, angels do not marry.

8. What name did Abraham give to the place where an angel of the Lord stopped him from killing Isaac?

9. In Zechariah 5, what does the angel show the prophet?

10. What did Gabriel say about himself to Mary?

11. In which month of Elizabeth's pregnancy did God send the angel Gabriel to Mary?

12. In his speech in Acts what did Stephen say was put into effect by angels?

13. According to Matthew where did the angel tell Joseph to take Mary and Jesus?

14. Fill in the missing word: "If I speak in the tongues of ____ and of angels, but have not love..."

15. According to the angel, Zechariah's son would be filled with what from birth?

Answers

1. South, to the Jerusalem to Gaza road **2.** Jesus **3.** Blindness **4.** David took a census of the fighting men **5.** Twice **6.** It was consumed by fire **7.** True (Matthew 22:30) **8.** The Lord will provide **9.** A measuring basket **10.** "I am Gabriel. I stand in the presence of god" **11.** The sixth month **12.** The Law **13.** To Egypt **14.** Men **15.** The Holy Spirit

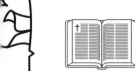

Facts 1

The Greek word *"angelos"* really means "messenger." It is translated in this way in the New Testament when it refers to a human being (e.g. Luke 7:24). However the word usually refers to a separately created order of heavenly beings.

"Cherubim" comes from the Hebrew *"kerub"* and probably means "fullness of knowledge" or "one who intercedes."

The name Gabriel means "hero of God" or "mighty one."

The idea that angels had wings evolved in the fourth century. Prior to that they were usually considered to be wingless.

Mark is the only gospel not to mention angels.

According to 2 Kings 19, the angel of the Lord killed 185,000 Assyrians.

Thanks to the intervention of the angels three people survived the destruction of Sodom: Lot and his two daughters.

There is nothing in the Bible to suggest that angels were ever human beings elevated to angelic status. Rather, angels are spiritual beings who were specially created by God (Hebrews 1:7).

In the time of Jesus the Sadducees did not believe in angels but the Pharisees did.

In both the Old and New Testaments the first accounts of visits from angels are to women – Hagar and Mary.

The idea of guardian angels describes God's watchful care over his people and this is mentioned occasionally in the Bible (Matthew 18:10; Hebrews 1:13-14). There are many examples of God's followers being helped by angels. Jesus himself was frequently helped by them.

Dreams, Visions and Prophecies

Quiz #1

I. According to Genesis, who did God promise to make the father of a great nation?

2. In the book of Revelation, which is the first Church that is given a prophetic message?

3. In Numbers, who did Balak ask to prophesy against the Israelites?

4. In which chapter of Deuteronomy does Moses predict the coming of another prophet?

5. According to Matthew, how did an angel first appear to Joseph?

6. In Isaiah 5 there is a song concerning what?

7. Which prophet was the son of Hilkiah?

8. In the Old Testament, which child received a prophesy concerning the sons of Eli the priest?

9. In his address on the day of Pentecost, Peter begins by quoting from which prophetic book?

10. What was the profession of Cornelius who was given a vision in Acts 10?

11. How many baskets did Pharaoh's baker see in a dream?

12. Which chapter of Ezekiel records the prophet's call?

13. In which chapter of Luke is Jesus met by a prophetess?

14. True or false? Elijah prophesied that there would be no rain in Israel for five years.

15. How many chapters are there in the book of the prophet Jeremiah?

---

15. 52

13. Chapter 2 **14.** False, he prophesied there would be a drought for three and a half years (James 5:17)

6. A vineyard **7.** Jeremiah **8.** Samuel **9.** Joel **10.** Soldier **11.** 3 **12.** Chapter 12

1. Abram **2.** The Church at Ephesus **3.** Balaam **4.** Chapter 18 **5.** In a dream

Answers

Quiz #2

1. In Genesis, what does Joseph see in his first dream?

2. Who, according to Peter on the day of Pentecost, will prophesy?

3. According to Revelation, where was John when he received the heavenly vision?

4. In the New Testament, who imprisoned the prophet John the Baptist?

5. According to Ezekiel 14, how many days was the prophet to bear the sin of Israel?

6. True or false? Jesus considered the Old Testament character Abel a prophet.

7. Which Old Testament character, who excelled in interpreting dreams, refused to eat from the king's table?

8. According to Isaiah's prophecy, what name would the virgin give to the child?

9. What is the name of the angel seen in Daniel 8?

10. In the Old Testament, whilst he was in prison, what interpretation did Joseph give to the baker's dream?

11. In which chapter of his prophecy does Ezekiel talk of shepherds and sheep?

12. Which Old Testament prophet had a father called Beeri?

13. According to 1 Kings 14, who prophesies against King Ahab?

14. Who was told to draw a picture representing Jerusalem on a clay tablet?

15. How many chapters are there in the book of Zechariah?

Answers

1. Sheaves of corn **2.** Your sons and daughters **3.** On the island of Patmos **4.** Herod
5. 390 days **6.** True (Luke 11:50,51) **7.** Daniel **8.** Immanuel **9.** Gabriel
10. He would be killed and hung on a tree, where the birds would eat his flesh **11.** Chapter 34
12. Hosea **13.** Micaiah **14.** Ezekiel **15.** 12

DREAMS, VISIONS AND PROPHECIES

Quiz #3

1. According to 1 Samuel 2, a man of God gave a prophecy concerning whose wicked sons?

2. True or false? Matthew tells us that an angel warned the wise men not to return to Herod in a dream.

3. In chapter 10 of his book, Daniel is standing by a river when he has a vision. Which river is it?

4. In which chapter of Genesis does God first promise to make Abram the father of a great nation?

5. True or false? According to 1 Kings 14 the house of king Jeroboam was destined to be burnt as if it were dung.

6. What does Nebuchadnezzar dream about in Daniel 4?

7. How many chapters are there in the prophecy of Ezekiel?

8. In the book of Revelation which is the last Church to receive a prophetic message?

9. True or false? The prophet Amos sees a tree of ripe fruit in the eighth chapter of his prophesy.

10. In which chapter of Isaiah do we find the question, "Who has believed our message?"?

11. How many chapters are there in the Old Testament prophecy of Obadiah?

12. According to the Old Testament, what new name was given to Daniel?

13. In 1 Kings 14 Ahijah prophesies against which evil king of Judah?

14. Which two birds are seen in Ezekiel 17?

15. According to Joseph what was the correct interpretation of Pharaoh's dreams?

---

14. 2 eagles 15. 7 years of plenty would be followed by 7 years of famine
11. 1 12. Belteshazzar 13. Jeroboam
8. The Church at Laodicea 9. False, he sees a basket of ripe fruit (Amos 8:1) 10. Chapter 53
3. The Tigris 4. Genesis 12 5. True (1 Kings 14:10) 6. A tree 7. 48
1. Eli's 2. False, there is no mention of an angel in their dream (Matthew 2:12)

Answers

Quiz #4

1. In Genesis, which officials of Pharaoh had dreams when they were in prison?

2. What is burnt in Jeremiah 36?

3. Who burnt the prophet's property in Jeremiah 36?

4. Which prophet saw visions in the "thirtieth year, in the fourth month on the fifth day"?

5. Who was the father of the prophet Joel?

6. In the Old Testament, Elijah defeated the prophets of which false god?

7. True or false? The book of Obadiah contains a prophecy for Midian.

8. When Jesus rode into Jerusalem on a donkey, whose words was he fulfilling?

9. Which prophetic book of the Old Testament begins with an invasion of locusts?

10. In Ezekiel 37 the prophet sees a valley of dry what?

11. In the vision of Revelation, which Church is described as being neither hot nor cold?

12. Which reluctant Old Testament prophet was the son of Amittai?

13. In the Old Testament what is the fate of the tree in Nebuchadnezzar's dream?

14. According to Luke, with what words did the prophet John the Baptist welcome those who came to him to be baptised?

15. In the Old Testament, Daniel has a vision of a man during the reign of which king?

Answers

1. Cup bearer and Baker 2. Jeremiah's scroll 3. Jehoiakim 4. Ezekiel
5. Pethuel 6. Baal 7. False, for Edom (Obadiah 1) 8. Zechariah's 9. Joel
10. Bones 11. The Church at Laodicea 12. Jonah 13. It is cut down
14. "You brood of vipers" 15. Cyrus

Quiz #5

1. What "geographical feature" does John see in Revelation 22?

2. In the Old Testament when Joseph was questioned concerning Pharaoh's dreams he said only one person could interpret them. Who was that person?

3. In Acts 10, at whose house was the apostle Peter staying when he had a vision?

4. Who did Stephen see in a vision at his trial?

5. When the prophet Ezekiel lay on his left hand side, what did this action signify?

6. According to God's promise to Abram his descendants would be ill-treated in a strange country for how many years?

7. In which chapter of Isaiah does the prophet receive his commission?

8. True or false? In the book of Daniel when Nebuchadnezzar told his wise men his dream they were unable to interpret it.

9. Which Old Testament prophet had a wife called Gomer?

10. According to Numbers what did the donkey of Balaam the prophet see?

11. In Ezekiel 37 what is the prophet told to do to the dry bones?

12. True or false? The prophet Jonah boarded a ship bound for Joppa.

13. In which chapter of the book of Revelation does John see a vision of the scroll and the lamb?

14. Cushi was the father of which Old Testament prophet?

15. In the Old Testament Daniel has a vision of a man wearing a belt made of what material?

Quiz #6

1. True or false? On his release from prison Pharaoh's cup bearer immediately informed his master of Joseph's ability to interpret dreams.

2. "For to us a child is born, to us a son is given." Who wrote these words?

3. Which Old Testament prophet was called with the words, "Before I formed you in the womb I knew you"?

4. In which chapter of Zechariah's prophecy does a flying scroll appear?

5. In Revelation 6, how many seals does John see in his vision?

6. According to Matthew, what were the wise men advised to do in a dream, after they had seen the baby Jesus?

7. Which prophetic book lies between Obadiah and Micah?

8. According to Jeremiah 31, the fathers have eaten which sour fruit?

9. Which prophetic book of the Old Testament promises the outpouring of the Spirit?

10. According to Daniel's interpretation of Nebuchadnezzar's dream of a tree, what would the king soon be eating?

11. How many Churches receive heavenly messages in the book or Revelation?

12. According to Acts 10, at what time of day did Peter receive his vision?

13. According to Hosea 1, what name did the prophet give to his first child?

14. What is the name of the prophetess who greets Mary and Joseph in Luke 2?

15. According to Daniel's prophecy at the end of his book what is the name of the great prince?

---

10. Grass **11.** 7 **12.** About noon (Acts 10:9) **13.** Jezreel **14.** Anna **15.** Michael
4. Chapter 5 **5.** 7 **6.** Not to return to Herod **7.** Jonah **8.** Grapes **9.** Joel
1. False. He forgot about Joseph (Genesis 40:23) **2.** Isaiah **3.** Jeremiah

Answers

Quiz #7

1. What, according to Pharaoh's dream in Genesis 41, scorched the seven thin ears of corn?

2. In his prophetic message John the Baptist said that God could make the children of Abraham from what?

3. Who was the father of the prophet Isaiah?

4. According to Revelation 22, what is heaven's light source?

5. In Genesis 40, what plant did the cup bearer see in his dream?

6. In the New Testament, who saw Nathaniel while he was sitting under a fig tree?

7. In the Old Testament, who took Daniel to Nebuchadnezzar so he could interpret the king's dream?

8. God told Abram his people would return to the Promised Land when the sin of which people reached full measure?

9. In the book of Revelation, which Church was told to open the door to Christ?

10. In Acts, when Philip met the Ethiopian eunuch, from which prophetic book was he reading?

11. Who was the father of the Old Testament prophet Zechariah?

12. In Revelation 6, what did John see when the first seal was opened?

13. What was the occupation of the prophet Amos?

14. According to Acts 10, what did Peter see being dropped down from heaven?

15. Which prophet received his commission in the year King Uzziah died?

Answers

1. The east wind 2. Stones 3. Amos 4. God himself 5. A vine
6. Jesus 7. Arioch, the commander of the king's guard 8. The Amorites
9. The Church at Laodicea 10. Isaiah 53 11. Berekiah 12. A white horse 13. Shepherd
14. A large sheet 15. Isaiah

Quiz #8

1. In John's vision in Revelation 7 what do four angels hold back?

2. According to Daniel 2, what did Nebuchadnezzar see in his dream?

3. True or false? The Church at Thyatira is the third one to receive a message in the book of Revelation.

4. According to Peter on the day of Pentecost, who will see visions?

5. God asked Jonah to prophesy in which city?

6. Daniel had a dream of four beasts during the reign of which king?

7. According to Genesis, what was the first thing Pharaoh saw in his second dream?

8. Which is the last prophetic book of the Old Testament?

9. How many adulterous women are seen in Ezekiel 23?

10. God told Abram that his people would return to the Promised Land after how many generations?

11. In his confrontation with the prophets of Baal how many large jars did Elijah use?

12. What was the head of the statue in Nebuchadnezzar's dream made of?

13. According to the book of Numbers how many oracles did the prophet Balaam speak?

14. According to the book of Jonah how many people lived in Nineveh?

15. Where did the Old Testament prophet Amos live?

Quiz #9

1. According to Joseph, who would be killed by Pharaoh, the cup bearer or the baker?

2. Who had a show of strength with the prophets of Baal in 1 Kings?

3. In the Old Testament Isaiah records his vision during the reign of how many kings?

4. Which woman laughed when it was prophesied that she would have a son in her old age?

5. True or false? According to Revelation the temple in heaven is more glorious than the earthly temple.

6. What was the first beast seen in Daniel 7?

7. The first beast seen in Daniel 7 had wings of which bird?

8. Who was Ezekiel among when he first saw visions of God?

9. According to the prophetic book of Jonah, who declared a fast at the city of Nineveh?

10. In his dream at Bethel God tells Jacob that his descendants will be like what?

11. In his dream what does Pharaoh's cup bearer do?

12. Which name, meaning "Not my people," did God tell the prophet Hosea to give to his child?

13. According to Daniel 2, what were the belly and thighs of the statue in Nebuchadnezzar's dream made of?

14. According to Revelation 8 what does John hear when the seventh seal is opened?

15. In which chapter of his prophecy is Ezekiel asked to cook?

Quiz #10

1. According to 1 Kings 14, which prophet spoke against Jeroboam?

2. In Jacob's dream at Bethel, what was going up and down the ladder?

3. True or false? The statue in Nebuchadnezzar's dream had toes made of wood and clay.

4. According to Ezekiel 47 what flows from the temple?

5. In Daniel's dream concerning the four beasts what was the bear holding in his mouth?

6. According to Genesis, what was the first thing Pharaoh saw in his first dream?

7. What did the prophet John the Baptist say the man with two tunics was to do?

8. In Daniel's dream concerning the four beasts, how many ribs was the bear holding in its mouth?

9. According to Ezekiel, the word of the Lord came to him during the exile of which king?

10. True or false? Saul was still a long way away from Damascus when he had his vision of Jesus.

11. According to Joseph in Genesis 40, what did the three branches in the cup bearers dream signify?

12. In John's vision, as recorded in Revelation 11, how many witnesses does he see?

13. What was the name of Bethel, before Jacob renamed it after his dream?

14. According to Jesus in Luke, which Old Testament prophet was killed between the altar and the sanctuary?

15. How many chapters are there in the prophecy of Hosea?

---

13. Luz 14. Zechariah 15. 14

9. Jehoiachin 10. False. He was nearly at the city (Acts 9:3) 11. 3 days 12. 2

4. A river 5. Ribs 6. 7 fat cows 7. Share them with the person who had none 8. 3

1. Ahijah 2. Angels of God 3. False, they were made of iron and clay (Daniel 2:33)

Answers

Quiz #11

1. In Genesis what does Jacob see in his dream while traveling to Haran?

2. True or false? Jeremiah has a vision of three baskets of figs.

3. In Genesis 41, how many animals does Pharaoh see in his first dream?

4. What personal tragedy strikes the prophet Ezekiel?

5. Which book comes immediately before the prophecy of Ezekiel?

6. According to Matthew, Joseph was told to take Mary and Jesus to which country in a dream?

7. How many chapters does the Old Testament prophecy of Haggai contain?

8. According to the book of Revelation, which church tolerated "that woman Jezebel"?

9. Which prophetic book contains the "Servant Songs"?

10. What did the seraph place on the lips of the prophet Isaiah?

11. In Genesis 28 Jacob has a dream while traveling to where?

12. Which Old Testament prophetic book contains the words, "But you, Bethlehem Ephrathah, though you are small among the clans of Judah..."?

13. What request did the man of Macedonia make to Paul when he appeared to him in a vision?

14. Who was the king of Israel when Amos received his prophecy?

15. According to 2 Kings 19 who prophesied the fall of Sennacherib?

Quiz # 12

1. In which chapter of his prophecy does Jeremiah speak of a Righteous branch?

2. Which two prophets does Mark quote at the beginning of his Gospel?

3. True or false? Jeremiah 31:1 reads: "Woe to those who go down to Egypt for help."

4. In the Old Testament which group of prophets cut themselves during a competition between rival gods?

5. How many chapters does the Old Testament prophecy of Micah have?

6. In the New Testament, how many of Joseph's dreams are recorded?

7. According to Revelation there were followers of the Nicolatians in which Church?

8. Which Old Testament book lies between Habakkuk and Haggai?

9. According to Isaiah 61, the Spirit of God was on the prophet to preach good news to whom?

10. When Jacob had his famous dream in Genesis 28 he was traveling from which city?

11. In his vision in Acts 9, Ananias was told that Saul would appear before which three groups of people, for the sake of God?

12. The word of the Lord came to the prophet Haggai in which year of Darius' reign?

13. According to Peter in Acts 2 what will happen to the sun?

14. True or false? The prophet Haggai called for the house of the Lord to be built.

15. On the night of his famous dream what did Jacob use as a pillow?

Answers

1. Chapter 23 2. Isaiah and Malachi 3. False, it appears in Isaiah 31:1
4. The prophets of Baal 5. 7 6. 4 7. The Church at Pergamum 8. Zephaniah 9. The poor
10. Beersheba 11. The Gentiles, their kings and the people of Israel 12. The second
13. It will be turned to darkness 14. True (Haggai 1:4) 15. A stone

Quiz # 13

1. Isaiah makes a poultice of what?

2. Why does Isaiah make this poultice?

3. Which king asked Jeremiah to enquire of the Lord about Nebuchadnezzar attacking Jerusalem?

4. According to Revelation 16 who gathers together at Armageddon?

5. Which builder's item is seen by Amos?

6. In Ezekiel's prophecy, what does the cedar in Lebanon represent?

7. In Joseph's second dream what bows down to him?

8. In the Old Testament, whose prophecy comes after the book of Zechariah?

9. John the Baptist prophesied that Jesus would baptize with the Holy Spirit and with what?

10. In Acts, Ananias was told in a vision to go to whose house?

11. In Daniel how many horns does the fourth beast of Daniel's dream have?

12. Who ordered the execution of the prophet John the Baptist?

13. Which Roman centurion had a vision in Acts 10?

14. What was the significance of placing the live coal on Isaiah's lips?

15. According to Daniel 2, what does the rock in Nebuchadnezzar's dream become?

Facts 1

Genesis 3:15 is the first verse in the Bible which is sometimes understood as a prophecy about Jesus' life.

Abraham is the first person in the Bible to be called a prophet (Genesis 20:7).

The wife of Isaiah was called the prophetess, probably by association with her husband (Isaiah 8:3).

The ministry of the prophet Jeremiah spanned the reigns of five kings: Josiah, Jehoahaz, Jehoiakim, Jehoiachin and Zedekiah.

The name of Micah the prophet means "Who is like Yahweh?"

The transfiguration of Jesus is mentioned only in the synoptic Gospels (Matthew, Mark and Luke).

Isaiah, Jeremiah, Ezekiel and Daniel are called the Major Prophets.

In his gospel Matthew mentions 22 times that Old Testament prophecies have been fulfilled.

The first two kings of Israel, Saul and David, were both prophets. The combination of the roles of king and prophet did not continue beyond them.

The name of the prophet Zephaniah means "Yahweh has hidden."

Isaiah is sometimes called the evangelical prophet because the word *"euangelizomai"* meaning "to proclaim good news", appears in Greek translations of Isaiah 40:9

Facts 2

Moses was considered the archetypal prophet with whom Jesus himself would be compared (Deuteronomy 18:15-19).

Daniel, Ezekiel, Obadiah and Nahum all prophesied during the period of exile in Babylon.

The first dream recorded in the Bible is that of Abimelech which warned him that Sarah and Abraham were really husband and wife (Genesis 20:3).

Joseph's brothers nicknamed him "dreamer" because of the dreams he had which implied he would become their superior (Genesis 37:19).

God spoke to Joseph, the father of Jesus, four times through dreams.

Philip's four unnamed daughters were all prophetesses (Acts 21:9).

Matthew's Gospel refers to the Old Testament prophet Jeremiah on three occasions (Matthew 2:17; 6:14; 27:9).

The name of the prophet Ezekiel appears only twice in the Bible (Ezekiel 1:3; Ezekiel 24:24).

The god against which the prophet Elijah fought and spoke was Baal-melqart, the protective god of Tyre.

Only two passages from the book of Amos are quoted directly in the New Testament. Amos 5:25-27 is quoted in Acts 7:42-43, and Amos 9:11-12 is quoted in Acts 15:16-17.

The prophecy of Obadiah is the shortest book in the Old Testament having only 21 verses.

Facts 3

In Judges 7 a Midianite soldier interprets the dream of his friend and fellow soldier. It is the only one occasion in the Bible where the correct interpretation of a dream is given by a non-Israelite.

The only dream given to a woman in the New Testament is the dream of Pilate's wife (Matthew 27:19).

According to Jewish tradition the prophet Isaiah was sawn in two during the reign of king Manasseh.

The oldest surviving complete copy of Isaiah was found in Cave 1 at Qumran near the Dead Sea.

In the 1st Century A.D. there were attempts to ban the book of Ezekiel from public use partly because of the unsavory contents of chapter 16.

Daniel 2:4-7:28 is written in Aramaic, but the rest of the book is written in Hebrew.

Joshua, Judges, 1 and 2 Samuel and 1 and 2 Kings are sometimes known as the Former Prophets.

Although the prophet Amos lived in the kingdom of Judah he preached to the northern kingdom of Israel.

The first instance of Jesus reading a passage of the Old Testament is recorded in Luke 4:17 where he is reading from Isaiah 61:12.

The Greek word "*apokalypto*" from which the English word "apocalyptic" is derived, means "unfolding" or "revealing."

Facts 4

Obadiah means "servant of Yahweh" or "worshipper of Yahweh.

In addition to "foretelling" the future, the role of the Old Testament prophet was to "forth-tell" the word of God as it applied to the immediate situation.

The name of the prophet Elisha means "God is salvation."

According to Jewish tradition the prophet Isaiah was of royal blood.

Jesus identified John the Baptist as the Old Testament Elijah who was to come (Matthew 11:14).

The books of Isaiah, Obadiah, Micah and Nahum all begin with the assertion that the writer had a vision.

In the New Testament Luke shows great interest in visions. He records the visions of Zechariah (Luke 1:22), Ananias (Acts 9:10), Cornelius (Acts 10:3), Peter (Acts 10:10) and Paul (Acts 18:9).

Jeremiah is directly quoted forty times in the New Testament, half of these quotations coming in the book of Revelation.

The name of Jonah the prophet means "dove".

Jacob is the first of God's chosen people in the Bible who has a dream (Genesis 28).

Miriam, the sister of Moses, was called a prophetess (Exodus 15:20).

Earth, Wind and Fire

Quiz #1

1. According to Genesis, what did God create on the first day?

2. In 1 Kings 17, who did the prophet Elijah inform that there would be no rain for three years?

3. In the Sermon on the Mount, who did Jesus say rain fell upon?

4. True or false? According to Exodus, the quail appeared each morning.

5. In Acts, at which city did Paul draw attention to God's kindness in sending rain?

6. Ezekiel prophesies an earthquake when Israel is attacked by whom?

7. What was the first plague with which Moses struck Egypt?

8. According to Zechariah 14:17, why will God withhold rain?

9. What did God send to make the waters recede after the flood?

10. According to Psalm 1, what does the wind blow away?

11. In the first chapter of Ecclesiastes the writer says that generations come and go, but something endures for ever. What is it?

12. What, according to the vision in Daniel 2, was swept away by the wind?

13. Jesus says that a cloud rising in the west means what is coming?

14. In which Old Testament prophetic book do we find the words, "Your love is like the morning mist, like the early dew that disappears"?

15. How many times did God call Moses' name from the burning bush?

Answers

1. Light **2.** Ahab **3.** The righteous and the unrighteous **4.** False. They appeared in the evening (Exodus 16:13) **5.** Lystra **6.** Gog **7.** The Nile turning to blood **8.** If people fail to go to Jerusalem to worship **9.** A wind **10.** Chaff **11.** The earth **12.** Fragments of the statue **13.** Rain **14.** Hosea **15.** Twice

Quiz #2

1. In which chapter of the Gospel of John does Jesus say that the wind blows where it pleases?

2. On which day was the sky created?

3. When Moses saw the burning bush what was he forbidden to do?

4. According to Song of Songs, what burns like blazing fire?

5. What, according to Jesus, is clothed one day and thrown into the fire the next?

6. Which New Testament book refers to Elijah praying that it would not rain?

7. According to Revelation 9, what proportion of mankind is killed by plagues of fire, smoke and sulfur?

8. According to Exodus, what did the Israelites see each morning in the desert?

9. What did the Israelites set up to mark the place where they had crossed the river Jordan?

10. When the Lord descended to Mount Sinai, what was it covered with?

11. Fill in the missing word: "They sow the wind and reap the ___"?

12. According to Amos 5, what should "roll on like a river"?

13. True or false? The top of mount Sinai was not visible from the plain below.

14. According to Exodus, what was the second plague suffered by the Egyptians?

15. According to Joshua 10 the moon stood still over which valley?

Answers

1. Chapter 3 2. Day 2 3. Come any closer 4. Love 5. Grass 6. James
7. One third 8. A layer of dew 9. 12 stones 10. Smoke 11. Whirlwind
12. Justice 13. False. It was visible (Exodus 19:16) 14. Frogs 15. Aijalon

Quiz #3

1. In the Old Testament, on which day were the Israelites forbidden to light fires?

2. In Judges, who fastened torches to foxes' tails?

3. As recorded in Genesis what did God create on the third day?

4. According to the book of Esther, why was King Xerxes angry with Vashti?

5. According to Jesus, what is more important than burnt offerings and sacrifices?

6. How many times did Elijah call down fire on messengers sent by king Ahaziah?

7. According to the Old Testament, what was the name of the ravine where Elijah was miraculously fed by ravens?

8. In Acts, who went to the river outside Philippi expecting to find a place of prayer?

9. According to Genesis 41, what was scorched by an east wind?

10. As recorded in 1 Samuel 5 which towns were afflicted with plagues of tumors?

11. In Revelation 15 John sees fire mixed in a sea made of what material?

12. In which prophetic book does God send rain on one town but not on another?

13. Which Old Testament character had to choose a punishment from three years famine, three months of military defeats or three days of plague?

14. Which form of punishment listed in the previous question was choosen?

15. The greatest earthquake known to man is prophesied in which chapter of Revelation?

Answers

1. The Sabbath 2. Samson 3. Dry land, the sea and vegetation
4. She refused to go to him 5. Loving God and one's neighbor 6. Twice 7. Kerith
8. Paul and his companions 9. Ears of corn in Pharaoh's dream 10. Ekron and Ashdod 11. Glass
12. Amos 13. David 14. 3 days of plague 15. Chapter 16

Quiz #4

1. According to Hosea 12, who feeds on the wind?

2. In Joshua 8 a covenant of renewal takes place upon which mountain?

3. During Paul's sea journey mentioned in Acts 27 what was not seen for many days?

4. What did God create on the fourth day?

5. In Revelation 8 a star is given a name. What is it?

6. Which chapter of Isaiah's prophecy makes ironic comparisons between an idol and firewood?

7. According to Jesus in Luke 17, sulfur and fire rained down upon which city?

8. What did the voice from the burning bush command Moses to do?

9. Which Old Testament commander was lured to the Kishon river in Judges?

10. Jesus, speaking in Matthew 7, says that something is thrown on the fire. What is it?

11. According to Exodus, what happened to the manna when the sun grew hot?

12. In the book of Numbers, who made an offering of unauthorized fire?

13. In John's account of Jesus walking on water, where does he say the disciples were heading in their boat?

14. According to Judges 19 whose companions threatened to burn his house if he did not explain a riddle to them?

15. Which Old Testament prophetic book begins with what the prophet saw two years before an earthquake?

Answers

1. Ephraim **2.** Ebal **3.** The sun and the stars **4.** The sun, moon and stars **5.** Wormwood **6.** Chapter 44 **7.** Sodom **8.** Remove his sandals **9.** Sisera **10.** A tree bearing bad fruit **11.** It melted away **12.** Nadab and Abihu **13.** Capernaum **14.** Samson's **15.** Amos

Quiz #5

1. According to Exodus the Israelites could collect double the usual amount of manna on which day?

2. What was the origin of the wind on the day of Pentecost?

3. By what name is the lake of fire of Revelation 20 also known?

4. Which king did David defeat when he restored his control along the Euphrates?

5. True or false? On the fifth day God created all creatures.

6. In Genesis, which flaming object guarded the way to the tree of life?

7. Which was the only northern city Joshua burnt to the ground?

8. In the book of Hosea who says, "I will be like the dew to Israel"?

9. In Genesis 19 who sees smoke rising from the destroyed cities of Sodom and Gomorrah?

10. According to Exodus 10 what was brought to Egypt by an east wind?

11. As specified in Numbers 28, how many lambs were to be prepared as burnt offerings each day?

12. In the New Testament why couldn't Jesus' disciples heal the boy who kept on falling into fire and water?

13. What, according to Jeremiah 10, does God send with rain?

14. Which king of Judah burnt incense at the altar when he should not have done so?

15. True or false? According to Passover regulations the meat was to be boiled and eaten.

10. Locusts 11. 2 12. They lacked faith 13. Lightning 14. Uzziah 15. False. It was to be roasted (Exodus 12:9)

5. False, he created only the fish and the birds 6. A sword 7. Hazor 8. God 9. Abraham

1. Sixth day 2. Heaven 3. The second death 4. Hadadezer

Answers

344

Quiz #6

1. On which island did the apostle Paul and his companions receive a warm welcome because of the rain?

2. According to Acts, who did Paul meet by the river outside Philippi?

3. In the words of Psalm 11 a scorching wind will be whose lot?

4. King Saul and his sons died on which mountain?

5. How many times a day was Elijah fed by ravens?

6. Whose armies were defeated by hailstones according to the book of Joshua?

7. Which Old Testament king threw Jeremiah's scrolls onto a fire?

8. Zechariah 14 records an earthquake that took place during the reign of which king?

9. In the Old Testament how many of Korah's rebellious followers were devoured by fire?

10. Which disciple warmed himself by a fire after Jesus' arrest?

11. What did God create on the sixth day?

12. According to Exodus 16 for how long did the Israelites eat manna?

13. In the Old Testament, what guided the Israelites by day during the Exodus?

14. What insect plagued the Egyptians after the mosquitoes had gone?

15. In the book of Jonah how did the sailors calm the fierce storm?

Quiz #7

1. Moses gave the name "Massah" to the place where he obtained water from the rock. Why?

2. In Acts 27, Paul and his companions were propelled by a storm to the lee of which small island?

3. In Revelation 12, what swallows the river spewed out by the dragon?

4. In the Old Testament, which animals were to provide the burnt offering at the Passover?

5. The writer of which book continually laments that life is like chasing after the wind?

6. According to Luke 16, who told Abraham that he was in agony in the fire?

7. What, according to the Psalmist, vanishes like smoke?

8. In which direction could the Garden of Eden be found?

9. In the book of Joshua who looked back to see their city on fire?

10. In the Old Testament what was the sixth plague brought upon the Egyptians by God?

11. Whose hearts burned within them when Jesus opened the scriptures to them?

12. Which king ordered three Israelites to be thrown into a fiery furnace when they disobeyed his command?

13. Which king of Judah was punished with leprosy for burning incense in the temple?

14. In the book of Job, who asks, "Who fathers the drops of dew?"?

15. How many people were on the mount of transfiguration altogether?

Answers

1. It means "testing", because the Israelites tested the Lord 2. Cauda
3. The earth 4. 2 young bulls, 1 ram and 7 male lambs 5. Ecclesiastes
6. The rich man 7. The Psalmist's days 8. East 9. The men of Ai 10. Boils
11. Cleopas and his friend 12. Nebuchadnezzar 13. Uzziah 14. The Lord 15. 6

Quiz #8

1. For how many nights were Paul and his companions caught in the storm of Acts 27?

2. According to Genesis, what geographical feature is found in the valley of Siddim?

3. According to James, what virtue helps a farmer wait for the autumn and spring rains?

4. In Exodus 32, what made Moses burn with anger when he approached the Israelite camp?

5. After his resurrection Jesus prepared a fire for which meal?

6. True or false? The seventh plague consisted of locusts.

7. In the Old Testament how many bulls were to be presented as a burnt offering on the first day of the Feast of Tabernacles?

8. Which Psalm contains the line "He hurls down hail like pebbles. Who can withstand his icy blast"?

9. In 1 Kings 18 how many times did Elijah go and tell his servant to go and look towards the sea?

10. Which ingredient did Jesus use to heal a blind man according to John 9?

11. Which raw material did God use to create woman?

12. According to Leviticus 1, which two birds could be presented as a burnt offering?

13. What did the disciples see on the Day of Pentecost?

14. According to 2 Kings 25 which invader set fire to Jerusalem?

15. In Acts 16 a violent earthquake caused the prison doors to do what?

Answers

1. 14 2. The Salt Sea 3. Patience 4. The golden calf 5. Breakfast
6. False. It was a hailstorm (Exodus 9:18) 7. 13 8. Psalm 147:(17) 9. 7 times
10. Mud 11. Adam's rib 12. Dove or pigeon 13. Tongues of fire 14. Nebuchadnezzar 15. To fly open

Quiz #9

1. In Ezekiel 5, what is the prophet told to scatter to the wind?

2. At what time of the day did the waters of the Red Sea return to normal?

3. "It is as if the dew of Hermon were falling on Mount Zion," is a quotation from which Psalm?

4. Which tribe did Moses bless saying, "may the Lord bless his land with the precious dew from heaven above"?

5. According to 2 Peter 2 what returns to wallow in the mud?

6. In the book of Job who was killed by a mighty wind striking a house?

7. Where was Jesus when he turned water into wine?

8. By what name is the Sea of Galilee also known?

9. Which Old Testament book records a public gathering thrown into confusion by rain?

10. According to the curse of Genesis which creature will eat dust all the days of its life?

11. Psalm 48 says that something is shattered by an east wind. What is it?

12. What type of snake emerged from a fire and bit the apostle Paul?

13. In Revelation 6 the moon turns to what?

14. According to Genesis 8, when did the mountain tops become visible during the flood?

15. At his transfiguration the face of Jesus shone like what, according to Matthew?

Answers

1. His hair 2. Daybreak 3. Psalm 133 4. Joseph 5. A sow
6. Job's sons and daughters 7. Cana 8. Tiberias 9. Ezra 10. Serpent 11. The ships of Tarshish
12. A viper 13. Blood 14. The first day of the tenth month 15. The sun

Quiz #10

1. In the first chapter of Job, he is told that fire fell from the sky burning what?

2. According to John the Baptist, Jesus would baptize with fire and what else?

3. Which Old Testament leader commanded the sun to stand still?

4. In Exodus, God promised to rain down what from heaven?

5. What is the biblical reference for "Do not put out the Spirit's fire"?

6. In the plagues of Egypt which creature came from the dust?

7. What was Jesus doing during the storm on the lake, according to Mark?

8. How many times was the apostle Paul shipwrecked at sea?

9. Which Old Testament prophet was thrown into a cistern and sank into the mud?

10. According to 1 Kings 19, what did Elijah experience after the powerful wind on the mountain of God?

11. What did Aaron claim emerged from the fire after he threw jewelry onto it?

12. 2 Samuel records that Absalom set fire to whose barley field?

13. The pregnant woman in the vision of Revelation 12 was clothed with what?

14. To whom did the prophet Elijah say, "Go, eat and drink, for there is the sound of a heavy rain"?

15. Which river did the Israelites have to cross before entering the Promised Land?

Answers

1. Sheep and servants **2.** The Holy Spirit **3.** Joshua **4.** Bread
5. 1 Thessalonians 5:19 **6.** Gnats **7.** Sleeping **8.** 3 **9.** Jeremiah **10.** An earthquake
11. The golden calf **12.** Joab's **13.** The sun **14.** Ahab **15.** Jordan

Quiz #11

1. In which chapter of Exodus are manna and quail first mentioned?

2. What was the name of the king of Judah who sacrificed his son in the fire?

3. According to Revelation 11, how many people will be killed by an earthquake?

4. True or false? The magicians of Egypt were able to replicate the plague of gnats Moses inflicted upon them.

5. In the Old Testament who stood in the river Jordan while the people crossed into the Promised Land?

6. On which mountain did Moses receive the ten commandments?

7. Which king received a sign in which a shadow went back ten steps?

8. According to Job 24, what do heat and drought snatch away?

9. According to 2 Kings 21, which wicked king sacrificed his son in the fire?

10. What was unusual about the darkness of the ninth plague to strike Egypt?

11. According to Judges 12, who wanted to burn down Jephthah's house?

12. In Daniel's vision of a river flowing from the Ancient of Days, what was the river composed of?

13. When Joshua commanded the sun to stop still, for how long did it remain so?

14. In the Song of Solomon, whose head was drenched with dew?

15. The pregnant woman in the vision of Revelation 12 had what under her feet?

Answers

1. Chapter 16 2. Ahaz 3. 7,000 4. False (Exodus 8:18)
5. Priests 6. Sinai 7. Hezekiah 8. Melted snow 9. Manasseh 10. It could be felt
11. The men of Ephraim 12. Fire 13. A day 14. The Beloved 15. The moon

Facts 1

Dew is mentioned 36 times in the Old Testament.

There is only one specific record of rain falling in the book of Acts (Acts 28:2).

"Matar", *"gesem"* and *"zarem"* are all Hebrew words used to signify violent rain.

The "west wind", *"ruah yam"*, was considered to be the father of rain (1 Kings 18:44-45).

Sun worship, although forbidden (Deuteronomy 4:19), was practised in the Old Testament (2 Kings 23:11).

In the Bible, lightning is frequently associated with theophanies (that is, appearances of God). For example; Exodus 19:16; Ezekiel 1:13-14; Revelation 4:5.

There are four seas named in the Old Testament, the Red Sea, the Dead Sea, the Sea of Galilee and the Mediterranean Sea.

The lowest point on land mentioned in the Bible is the Dead Sea.

The first expression of God's holiness in the Bible occurs in the story of Moses and the burning bush (Exodus 3).

"Yarden", the Hebrew word for the river Jordan, means "descender".

The surface of the Dead Sea is an average of 1365 ft. below sea level.

Facts 2

St. Catherine's Monastery is now situated below Jebel Musa, at the site traditionally regarded as being Mount Sinai of the Old Testament.

During the Feast of Tabernacles 71 bulls or young bulls were to be offered as burnt sacrifices (Numbers 29).

15 rams were burnt as sacrifices during the Feast of Tabernacles in the Old Testament (Numbers 29).

The first recorded earthquake in the Bible is mentioned in 1 Kings 19:11 when the Lord appears to Elijah.

In Hebrew the words *"rebibim"* and *"resisim"* are used to describe showers and gentle types of rainfall.

In the Bible thunder is frequently associated with the voice of God (Psalm 77:18; Psalm 104:7).

According to Genesis, after the flood reached its maximum, the waters receded for 74 days until the mountain tops became visible (Genesis 8:5).

The deepest point of the Dead Sea lies more than 2,600 feet below sea level.

Two kings in the Old Testament sacrificed their sons in fire: Ahaz and Manasseh.

The direct distance of 72 miles from Lake Hulah to the Dead Sea is doubled by the river Jordan's meander.

The Dead Sea is 44 miles long and nearly 9 miles wide at places.

Facts 3

There are eleven earthquakes recorded in the New Testament.

Hail is often known to accompany the violent thunder storms that usually strike Israel between December and March.

The Hebrew word *"mabbul"*, used to describe the Flood in Genesis, occurs only once outside the flood narratives in the Bible (Psalm 29:10).

Noah sent the dove from the ark 264 days after the flood had first begun.

Mountains in the Bible were sometimes used as symbols denoting difficulty and obstacles (Matthew 21:21).

Mount Nebo, the site from which Moses viewed the promised land before his death, is 2,739 feet high.

The River Euphrates is the largest river in West Asia, being 1,510 miles long.

Of the Gospel writers, only Matthew and Mark mention John the Baptist's activity in the River Jordan (Matthew 3:6; Mark 1:5).

The Bible often describes the disease of leprosy as one which turns the skin white like snow (Exodus 4:6).

The word sun is mentioned most times in the book of Ecclesiastes where it appears 35 times.

Noah was the first person in the Bible to make a burnt offering (Genesis 8:20).

Facts 4

Revelation is the only book in the New Testament to mention the word "rainbow" which it does on two occasions (Revelation 4:3; 10:1).

The Hebrew word for dew, *"tal"*, means "sprinkled moisture".

The "north wind", *"ruah sapon"*, was associated with cold weather conditions in the Old Testament (Job 37:9).

In the Old Testament the mountains were considered to be the oldest created objects (Job 15:7; Proverbs 8:25).

Mount Carmel, where Elijah triumphed over the prophets of Baal, is 1,740 feet high.

The headwaters of the River Jordan collect into Lake Hulah, which is 230 feet above sea level.

The Dead Sea is also called the Salt Sea (Genesis 14:3), the Eastern Sea (Ezekiel 47:18) and the sea of Arabah (Deuteronomy 4:49).

The New Testament book mentioning the sun most frequently is Revelation where it occurs twelve times.

Three constellations that are recognized today are mentioned in Job, The Bear, Orion and Pleiades (Job 38).

The earliest mention of rain occurs in Genesis 2:5.

"Ruah sapon", called the "whirlwind" or "south wind" in the Bible, could be either tempestuous (Isaiah 21:1) or gentle (Acts 27:13).

Elijah, Your Chariot Is Waiting

Quiz #1

1. Who escaped, by night, in a basket down a city wall when he heard that the Jews plotted to kill him?

2. Who was in danger of being killed by fire and water by his convulsions?

3. What name does Revelation 6:8 give to the rider of the pale horse?

4. Which godly man, in the middle of great suffering, cursed the day he was born?

5. After David had killed Goliath, the Shaaraim Road from Gath to Ekron was lined with the dead bodies of which people?

6. Everyone in Israel mourned for their king-maker and buried him in his home town of Ramah. Who was he?

7. In the New Testament who did some Jews seize in the temple courts and nearly kill?

8. Which Old Testament book says that there is a time to kill and a time to heal?

9. How did Hazael assassinate the sick Ben-Hadad and so become king?

10. Which two brothers murdered Abner?

11. Who falsely claimed that he killed Saul in accordance with Saul's request?

12. In which valley did David strike down 18,000 Edomites?

13. Who said of the people of Gog that every man's sword would be against his brother?

14. Who killed Solomon's brother Adonijah on Solomon's orders?

15. Who said that if anyone killed Cain he would suffer vengeance seven times over?

Answers

1. Paul 2. The deaf, mute boy who was brought to Jesus for healing 3. Death
4. Job 5. The Philistines 6. Samuel 7. Paul 8. Ecclesiastes 9. He suffocated him with a thick wet cloth
10. Joab and Abishai 11. An Amalekite young man 12. The Valley of Salt
13. Ezekiel 14. Benaiah 15. The Lord

Quiz #2

1. What did Sennacherib's two sons, Adrammelech and Sharezer, do while he was worshiping his god Nisroch?

2. Who saved Israel by killing 600 Philistines with an ox-goad?

3. How many of the Arameans who helped Hadadezer were killed by David's army?

4. Which judge "on one stone murdered his seventy brothers"?

5. Who killed thirty men at Ashkelon?

6. Who with ten men assassinated Gedaliah?

7. Which army had more people killed by large hailstones than by the swords of the Israelites?

8. For how long did the Israelites mourn Aaron?

9. Who was killed by being stabbed in the stomach while he was lying down at midday?

10. When Saul's armor-bearer saw that Saul was dead after falling on his own sword, what did he do?

11. Who told his wife to say that she was his sister because he feared that Pharaoh might kill him?

12. Who plotted to arrest Jesus and in some underhand way to kill him?

13. Who did God tell in a dream that he was as good as dead because he had taken a woman who was married?

14. Who died at Kiriath Arba and was wept over by Abraham?

15. Who was dead but is now alive for ever?

Answers

1. Killed him with swords 2. Shamgar 3. 22,000 4. Abimelech
5. Samson 6. Ishmael 7. The Amorites 8. 30 days 9. Ish-Bosheth 10. He fell on his own sword
11. Abraham 12. The chief priests and the elders of the people
13. Abimelech 14. Sarah 15. The risen Lord Jesus Christ

Quiz #3

1. How many suicides are recorded in the Bible?

2. Who predicted that brothers would betray brothers to death and that children would even rebel against their parents and have them put to death?

3. True or false? In the Old Testament someone convicted of murder could offer a ransom in return for his death sentence being commuted.

4. Who slaughtered 80 men and then threw their bodies into a cistern in Jerusalem?

5. Which prophet records that God compared the unfaithful officials in Jerusalem to wolves tearing their prey and shedding blood in order to make money?

6. Who, according to one of God's commands, had to be stoned or shot with arrows but couldn't have a hand laid on him?

7. Which person who had eleven brothers was embalmed and put in a coffin in Egypt?

8. According to Psalm 116:15, what is precious about God's saints?

9. Where did Moses say a blasphemer should be stoned?

10. Where in the Bible does it say that nobody has power concerning the day of their death?

11. Who committed his spirit into God the Father's hands as he died?

12. Which woman said to her mother-in-law that she would die where she died and would be buried where she was buried?

13. Where, according to the book of Revelation 21:1-4, will there be no more death?

14. Who warned his hearers to be more concerned about the one who could kill the soul than about those who could kill the body?

15. Which Old Testament prophet records the words, "I will destroy her ruler and kill all her officials"?

Answers

1. 7 **2.** Jesus **3.** False. This is specifically forbidden in Numbers 35:31 **4.** Ishmael **5.** Ezekiel **6.** Any person who touched Mount Sinai **7.** Joseph **8.** Their death **9.** Outside the camp **10.** The book of Ecclesiastes **11.** Jesus **12.** Ruth **13.** In the new heaven **14.** Jesus **15.** Amos

Quiz #4

1. True or false? Two brothers had all the people of Shechem killed for the sake of one woman whose name was Esther.

2. Which king of Judah sacrificed his own children by burning them before pagan gods?

3. Which of Joseph's brothers did not want to kill him?

4. Which of Jesus' disciples said that the disciples should go with Jesus and die with him?

5. After the downfall of Haman, who became second in rank to King Xerxes?

6. Which Israelite commander was killed at the gates of Hebron?

7. When Pharaoh heard that Moses had killed an Egyptian, what did he try to do to Moses?

8. True or false? The Israelites were given a law by God stating that murderers should be put to death.

9. Which woman murdered her whole family, except one grandson?

10. Which king of Israel was burned to death after he set fire to his own palace?

11. What were the four kinds of destroyers God promised he would send on the unrepentant people of Jerusalem?

12. Who said, "Don't kill us! We have wheat and barley, oil and honey, hidden in a field"?

13. Which Old Testament book opens with the words, "After the death of Moses the servant of the Lord..."?

14. Who described himself to Saul as "a dead dog"?

15. To whom did Elijah send a letter which said, "You have murdered your own brothers, men who were better than you"?

Quiz #5

1. Who was assassinated at Beth Millo?

2. Who rashly promised that if he won his battle against the Ammonites he would sacrifice the first living thing that came out of his property, and then did so when his daughter came out to greet him?

3. Who gave orders that all Hebrew baby boys should be killed while girls were allowed to live?

4. Who ordered a baby to be cut in two so that one half of the baby could be given to two women?

5. Who did Shemaiah tell to hide in the temple because men were planning to kill him at night?

6. In which poetic book of the Old Testament is the verse, "Bloodthirsty men hate a man of integrity and seek to kill the upright" ?

7. Which of David's sons was murdered at a party?

8. Which Old Testament prophet asked God not to forgive the crimes of those who sought to kill him?

9. Who told Moses to say to Pharaoh that his firstborn son would be killed?

10. In which Old Testament book is it written, "Cursed is the man who accepts a bribe to kill an innocent person"?

11. Who prevented soldiers from killing Paul and other prisoners on board a boat?

12. After he had been killed in battle who had his head and his body attached to the wall of a town called Beth Shan?

13. A tornado killed whose ten children?

14. Which biblical book pictures all of the dead, both great and small, standing before God's throne as books are opened?

15. Who is going to end up by being thrown into a lake of burning sulfur?

---

11. A centurion 12. King Saul 13. Job's 14. The book of Revelation 15. The devil
5. Nehemiah 6. Proverbs 7. Amnon 8. Jeremiah 9. The Lord God 10. Deuteronomy
1. Joash 2. Jephthah 3. The King of Egypt 4. Solomon

Answers

Quiz #6

1. In the book of Genesis, who killed his brother, Abel?

2. In the book of Genesis, how did God destroy the cities of Sodom and Gomorrah?

3. True of false? In the Old Testament, God destroyed the cities of Sodom and Gomorrah because he could not find even ten good people living there.

4. Which Old Testament character was turned into a pillar of salt?

5. In the book of Genesis, who narrowly escaped death when Abraham was about to sacrifice him?

6. Whose brothers hoped he would meet a sticky end when they threw him into a well and abandoned him?

7. Joseph's brothers showed Jacob Joseph's blood-stained coat. What did Jacob think had happened to Joseph?

8. In the book of Genesis, what happened to Pharaoh's baker, who was imprisoned with Joseph and told him his dream?

9. In the book of Genesis, what dream did the baker tell Joseph that he had?

10. In the book of Exodus, what fate did Pharaoh decree for every male child born to a Hebrew woman?

11. Which Old Testament character was saved from a certain death because his mother hid him among the bulrushes on the banks of the Nile?

12. Who rescued baby Moses from the river Nile?

13. In Exodus, who met their deaths in the tenth plague?

14. How did the Israelites escape the angel of death?

15. In the book of Exodus, who was drowned in the Red Sea?

Answers

1. Cain 2. He rained burning sulfur on them 3. True (Genesis 18:32) 4. Lot's wife 5. Isaac
6. Joseph 7. He had been killed by a wild animal 8. He was hanged three days later
9. The baker said that birds ate out of a basket that was on his head
10. They were to be killed 11. Moses 12. Pharaoh's daughter 13. The firstborn of Egypt 14. They daubed lamb's
blood on the lintels of their homes. 15. All of Pharaoh's men who were pursuing the Israelites

Quiz #7

1. Why didn't the Israelites starve as they wandered in the desert?

2. Which Old Testament city was destroyed when its walls fell to the ground?

3. When Joshua destroyed the city of Jericho, he cursed any man who might try to rebuild it. In the book 1 Kings, who unwisely rebuilt the city?

4. In the book of Judges, who killed Sisera by driving a tent peg through the temple of his head?

5. At which cave did 3,000 men try to kill Israel's most famous judge?

6. Which Old Testament character met his death when he single-handedly destroyed a Philistine temple?

7. In which book of the Bible does the account of Samson's death appear?

8. True or false? When Samson's hair was cut off he lost his strength for ever.

9. In the book 1 Samuel, who died suddenly when he heard the news that the Ark of the Covenant had been captured by the Philistines?

10. What were the names of Eli's two sons who were killed in battle against the Philistines?

11. Which Old Testament character died when he was hit on the forehead by a stone from a sling?

12. Who narrowly escaped being killed when King Saul threw a spear at him?

13. In 1 Samuel, how did King Saul die?

14. Which Old Testament king was warned of his imminent death by the witch of Endor?

15. Who was a close friend of David and died with his father Saul in a battle against the Philistines?

Answers

1. God sent manna for them to eat 2. Jericho 3. Hiel of Bethel 4. Jael 5. Etam
6. Samson 7. The book of Judges 8. False. Samson regained his strength when his hair grew
again (Judges 16:22) 9. Eli 10. Hophni and Phineas 11. Goliath 12. David
13. He was wounded in battle, then killed himself by falling on his sword 14. Saul 15. Jonathan

Quiz #8

1. In 2 Samuel, what was the name of Bathsheba's husband whose death in battle King David arranged?

2. To whom did the prophet Nathan say, "The Lord says: 'Out of your own household I am going to bring calamity on you' "?

3. Which Old Testament character came to a sticky end when he was caught by his head in the branches of an oak tree?

4. Who killed a man hanging from the branches of a tree?

5. In 1 Kings, who was stoned to death after he refused to sell his vineyard to King Ahab?

6. Which infamous Old Testament queen died when she was pushed out of a window?

7. According to the book of Jeremiah, what happened to many of the people of Jerusalem after the city was defeated by Nebuchadnezzar, king of Babylon?

8. Which prophet falsely said that Nebuchadnezzar's grip on Jerusalem would be broken?

9. Which three people escaped death when they were thrown into Nebuchadnezzar's fiery furnace?

10. Which Old Testament character saw a hand writing on the wall and was slain later that night?

11. Who was saved from being mauled to death in the lions' den?

12. Why was Daniel condemned to death in the lions' den?

13. What happened to King Darius' wicked officials who had plotted against Daniel?

14. In the book of Esther, what was the name of the chief minister who plotted to have all Jews put to death?

15. Which Old Testament character's sticky end is described thus: "But when they went out to bury her, they found nothing except her skull, her feet and her hands"?

Answers

1. Uriah the Hittite 2. King David 3. Absalom 4. Joab, commander of David's army
5. Naboth 6. Queen Jezebel 7. They were taken into exile 8. Hananiah 9. Shadrach, Meshach and Abednego
10. King Belshazzar 11. Daniel 12. Because he continued to worship God and not King Darius
13. They were thrown to the lions themselves 14. Haman 15. Jezebel

Quiz #9

1. True or false? Jonah met his death when he was swallowed by a giant fish.

2. True or false? The people of Nineveh did not listen to the prophet Jonah's warning that they should repent, so their city was destroyed.

3. Whose head was presented to Salome on a platter?

4. How had John the Baptist offended Herod and his wife?

5. In the New Testament, who ordered that all baby boys in Bethlehem under the age of two should be killed?

6. According to tradition, which of the disciples died by being crucified upside down?

7. Which group of animals rushed into the lake and were drowned when Jesus healed a man who was possessed by demons?

8. Which of Jesus' parables features a traveler who was attacked and left half-dead on his way to Jericho?

9. True or false? In Jesus' Parable of the Good Samaritan, three men passed by the injured traveler before the Samaritan stopped to help him.

10. In Jesus' story of the rich man and the beggar Lazarus, what happens to the rich man when he dies?

11. In Jesus' Parable of the Talents, why did the master take the third servant's one talent away and throw him out of the house?

12. Which New Testament character said, shortly before his death, "I have sinned... for I have betrayed innocent blood"?

13. What was the name of the first Christian martyr whose death is described in Acts?

14. According to the book of Acts, which disciple, brother of John, was "put to death with the sword" by King Herod?

15. In the book of Acts, who fell out of a window to his death, but was brought back to life by Paul?

Answers

1. False. Jonah was swallowed by a fish, but didn't die (Jonah 1:17)
2. False. They repented and God spared their city (Jonah 3:10) 3. John the Baptist 4. John the Baptist said in public that they had married unlawfully 5. King Herod 6. Peter 7. Pigs 8. The Parable of the Good Samaritan
9. False. Only two men passed by (Luke 10:31-32) 10. He is sent to hell
11. Because he had not done anything with the money 12. Judas 13. Stephen 14. James 15. Eutychus

Facts 1

When Joseph died the Egyptians mourned for him for seventy days. The length of the mourning period depended on the importance of the person who had died. The Egyptians treated Joseph like royalty by observing such a long time of mourning for him.

The Bible does not say that Enoch "died", but that he was "taken". The implication is that he was taken to heaven, to God's presence, without experiencing death.

When Ahithophel realized that his advice was not going to be taken, he went home and took his own life by hanging himself. He probably thought that the rebellion he had conspired in would fail and he would be branded a traitor.

Pilate allowed Jesus to be crucified even though he knew that Jesus was innocent. In both John's Gospel and in Luke's Gospel the fact that Pilate found no basis for any charges against Jesus is recorded three times.

The risen Jesus told Peter that when he was old he would stretch out his hands, be dressed by somebody else and go where he did not want to go (John 21:18). From the days of the early church this has been taken as a reference to Peter's own martyrdom by crucifixion.

Joab stabbed Abner to death. He did this to avenge the death of his brother Asahel. But as Abner had killed Asahel in a battle, Joab's action can hardly be classed as justifiable blood revenge. It was murder.

When Jesus told his would-be followers that they had to take up their crosses if they wanted to be his disciples, it was no mere figure of speech. Jesus was saying that being his follower could lead to being put to death, since the cross was an instrument of death.

Ebed-Melech heard that Jeremiah had been left to die in a muddy cistern. Ebed-Melech went and told King Zedekiah about this as the king was sitting in the Benjamin Gate. This gate served as a courtroom and Zedekiah may have been dealing with legal cases when Ebed-Melech arrived.

"Thou shalt not kill" (Exodus 20:13 KJV) is one of the Ten Commandments. The NIV has "You shall not murder" because the Hebrew verb implies a deliberate and premeditated act.

Facts 2

Amos condemned the Moabites for burning the bones of the king of Edom (Amos 2:1). This prevented the spirit of the king ever finding rest as it was then believed that bodies decently buried found rest.

Jesus saved an adulterous women from being stoned (John 8:1-11). The teachers of the law and the Pharisees had conveniently forgotten that the law stated that both parties, the man and the woman, should be executed.

The Israelites were told that they would die if they walked up Mount Sinai or even touched it. This was to teach them about God's holiness. Mount Sinai was holy because of God's presence there.

Joshua 7:25 says that "all Israel" stoned Achan and then burned his body. God had ordered anyone who broke his covenant to be stoned. His body was burned as a sign that the land was being purged of evil.

The Bible states that Joseph was 110 years old when he died (Genesis 50:26). Some very old Egyptian records reveal that 110 years was considered to be an ideal life span. The Egyptians would have thought that Joseph was greatly blessed to have lived to that exact age.

Two of Aaron's sons, Nadab and Abihu fell dead because they made an offering of unauthorized fire. In some unexplained way they used fire in a way not permitted by God. This incident illustrates the dire consequences of disobeying God.

Some parts of the Bible appear to teach that the wicked will be annihilated. However, Revelation 14:11 does not seem to support this . "And the smoke of their torment ascendeth up for ever and ever: and they [those who worship the beast] have no rest day or night" (KJV).

The Bible does not say that Elijah died but that he was carried into heaven by a whirlwind. Elijah never experienced physical death but was taken bodily into heaven.

Jeroboam's wife was told by Ahijah that her son would die as soon as she returned to her house. This did indeed take place. However, her son was spared the utter disgrace which befell his father's house.

According to the book of Genesis everyone is made of dust and after death will return to being dust. In the Bible dust often stands for human frailty.

Facts 3

The phrase "a second death" is mentioned only in the book of Revelation. It is defined as the "Lake of Fire".

2 Samuel 12:14 states that because of David's sin the baby son born to Bathsheba would die. David was disciplined in this way by God, but was himself spared the usual death penalty for murder and adultery.

Adoniram, who was in charge of forced labor in King Rehoboam's time, was stoned to death by the Israelites (1 Kings 12.18). But he was in this post under both David and Solomon and the people really only vented their fury on him because Rehoboam escaped.

Hebrews 11:37 says that some of God's faithful followers in the Old Testament were martyred by being sawn in two. While the Bible does not say who this refers to there is an old tradition that it alludes to the way Isaiah was killed, by order of wicked King Manasseh.

When Josiah died, Jeremiah composed laments for him (2 Chronicles 35:25). This is one of the arguments for supporting Jeremiah's authorship of the book of Lamentations.

The Israelites had a law that anyone accused of murder could not be convicted on the evidence of a single witness (Numbers 35:30). There had to be 2 or 3 witnesses before anyone could be put to death for murder.

Hebrews 11:37 mentions that some of God's people were stoned to death in the Old Testament. One such faithful prophet was Zechariah who was stoned to death by order of King Joash in the courtyard of the temple.

Some valiant men from Jabesh Gilead retrieved Saul's dead body from Beth Shan and burned it. Cremation was not a normal practice among the Jews, but was probably done in this instance to prevent Saul's corpse being further abused.

Aaron died on top of Mount Hor in full view of all the Israelites. Just before he died, Moses placed Aaron's priestly garments on his son Eleazar. Aaron's death marked the passing of a generation.

Facts 4

1 Kings 13 records the death of an old man of God. A lion killed him as he traveled by donkey. God's hand is seen here because when a prophet arrived on the scene he found that the donkey had not run off and the body had not been mauled.

The Living One holds the keys of death and Hades (Revelation 1:18). This emphasizes Christ's complete control over the domain of life and death.

Ecclesiastes 3:2 says there is a time to be born and a time to die. This teaches that birth and death are ultimately in God's hands and are by divine appointment.

Jesus promised one of the dying criminals beside him on the cross that he would be with him in paradise. The word "paradise" only occurs three times in the New Testament and refers to a state of rest and a time of bliss between death and resurrection.

Paul states in 1 Corinthians 15:26 that death is the last enemy that will be destroyed. This will happen at Jesus' return when all his enemies will be conquered.

The church at Smyrna are encouraged to be faithful to God even if this involves martyrdom (Revelation 2:10). They are promised the "crown of life," a reference to the garland or wreath won for endurance at athletic contests.

Eliphaz, one of Job's so-called comforters, maintains that resentment kills a fool (Job 5:2). By this he was implying that Job faced his difficulties because of his resentment against God.

Jesus warned his disciples that the day would come when they would be killed for being his followers and that those who did this would think that they were serving God. Throughout history this has been proved true as religious people have often been the greatest persecutors of Christians.

Jesus said Old Testament martyrs ranged from Abel to Zechariah. Abel's murder comes in Genesis, but Zechariah's murder is recorded in 2 Chronicles. The Jews placed 2 Chronicles last in the Old Testament.

Gideon ordered his son Jepher to kill Zebah and Zalmunna. Jepher refused because he was only a boy and was afraid to do this (Judges 8:20). It was probably considered a great disgrace to be killed by a child.

Facts 5

Ishmael assassinated Gedaliah (Jeremiah 41:1). As Gedaliah had been left in charge of Jerusalem as a puppet ruler controlled by the Babylonians, and since Ishmael was himself of royal blood and had been one of King Zedekiah's officers, Ishmael may have acted out of loyalty to Zedekiah.

While Jesus was eating in the home of Simon the Leper a woman poured very expensive perfume on him which the guests said was a waste (Mark 14:3-9). Jesus said that it was in preparation for his burial. Jews anointed their corpses with aromatic oil as part of their funeral preparation.

Methuselah was 969 years old when he died (Genesis 5:27). He had "lived 187 years" when his son Lamech was born; Lamech had "lived 182 years" when Noah was born; and Noah was 600 years old when the flood came. So Methuselah died in the year of the flood.

Job asked the question, "If a man dies, will he live again?" (Job 14:14) In the Old Testament there appears to have been less certainty about resurrection life than there is in the New Testament.

Herod, grandson of Herod the Great, died by being struck down by God's angel and then being eaten by worms. Acts 12:23 indicates that this happened suddenly, just after people had hailed him as a god.

Isaiah prophesied that the Lord Almighty would swallow up death for ever. So, death, which has been called "the great swallower" will itself be swallowed up. Paul uses this verse to great effect in 1 Corinthians 15:54.

Jeremiah, personifying death, talked about death climbing in through their windows (Jeremiah 9:21). In a similar way Habakkuk says that death is never satisfied (Habakkuk 2:5).

The book of Lamentations records instances of mothers cooking their own children for food (4:10). When all the food in Jerusalem ran out during the Babylonian siege of 586 B.C. people were driven to cannibalism.

Apocalypse Now

Quiz #1

1. Name the final battle between the forces of good and evil to take place at the end of the world.

2. When Jesus said that there will be no marriage in heaven, who was he talking to?

3. To what assembly did Paul say, "He [God] has set a day when he will judge the world with justice"?

4. How many horsemen are there in Revelation 6 ?

5. True or false? Jesus said that he would return in the same way in which he ascended into heaven.

6. In the light of God's coming judgment, who wrote that Christians live as "strangers" in "reverent fear"?

7. From where will people come to take their places at the feast in the kingdom of heaven?

8. Which book of the Bible says that the dead "were judged according to what they had done as recorded in the books"?

9. In Jesus' parable about all the nations being collected together and separated into two groups, the sheep were separated from what other animal?

10. True or false? In Mark 13, Jesus said that before the end of the world there would be an outbreak of unprecedented global peace between the nations.

11. What is the name of the city where, according to the author of Hebrews, there will be "thousands upon thousands of angels in joyful assembly"?

12. In John's apocalyptic vision, who sang, "Worthy is the lamb who was slain"?

13. When did Jesus say, "You will see the Son of Man sitting at the right hand of the Mighty One, and coming on the clouds of heaven"?

14. What was written on the foreheads of the 144,000?

15. In the face of what threatened destruction did Abraham ask, "Will not the Judge of all the earth do right?"?

---

1. Armageddon 2. The Sadducees 3. To a meeting of the Areopagus in Athens
4, 5. False. The angels said this (Acts 1:11) 6. Peter 7. From all 4 points of the compass
8. The book of Revelation 9. Goats 10. False. He spoke of wars and rumors of wars (Mark 13:7) 11. Heavenly
Jerusalem, the city of the living God 12. Thousands upon thousands of angels 13. When he was on trial before the
Sanhedrin 14. The name of the Lamb and of the Father 15. The destruction of Sodom and Gomorrah

Answers

372

Quiz #2

1. Supply the missing word from this verse in Psalm 58: "Surely the righteous still are rewarded; surely there is a God who ___ the earth."

2. Which New Testament book is sometimes called the Apocalypse?

3. Who, according to Revelation 20, is going to be bound by an angel for 1,000 years?

4. In Revelation 21, John records that God will wipe away every tear. He lists four things that will be "no more." Name one of the four.

5. In Isaiah's prophecy of peace in nature, who will live with the lamb?

6. Which New Testament author wrote that Jesus "would appear a second time, not to bear sin, but to bring salvation"?

7. True or false? Jesus taught that God the Father would not judge anyone as all judgment has been entrusted to the Son.

8. At Jesus' return, what will happen to the person who is ashamed of Jesus and his words?

9. Fill in the missing two words from Paul's second letter to the Corinthians: "For we must all appear before the ___ ___ of Christ."

10. True or false? The one thing that is not found in the sermons of the first Christians is any mention of God's judgment.

11. According to Isaiah's prophecy, in the year of the Lord's favor, what will happen to the ancient ruins?

12. In which of his letters does Paul write that at Jesus' second coming, God "will pay back trouble to those who trouble you"?

13. In Jesus' parable, why was the rich farmer exceedingly foolish?

14. Supply the missing word in this song sung by the great multitude in heaven: "Hallelujah! For our Lord God Almighty ___."

15. Who saw a vision of Jesus and wrote that from the waist up he looked like glowing metal, from the waist down he looked like glowing fire, and brilliant light surrounded him?

Answers

1. Judges **2.** The book of Revelation **3.** The devil **4.** Death, mourning, crying, pain **5.** The wolf **6.** The author of Hebrews **7.** True (John 5:22) **8.** The Son of Man will be ashamed of him **9.** judgment seat **10.** False (Acts 10:42) **11.** They will be rebuilt **12.** 2 Thessalonians **13.** Because though he had barns full of corn, he was spiritually bankrupt, and that night he was going to die **14.** Reigns **15.** Ezekiel

Quiz #3

1. Who said that Jesus' second coming would be as visible as lightning which comes from the east but is also seen in the west?

2. According to Isaiah, in the last days, which mountain will be chief among the mountains?

3. Who wrote, "He will judge the world in righteousness and the peoples with his truth"?

4. In the symbolic imagery used by John in Revelation 21, what is the bride of the Lamb?

5. The bride of the Lamb is bedecked with jewels, and given fine linen to wear. According to Revelation 19, what does the fine linen stand for?

6. Wide is the gate and broad the road that leads where?

7. Give the color of the first horse mentioned in Revelation 6.

8. The rider of the first horse mentioned in Revelation 6 had what in his hand?

9. What, according to Revelation 13, is going to be limited to 42 months?

10. In Revelation 20:4, what has been given to the souls of beheaded Christian martyrs?

11. In whose house did Peter say, "He [Jesus] is the one whom God appointed as judge of the living and the dead"?

12. According to Paul, when the Lord Jesus is revealed from heaven in blazing fire, who will be with him?

13. True or false? Jesus said that the righteous would live in heaven for 10,000 years.

14. Which New Testament author says that his readers should be patient and stand firm because the Lord's coming is near?

15. In the last days, when there is peace among the nations, what, according to Micah, will be beaten into pruning forks?

Quiz #4

1. In Jesus' Parable of the Sheep and the Goats, where are the sheep and goats standing?

2. The prophet Joel pictured the day of God's judgment as a day of darkness and gloom, like what sort of terrible plague?

3. What is the second name given to the child ruler in Isaiah 9?

4. According to Paul in 2 Thessalonians, why do people perish?

5. True or false? Jesus said that one of the signs of the end of the age would be that America would be defeated in a battle by Russia.

6. Where, according to Jesus, do moth and rust not destroy?

7. Supply the missing word from Paul's words to the Corinthians: "Wait till the Lord comes. He will bring to ____what is hidden in darkness."

8. Just before Stephen was martyred, what did he see as he looked up to heaven?

9. Who promised his readers that when the Chief Shepherd appears they would receive a never-fading crown of glory?

10. True or false? Jesus never spoke about eternal punishment.

11. Which Old Testament prophet wrote, "The sun will be turned to darkness and the moon to blood before the coming of the great and dreadful day of the Lord"?

12. In John the Baptist's prophecy of the coming of the Messiah, he used an image of a farmer. What does the Messiah have in his hand?

13. In John the Baptist's prophecy, what does the Messiah do with the wheat?

14. According to Isaiah, what will come up from the stump of Jesse (King David's father)?

15. True or false? Among the marks of godlessness in the last days (listed in 2 Timothy 3) people will be unforgiving.

---

13. He puts the wheat into his barn 14. A shoot 15. True (2 Timothy 3:3)

10. False. (Matthew 25:46)0 11. Joel 12. His winnowing fork

6. Heaven 7. Light 8. Stephen saw the glory of God and Jesus standing at the right hand of God. 9. Peter

4. Because they refuse to love the truth 5. False. But he does say nation will rise up against nation (Mark 13:8)

1. Before Jesus, who is sitting on his throne in glory 2. Locusts 3. Mighty God

Answers

375

Quiz #5

1. With reference to God's judgment, which Old Testament prophet said, "Not a root or branch will be left to them [the arrogant and evildoers]"?

2. Supply the missing four words from Malachi's prophecy: "For you who revere my name, the sun of righteousness will arise with ___ ___ ___ ___."

3. Paul does not use the word "Antichrist" but has another name for the same person. What is this name?

4. What is the name used in Revelation for the Antichrist?

5. When Jesus spoke to the Sadducees, he said that those who take part in the resurrection of the dead will not marry. What else will they not do?

6. What is the color of the second horse mentioned in Revelation 6?

7. In the vision in Revelation 6, what was given to the rider of the second horse?

8. The rider of the second horse was given power to do what?

9. True or false? Jesus said that anybody who said, "You fool," would be liable to the fire of hell.

10. To which of his friends did Paul write: "There will be terrible times in the last days"?

11. In Isaiah's prophecy of peace in nature, the lion will eat straw like what animal?

12. In Jude's account of the day of judgment, what sin had been committed by the angels chained up in darkness?

13. True or false? Peter wrote that when Jesus returns he will expose the motives of people's hearts.

14. Paul wrote that in the last days people will be lovers of themselves and what else?

15. Paul wrote that in the last days people will always be learning, and yet what will they not acknowledge?

Answers

1. Malachi 2. Healing in its wings 3. The Man of Lawlessness
4. The Beast 5. Die 6. Fiery red 7. A large sword 8. To take peace from the earth and to make men kill each other
9. True (Matthew 5:22) 10. Timothy 11. The ox 12. They did not keep their positions of authority but abandoned their own home (heaven) 13. False. Paul wrote this to the Corinthians (1 Corinthians 4:5)
14. Money 15. The truth

Quiz #6

1. In Isaiah's prophecy of peace in the new creation, what animal will the leopard lie down with?

2. Fill in the missing word from the Sermon on the Mount: "But I tell you that anybody who is ___ with his brother will be subject to judgment."

3. To which Christian minister did Paul say that Jesus' second coming should be a spur to his work?

4. Paul wrote to the Thessalonians that for non-believers the day of the Lord will come like what in the night?

5. In Revelation 20, the devil is called Satan, and he is also given the name of what mythological animal?

6. According to the prophets, in the future age, God's chosen king will be a descendant of which king of Israel?

7. Which New Testament writer wrote, "Dear children... as you have heard that the antichrist is coming, even now many antichrists have come"?

8. From the Sermon on the Mount, why should those who are persecuted and maligned for the sake of Jesus nevertheless be happy?

9. Supply the missing four words from chapter 12 of Hebrews: "[Jesus] for the ___ ___ endured the cross, scorning its shame, and sat down at the right hand of the throne of God."

10. True or false? In the Parable of the Vineyard Workers, the workers who worked all day were paid more than the workers who worked for only one hour.

11. Fill in the missing word from Daniel's prophecy: "Those who are wise will shine like the brightness of the heavens, and those who lead many to righteousness like the ___ for ever and ever."

12. Who wrote that scoffers would come in the last days?

13. What is the third name given to the child-ruler mentioned in Isaiah 9:6?

14. True or false? Jesus said that anybody who said to him, "Lord, Lord," would enter the kingdom of heaven.

15. In Revelation 6, what did the rider of the black horse have in his hand, symbolizing famine?

Quiz #7

1. In the book of Revelation, who has the number 666?

2. True or false? The Bible never speaks about "rewards" in heaven.

3. In order to stress the importance of obedience to God, who taught that it is better to tear out an eye than have two eyes but go to hell?

4. According to Mark 13, as well as false Christs, what other group of false people will appear in the lead up to the end times?

5. Who appealed to his readers as a fellow elder, a witness of Jesus' sufferings and as one who was going to share in the future glory?

6. True or false? When Jesus said to the repentant thief, "Today you will be with me in paradise," the thief replied, "Then save me from dying on this cross."

7. Which Old Testament prophet said that a time would come when the earth would no longer conceal her slain?

8. When Martha said to Jesus, "I know he will rise in the resurrection at the last day," who was she talking about?

9. In Isaiah's prophecy of future peace, who will lead the wild and tame animals?

10. Who wrote that at the Lord's coming the ungodly would be convicted of all the harsh words they had spoken against the Lord?

11. Matthew 24 records Jesus' warning that he would come again when his disciples were not expecting him. What did Jesus therefore tell them to do?

12. True or false? Peter wrote that he would prefer to be away from the body and at home with the Lord.

13. Supply the missing words from Paul's first letter to the Corinthians: "Therefore you do not lack any spiritual gift as you eagerly wait for ___ ___ ___."

14. In Jesus' Parable of the Wedding Banquet, why was one of the guests thrown out?

15. When did Jesus pray, "Father, I want those you have given me to be with me where I am and to see my glory"?

Answers

1. The Beast (Revelation 13:18) **2.** False. Christians will suffer loss or be rewarded according to what they have done (1 Corinthians 3:15; Revelation 22:12) **3.** Jesus **4.** False prophets **5.** Peter **6.** False. No reply from the thief is recorded (Luke 23:42-43) **7.** Isaiah (Isaiah 26:21) **8.** Her dead brother Lazarus **9.** A little child **10.** Jude **11.** Be ready! Keep watch! **12.** False. Paul wrote this (2 Corinthians 5:8) **13.** The Lord's return **14.** Because he was not wearing wedding clothes **15.** On the last night before he died

Quiz #8

1. In which Gospel are these words of Jesus recorded: "There is a judge for the one who rejects me and does not accept my words"?

2. True or false? Paul taught that at Jesus' second coming the Christians who are still alive will be raised up to meet Jesus in the air.

3. How many apocalyptic visions are recorded in the book of Zechariah?

4. What was seen in the first vision in the book of Zechariah?

5. What was the meaning of Zechariah's first vision?

6. Which Old Testament prophet spoke about God creating new heavens and a new earth and a time when "the former things will not be remembered"?

7. What did Paul pray for in connection with the coming of Jesus for the spirits, souls and bodies of the Christians in Thessalonica?

8. According to Isaiah, who will have good news preached to them in the year of the Lord's favor?

9. What is the color of the third horse mentioned in Revelation 6?

10. In Joel's prophecy of the day of the Lord, what will the sons and daughters do?

11. According to Peter, there will be a new heaven and a new earth which will be the home of what?

12. How many times is Jesus' return mentioned in the New Testament?

13. Who said that at the end of the age the wicked would be thrown into a "fiery furnace" where there would be "weeping and gnashing of teeth"?

14. What percentage of the Bible is made up of predictions about the future?

15. In the Parable of the Great Banquet, when the banquet was ready, the guests made excuses. Name one of the three excuses given.

Answers

1. The Gospel of John 2. True (1 Thessalonians 4:17) 3. 8
4. A man riding a red horse among myrtle trees, red, brown and white horses 5. Future restoration for God's people
6. Isaiah 7. That they should be kept blameless. 8. The poor 9. Black 10. Prophesy
11. Righteousness 12. 319 times 13. Jesus
14. 27 per cent 15. The purchase of a field; the purchase of 5 yoke of oxen; recent marriage

APOCALYPSE NOW

Quiz #9

1. In Zechariah's third vision, forecasting full restoration for God's people, Zechariah saw a man with a measuring line: what was he measuring?

2. In Revelation 19 John records a vision of a great white horse. The rider is called Faithful and True. What further name is he given?

3. The armies of the rider on the white horse are also on white horses. What are they wearing?

4. According to Jesus, what is it, that, if given to one of his little ones, will earn someone a reward in heaven?

5. Supply the missing word from Jeremiah's prophecy in chapter 23: "'The days are coming,' declares the Lord, 'when I will raise up to David a righteous ___.'"

6. According to Revelation 13, who gives the Beast his power?

7. How long will the child-ruler of Isaiah 9:6 reign?

8. Who, in torment in hell, saw Abraham?

9. What, according to the apostle Paul, are our light and passing troubles going to achieve for us?

10. What is the meaning of Zechariah's fourth vision in which the high priest's dirty clothes are replaced by rich, clean clothes?

11. Who predicted that Zion's future king would take away the war-horses from Jerusalem?

12. Paul wrote to Timothy that in the last days people would have a form of godliness, but what would they lack?

13. Supply the missing two words from the promise Jesus gave to his followers: "In my Father's house are many ___; if it were not so, I would have told you. I am going there to prepare a ___ for you."

14. According to Paul, where is our citizenship?

15. To whom did Paul write, "We eagerly await a Savior from there [heaven], the Lord Jesus Christ"?

Answers

1. Jerusalem 2. The Word of God 3. Fine linen, white and clean 4. A cup of cold water 5. Branch 6. The dragon (Satan) 7. For ever 8. The rich man, in Jesus' parable about Lazarus and the rich man 9. An eternal glory 10. Israel's cleansing; she will be restored as a nation of priests 11. Zechariah 12. The power of godliness 13. rooms, place 14. In heaven 15. The Christian church in Philippi

380

Quiz #10

1. From Jeremiah chapter 23, complete the name given to the future King who reigns wisely: "This is the name by which he will be called: The Lord Our ___."

2. True or false? Jesus compared heaven to a wedding banquet which a Pharisee prepared for his son.

3. In which of his letters does Paul say that Christians must not mind if their earthly bodies are destroyed because they have "a building from God, an eternal house in heaven"?

4. What does Paul say is a guarantee that Christians have an eternal house in heaven?

5. Who said that the day of the Lord would be like a launderer's soap?

6. What was the color of the fourth horse mentioned in Revelation 6?

7. According to Revelation 1, when Jesus returns, as well as all the peoples of the earth, who in particular will mourn because of him?

8. Who wrote that those who "do not obey the gospel of our Lord Jesus... will be... shut out from the presence of the Lord and from the majesty of his power" when he comes again?

9. Supply the missing word from Isaiah's prophecy about the child-ruler's reign: "Of the increase of his government and ___ there will be no end."

10. What symbols did Zechariah see in his fifth vision to remind him of God's mighty resources?

11. In Jesus' Parable of the Weeds, when will the weeds be separated from the wheat?

12. In Jesus' Parable of the Weeds, what do the weeds and wheat represent?

13. When Joel spoke of the day of the Lord, what did he say the young men would see?

14. According to John chapter 6, who will be raised up by Jesus at the last day?

15. Who, according to 1 Corinthians 15, are to be pitied more than all men?

APOCALYPSE NOW

Quiz #11

1. What was Paul's reason for writing that the Corinthians should not judge people before the appointed time, but wait until the Lord returns?

2. In Revelation 6, what was the name of the rider on the pale horse?

3. True or false? According to the book of Revelation, when Jesus returns, only his disciples will see him.

4. Supply the missing word from Jesus' declaration in Revelation 1: "Behold I am alive for ever and ever! And I hold the ____ of death and Hades."

5. What did Zechariah see in his eighth vision symbolizing worldwide divine judgment?

6. In Zechariah's prophecy of future restoration, what name will be given to Jerusalem?

7. In Jesus' words about future destruction, where will the Abomination of Desolation stand?

8. Who said that Israel could look forward to a time when their land would be renowned for its crops, and they would no longer be victims of famine?

9. According to Jesus, when nations see the Son of Man appear in the sky with power and great glory, what will they do?

10. In the year of the Lord's favor, instead of a spirit of despair, what will the people have?

11. In Jesus' Parable of the Rich Man and Lazarus, when the rich man was in hell, why did he want Lazarus to come to him?

12. True or false? In Jesus' Parable of the Rich Man and Lazarus, Abraham said that a great chasm had been fixed between the rich man and Lazarus and no one could cross it.

13. In the book of Revelation, John is shown a series of seven seals followed by two other series of seven things. Name one of them.

14. What followed closely behind the rider of the fourth horse mentioned in Revelation 6?

15. According to Hebrews chapter 9, human beings are destined to die once, and what comes after that death?

Facts 1

God's goal for his people is eternal life in his kingdom (Matthew 25:34). Hell was "prepared for the devil and his angels" (Matthew 25:43). To choose hell is to reject God's intended destiny.

In Old Testament times it was understood that at death people went to "Sheol," which meant "the place of shades." It was a place of waiting, rather than a place of punishment.

The New Testament translation of "Sheol" is "Hades." Jesus spoke of the unrepentant city of Capernaum which would "go down to the depths " (Matthew 11:23). Hades is not usually the place of final judgment.

Jesus said that "the gates of Hades will not overcome it [my church]" (Matthew 16:18). These "gates of Hades" represent the rallying point for Satan's armies, as city gates were rallying centers for a city's army.

The Jews believed that there were two compartments to Hades. The wicked dead went to one part of Hades, while the righteous dead went to another part of Hades, called Paradise.

The word "Gehenna" comes from the Greek meaning "Valley of Hinnom." This was the garbage dump outside Jerusalem, where children were once sacrificed by fire (Jeremiah 7:31).

In New Testament times, there were always fires in the Valley of Hinnom, burning up the rubbish left there. It became a metaphor for hell (e.g. Matthew 5:22; 25:41).

In the Bible, the phrase "the day of the Lord" refers to a time when God will act decisively in human history to implement the final stage of his redemptive plan for humankind.

The Old Testament speaks about God's judgment in terms of "the day of the Lord." On "that day" God will judge all peoples and nations, including Israel (Zephaniah 1:15).

In the Old Testament (Zechariah 14) and the New Testament, the day of the Lord refers to the second coming of Jesus. It has been calculated that the second coming is foretold 319 times in the New Testament.

"The day of the Lord" in 2 Peter 3:10-13, refers to a future climactic time when earth will be destroyed by fire. This will also be the moment that the new earth and new heavens are ushered in.

Facts 2

The New Testament uses three words for the return of Jesus, each with a slightly different emphasis. In classical Greek "parousia" referred to the arrival of someone of high rank. This is the usual word for the return of Jesus (Acts 1:11).

"Epiphaneia" means "appearance", and was used in Greek mythology of the appearance of a god, or of an emperor coming out before his people (2 Thessalonians 2:8).

"Apocalypse" means "uncovering," in the sense of revealing a hidden glory or splendor (2 Thessalonians 1:7). Apocalyptic writings describe mystical revelations from God. They are characterized by the use of codes, numbers and symbols.

Heaven is pictured as a place where there will be no sin (Revelation 21:27), no evil people (Revelation 21:8), no darkness and no sadness of any kind (Revelation 21:4).

There is an important division in Mark chapter 13. Verses 1-23 refer to events that will occur before Jesus' return, while verses 14-27 refer to events that will take place at Jesus' return.

"Paradise" is used metaphorically three times in the New Testament and describes the place where the spirits of God's people go when they die (Luke 23:43).

The New Testament talks of death as "sleep" (Acts 7:59-8:1), but does not teach that the spirit is unconscious until Jesus' return. It may be said that the body "sleeps," waiting to be reunited with the spirit.

The Westminster Confession refers to the "intermediate state" as a state in which "souls of the righteous [are]... received into the highest heaven where they behold the face of God... waiting for the full redemption of their bodies."

John teaches that the "Antichrist" is an evil person. His chief characteristics are the denial that Jesus is from God (1 John 4:3), and self-exaltation.

The spirit of antichrist is at work in the world, causing many "antichrists" to arise. But in the last days this spirit will be fully expressed in one final evil figure.

In Revelation the Antichrist is referred to as the Beast (Revelation 13), and in Paul's writings as the Man of Lawlessness (2 Thessalonians 2:3). He will be decisively destroyed by the coming of Jesus (2 Thessalonians 2:8)